TO HELL WITH PICASSO

and Other Essays

TO HELL WITH PICASSO
and Other Essays

Paul Johnson

Weidenfeld & Nicolson
LONDON

This book is dedicated
to John, Henry, Billy,
Maurice, George, Kingsley
and other old chums,
who have gone ahead

First published in Great Britain in 1996 by
Weidenfeld & Nicolson

The Orion Publishing Group Ltd
Orion House
5 Upper Saint Martin's Lane
London WC2H 9EA

A catalogue record for this book is available
from the British Library.

ISBN 0 297 81773 6

Printed in Great Britain by
Butler & Tanner Ltd
Frome and London

CONTENTS

The Art of Writing a Column

Writing can be more drudgery than pleasure, and journalism more degradation than duty. But to write a regular column on any subject that takes your fancy is surely one of the great privileges of life. When asked to contribute an article on 'Literature and Life' every week to the *Evening News* in 1907, Arnold Bennett called it 'the realisation of a dream I have dreamt for a long time'. George Orwell, given a similar weekly column by *Tribune* in December 1943, celebrated his delightful freedom by entitling it 'As I Please'.

I have been writing columns of one kind or another virtually all my professional life. I began in 1953, when I was twenty-four, contributing a weekly column from Paris to the *New Statesman* (often paralleled by another one in *Tribune* under the pseudonym 'Guy Henriques' – thus provoking the French Socialist leader Guy Mollet, a particular target of mine, to the angry query 'What sort of a Guy is this?'). I have written columns in the *Evening Standard*, the *Daily Telegraph*, the *Sun* and the *Daily Express*, in the *Catholic Herald* and the Paris weekly *L'Express*, in daily newspapers in Spain, Italy and Japan. For many years I wrote the 'London Diary' in the *New Statesman*, and since 1980 I have written a weekly column in the *Spectator*, from which this selection is drawn. In short, I know a bit about writing a column, though there is still a lot I do not know, and I find myself discovering new tricks and devices – and occasionally falling into new traps – almost every week.

One thing I have learnt is that the column is much older than most people realise. It antedates the newspaper, indeed. I am not going back to Roman times, though you could make a case for columnists of a sort existing even then. A more plausible birth-date is the 16th century, with Montaigne the founding-columnist and Francis Bacon his successor. Of course these were essays not columns, and were written neither to a fixed length nor for immediate publication. Montaigne began his *Essais* as a commonplace book for his own re-perusal; only some years later, in 1580, did he first print them as a collected volume. Bacon's *Essays* and *Apothogms* had a similar genesis. But both men produced columns in the sense that their reflections were short, regular, often topical, neatly turned and highly readable, and a satisfying blend of knowledge, argument, personal opinion, idiosyncracy and self-revelation. The subject-matter in both cases – calamities, education, repentance, conversation, thinking of death (Montaigne), and riches, youth and age, friendship, ambition, marriage versus single life, etc (Bacon) – crop up continually in columns written in the 1990s. These two experienced and clever men dealt with many, perhaps most, of the main problems which preoccupied worldlings in the 16th century, continue to interest and puzzle us today, and will be items of human intellectual furniture so long as our race endures. If, today, I were planning to write a column on death, I would certainly want to look up what Montaigne had to say in his essay 'Thoughts on Death' and Bacon in 'On Death'. And if I were writing about gardens I would begin by re-reading Bacon's marvellous little discourse 'On Gardens'. On such fundamental matters, nothing much changes in four centuries – or, I suspect, four millennia. And I like to think that Montaigne and Bacon are peering over my shoulder – albeit with quizzical, ironic or even faintly contemptuous expressions – as I sit at my desk columnising.

There were well-informed London gentlemen who wrote regular columns about life in the capital, for the information of country squires and lords, even in Shakespeare's day. But these were more newsletters than reflective essays. It was the 18th century which saw the birth of the column. The *Spectator* of Addison and Steele was a columnar periodical. So was Samuel Johnson's *Rambler*, his *Adventurer* and his *Idler*, and Coleridge's *Watchman*, though it only ran for ten issues, and his *Friend*, which lasted for 28. These columnists had all the trouble of seeing their work through the press, and collecting money from subscribers so that they could pay the printer. They were the columnists of the heroic age. By comparison, Coleridge's younger contemporaries, Charles Lamb and William Hazlitt, had it easy, turning in their copy to regular publications, leaving all the difficult money side to editor-proprietors. On the other hand, their essays or columns might well be censored, cut, held over or even rejected altogether. Some will hold that Lamb was not a columnist at all – his pieces appeared irregularly and varied enormously in length – and that Hazlitt's 'Table Talk' was the first true column. That may be so, but I turn, in search of inspiration or guidance, as often to Lamb as to Hazlitt, and regard both as mentors of the Great Columnar Tradition.

After these pioneers of the 1810s and 1820s, when Lamb and Hazlitt – and Leigh Hunt – wrote their best work, columnists come thick and fast, in endless succession until our own day. There are so many good ones it is not easy to award crowns. One has to bear in mind, too, that a column which is brilliantly suited to, say, the 1840s, may not work today at all. The columnist writes for tomorrow or this week, not for posterity, although the best satisfy both. One of the greatest American columnists, Ralph Waldo Emerson, the most highly-regarded and representative voice of the mid-19th century, from the eastern seabord to the Rockies, bores most readers now (though not me, as it happens). On the other hand, H.L. Mencken, perhaps the finest of all and hugely influential in his day, still comes through hot and strong in his six collections of pieces, *Prejudices* (1919–27).

My roll of honour would include G.K. Chesterton, who wrote columns of all kinds and shapes during his prolific life, often in pubs and cafés and in railway waiting-rooms and on trains, in true Grub Street fashion. The amount of genuinely original thought in his ephemera thus dashed off is truly awe-inspiring, and I find him a rich brantub from which to pick out specimens still capable of inspiring a columnist's thoughts half a century after his death. Bennett's *Evening News* columns have sunk without trace but those on writers and books which he later contributed to Beaverbrook's *Evening Standard* in the 1920s are classics of the art. Beaverbrook himself told me that publishing them gave him the greatest satisfaction of his entire career as a newspaper proprietor. The *Standard* has always had good columns. It ran Dean Inge of St Paul's, known as 'the Gloomy Dean', whose columns on religious abuses and the general decline of morals, collected in book form, make a favourite volume on my shelves. In my own day it broadcast Randolph Churchill's powerful, rough- edged and often prodigiously well-informed voice, shouting on politics, as well as an entire choir of clever women, from Maureen Cleave to Valerie Grove. The *Observer* is another columnists' newspaper. In the 1950s it had a mesmerising political column written by Hugh Massingham, who came from a family of fine columnists. He specialised in getting unsuspecting politicians to tell him their secrets. Then there was the urbanity of Harold Nicolson, with its faint whiff of malice, written by a man intended for diplomacy but really born to columnise.

About this time a clutch of outstanding arts columnists adorned the *Sunday Times*. They have never been excelled, in my view: Cyril

Connolly and Raymond Mortimer on books, Desmond Shawe-Taylor and Ernest Newman on music, Cyril Ray on the good life, Edward Sackville-West on gramophone records and James Agate on the theatre. These gifted men were an important part of my education, a sophisticated and enjoyable Sunday school of culture, the caviar and the pâté de foie gras of European civilisation slipping down one's throat with gratifying ease. Equally, while I was living in Paris as a young man, I devoured François Mauriac's famous 'Bloc Notes' on the back page of *L'Express*, Raymond Aron in *Figaro*, Albert Camus in *Combat* and Maurice Duverger in *Le Monde*. Some made more regular appearances than others, but all qualified for the title of columnist since they produced periodic discourses on important and usually topical issues of their choice. Jean-Paul Sartre, on the other hand, gave himself too much space in *Le Temps moderne* – he was the only journalist I have ever known who could write 20,000 words in a day without making himself ill – and was not therefore a columnist by my definition, more a verbal phenomenon, sometimes a verbose one.

The Americans produce more columns than any other nation, nearly all syndicated and many of poor quality. Walter Winchell's columns, immensely influential in their day, are unreadable now, and even Walter Lipmann, the outstanding pundit-columnist of the Truman–Eisenhower–Kennedy years, has not survived, his weekly digests of Washington wisdom seeming today flat, empty and composed of truisms. On the other hand, William Safire, who deals with words as well as issues in the *New York Times*, is a pundit in the Mencken mould, funny as well as shrewd and apposite. So the tradition carries on.

What makes a good columnist? In my view there are five essentials. The first is knowledge. I am not saying that a columnist ought to be a walking encyclopædia. Far from it. Nothing is more tedious than a man crammed with knowledge – especially facts – who is anxious to unburden his treasure on you. Some of the greatest bores are knowledgeable men. (Interestingly enough, women do not bore you with facts, more with opinions: I do not know of any woman columnist who crams too many facts into her offerings – the weakness of the sex is to supply too few.) But he who ventures to write a column must know a great deal, on a wide variety of subjects. His knowledge, however, should be stored and classified, kept up to date and dusted down regularly, but called on only sparingly, in small quantities, exactly according to the need of the piece. The good columnist's knowledge should be like a vast cellar of fine wine, cool and well-kept, constantly maturing and periodically replenished as fresh vintages become available. He invites the reader in to sip and to taste, in sufficient quantity to appreciate the quality of the wines available. But he never presses his guest to drink more than a glass on each occasion, so that these visits to his cellar retain their freshness and pleasure. But equally, no reader should be allowed to pass without some knowledgeable hospitality, be it ever so slight. I feel I have been short-changed if I finish a column without acquiring some useful or interesting or unusual little nugget – something I did not know and am glad to know.

No columnist will survive long without being to some extent a man or woman of the world. In theory a column can be written by an innocent and unworldly bystander, who makes a point of being out of it and not knowing what is going on. Given great literary ingenuity, this will do for a time, as a novelty or a journalistic paradox. But readers will not long be amused by someone even less well-informed than themselves or who merely mirrors their own vacuity. It is true that a columnist can, as it were, place himself in voluntary exile, and affect to survey society with disinterested detachment. J.B. Priestley in the 1950s wrote an admirable series of essays in the *New Statesman* called 'Thoughts from the wilderness', in which he criticised modern society from the viewpoint of a man, like Cicero, who had retired from the great game in London to his country estates, to sit things out for a while. But this only works if, like Priestley, you have once been in the thick of events, and intend to be so again.

Knowledge is composed of many things. Worldliness, of course: knowing how a prime minister conducts a Cabinet meeting or how the Booker Prize is awarded or why invitations to Mrs —'s luncheons are eagerly sought, while Lady —'s parties are ill-attended if something better is on offer. A columnist should have travelled far, especially to those key places which constantly crop up in the news and conversation. He should be familiar with Paris and New York and Rome and Venice, and have visited all the rest at least once. He needs to be able to distinguish a genuine exotic from a mere travel-agent's brochure material. Languages do not matter – it is the columnist's job to speak, write and understand English to perfection – but if he insists (on what must be rare occasions) on using foreign words, he must get them right.

A columnist ought to have known, and know, a huge range of

people, from the humble right up to the top. He who claims an extensive acquaintance with the common man or woman skates on thin ice, and I do not advise a display of demotic knowledge. Taxidrivers should never be quoted, at any rate on politics. On the other hand, gardeners can be put to use and, with skill, built up into a serviceable stock character – not to be brought in too often however. Kingsley Martin made splendid use of his Sussex gardener for over a quarter-century, employing him to impart wisdom and comment covering a much wider ground than mere horticulture. I have quoted gardeners myself – and their dogs, for that matter. Cleaning-women I do not advise. Butlers or valets are taboo, even if you have them. On the other hand, it is often convenient to have a well-informed and sensible detective-sergeant on tap: crime and criminals play a necessary part, these days, in a well-regulated column read by the middle classes. Personally I like to bring in an observant and well-connected foreigner to produce an outsider's view of English *mores*, especially if the language can be made quaint and amusing – I often employ Lady (Carla) Powell for this purpose. Quoting the great, the good and the bad is sometimes necessary but is always risky. Of course the columnist ought to know personally the principal rulers of the day, and if possible anyone else who is in and out of the news. But awareness of this extensive and grand acquaintance ought to filter through to the reader, as it were by accident, and should never be baldly claimed. Name-dropping is fatal to a good column. The sad example of Ali Forbes, Britain's Name-Dropper-in-Chief, ought to be in all our minds. But I like a name or two in each piece. Good journalism is always about people. An argument, an impression, is always more effective if it is pointed up by real men and women, cited or quoted or exemplified. And brush such characters in with an adjective or two, to bring them to life and persuade the reader that they are or were real persons to you, not just celebrities.

Knowledge of history is the most useful to the all-purpose columnist. It needs to be blended in, imperceptibly, with personal recall of the recent past. This is a difficult, subtle and essential business. The reader needs to feel that you comment on what is going on in the world not from theory or conjecture but from experience – that you have lived through anxious decades, near the centre of events, as well as studied more remote ones. I do not say a columnist needs to be old – far from it – but he or she must not be too young. It is one thing for a young man or woman to relate actual experiences, week by week, in a place we want to hear about – I am thinking of Zoë

Heller's column from New York in the *Sunday Times Magazine* – when all that is required is a busy life and literary skills. It is quite another to have someone in their twenties pontificate about the day and age from the perspective of a mere newspaper-reader. There are too many such columnists about nowadays, none of them worth tuppence.

Next to knowledge comes reading. Every good columnist carries a library around in his head. A column – not even a literary column – should not be bookish, which is fatal to the essential note of world-liness. One of the worst columns I can recall was the weekly *causerie* produced by Sir William Haley. As Haley had been Director-General of the BBC as well as Editor of the *Times*, and had made his way up from very humble beginnings, he ought to have had plenty to say. But he preferred to write in the *persona* of a bookman, and a notably old-fashioned one at that, fussing over ancient Everyman editions and World Classics and turn-of-the-century pocket stuff. It all smacked of *John O'London's Weekly*, a well-meaning journal for autodidacts which died a natural death from fustiness. No: the reading must be there – the more of it the better – but slipped into the column by sleight of hand, gracefully, economically, only when it is really needed. Whatever the topic is, the columnist ought to be able to make a long arm and neatly pull down the book from the recesses of his mind, when reference or quotation is apt. No showing-off. No erudition for its own sake. Poetry to be quoted only on rare occasions – and be certain the reader wants to hear it or be reminded of it. No Greek, ever. No Latin either, unless you are absolutely sure of yourself and your readers. I have many dictionaries of quotations on my study shelves, but these are for checking, not inspiration. Never quote unless the saying is already familiar to you. The best kind of literary reference in a column is one which makes the reader want to go out and buy the book, immediately. That means it must be apposite, interesting in itself, and skilfully worked into the theme of the piece.

The second function of wide reading is to produce ideas. I am a great browser of shelves, an assiduous dipper into volumes. I thumb a book through, read a page or two, then replace it. I do this in bookshops and libraries, and among my own shelves. At present I own (I think) about 12,000 volumes. Sometimes I have had more, sometimes less. Every few years, a shortage of shelf-space dictates a huge and painful purge, when meretricious or duplicate or dis-appointing works are weeded out. Then, all too quickly, fresh arrivals fill up the vacant spaces, and overflow them, and a new crisis develops. I receive many new books for review, or publishers send them to me, hoping for a mention. Most of these volumes go, speedily, to what I call the knacker's yard, which in my case is an admirable establishment near my house, called Notting Hill Books, run by that great and learned lady Sheila Ramage and her lovely assistant Pamela. However, Sheila also sells books, chiefly on art, at much reduced prices, so I usually emerge from her shop with many more volumes than I take in. The urge to buy books is a chronic disease, which is cured only by bodily annihilation. In my case, the consequences of the disease are dealt with by dividing my books into two libraries. Most are kept at my London house, into every cranny of which they have spread. But about 2,000 books on the history of art, the majority large quartos or folios, have been consigned to my Somerset house, where special shelves have been built to accommodate them. As a result, the book I particularly want at any one time is always 250 miles away. However, I can see no other solution.

I do not claim to have read all or even most of the books I own. Some I read many years after purchase, others never. But I have looked into all of them. I know what they contain. All are for potential use, as well as pleasure. Many are for reference or checking, and it is gratifying how often I refer to them. The advantage of having so many books, on all the topics that interest me, but chiefly history, literature, the world, travel, philosophy, politics and religion, is that they are there for a rainy day. By this I mean a deadline-day when I have not yet found a subject for a column. I peer along the shelves, hoping for inspiration. This is a dangerous procedure, for I may pick up a volume, become absorbed in it, and find at the end when I look at the clock, that it is not to my purpose, and meanwhile precious hours have flown. On the other hand, it has saved my journalistic bacon many a time. Besides, having so many books at hand often means that I can flesh out an existing idea, but a rather thin one, with a certain amount of scholarship, real or spurious.

The third key to column-writing is news-sense. A columnist may be a historian, as I am, or a playwright, like Keith Waterhouse, or a novelist, like Robert Harris. But he ought never to forget that, for this purpose, he is first and foremost a journalist. He should keep a fine nose for the news, and sniff it inquiringly before settling to his task. The reader's mind hankers after novelty, always. The best column is one which responds to novelty, links it to the past, carries it forward to the future and invests the topic with wit, wisdom and elegance. The novelty can be anything: geopolitics, home affairs, science, literature, fashion, art, the drama, society, religion. Its gravity is immaterial; what it must be is new, not some hackneyed theme which has been chewed over for weeks. A good columnist will spot some emergent topic just as it comes to the forefront of the news, and fire his guns before the battlefield is trampled over and lost in smoke. Just occasionally it is good tactics to take last week's theme and upend it, but only if you have something good and valid to say which runs counter to the conventional wisdom.

My method is to make three out of four columns topical in one way or another. In the fourth I please myself, and write about what I think matters, irrespective of what is in the papers, or will be. I write about the weather or the season or something I have done or seen or heard. These personal columns are the real test of whether you know how to do the thing. You have to marshal all your literary skills and make absolutely sure you can carry your readers with you to the end of the last paragraph. If you are not sure, beat a hasty retreat and stick to topicality. On the other hand, if you can pull it off, these eye-witness or autobiographical pieces are, I find, the ones that most delight the reader, stick in his or her mind, and find their way eventually into the anthologies. One word of caution: beware braggadocio or triumphalism. Such personal pieces should be seasoned with modesty, should be humble or if needs be ironic about one's claims to importance, and stress incompetence and failure – or discomfiture – rather than personal accomplishment. The reader is more likely to sympathise and identify with one who cheerfully endures misfortunes, than with one who effortlessly surmounts them. In the battle for life, the good columnist is a natural loser, albeit a perennially optimistic one.

The fourth point to be borne in mind is that your natural news-sense should take account of the need for variety. Most columns should never be too far from the events of the day, be they political, social or cultural. But, while being topical, the columnist should dodge about between these, and other, fields. I try never to write on domestic politics, or geopolitics, two weeks running, unless the news leaves me no choice. And if there is a big political news story, which rivets the attention of all writers, I am careful to consult with the editor about how he is handling it. If his coverage is comprehensive, I am often inclined to give the subject a miss and write on something completely different, even lightweight – that is, if he will let me. Or he may warn me off in the first place. If I write on painting, a subject which preoccupies me more and more, I will then leave it alone for at least six weeks, however great the temptation. I avoid discussing

TV if possible – it is too easy and obvious. I try not to write about religion more than four times a year, and never at Christmas or Easter, when everyone else is doing so. On the other hand, I never write less than four pieces a year with God in them. I do not write a foreign piece two weeks running. If I travel, I sometimes use my experiences for a column, but not often, and only when they merit it. Everyone travels nowadays, frequently, all over the world – or it is sensible to assume they do. No place is truly exotic any more, unless you are on the inside track there; and then you must beware of snobbery or in-grouping.

It is fatal to appear to condescend to your readers, just as it is impolitic to suck up to them, or hector them, or try to jolly them along. Remember, it is the easiest thing in the world for them to stop reading your article after the first paragraph, or half-way through, or at any stage. They do not even need to take a conscious decision. Their eye simply slips off the page. Or the piece is put down because the phone rings, and never taken up again. And if your column is not finished one week, it may not even be begun the next. Remember: you are always the suppliant, it is the reader who is the haughty beloved. Woo him or her, in every paragraph, in every sentence, with every word – and, hardest thing of all, never seem to do so. Never grab him by the lapels or thrust an importunate hand up a tightly gathered skirt or bellow into an indifferent ear. Love, but do not let your anxiety to be loved in return be evident. If you know how to stalk red deer, stalk. If you know what tickling trout is, tickle. But forget your shotgun: it does not work with this kind of game.

The reader will notice that I used the word 'I' a dozen times in the paragraph before last. Then I realised what I was doing and switched the tone. All good columns are about humanity and human nature, and they are personal. But they should never be egotistical. Vanity is the cardinal sin of the columnist. Next to that in heinousness is omniscience, vanity's younger brother. A know-all manner is a repellant. So is undue stress on insider knowledge. Never use phrases like 'I asked the Prime Minister' or 'a member of the Cabinet told me'. The personality of the columnist should always be present but it should rarely break out openly in the text. A good columnist is a submarine, prowling just below the surface of his prose, periscope up but inconspicuous.

On rare occasions it is just permissible to use your column to promote a personal cause or come to the rescue of a friend in distress or memorialise someone you knew who will otherwise receive no mention. But these topics should be broached entirely on their intrinsic merits, never because of their connection with yourself. Assume there is something inherently tiresome about your own personality or radically defective about your judgement where your personal interests are involved – or, better still, get yourself a wife with the courage to point these things out to you. (It is a fact that confirmed bachelors rarely make good columnists for long – and even Bernard Levin, the great exception, would have been a better one under regular wifely supervision.) And this brings me to the next, and most important, point: never exploit your power as a columnist for personal ends. No doubt the traffic cop was quite mistaken to stop you for speeding/careless driving, and his language was inexcusable. But the readers do not want to hear about it. Nor are they interested in the reasons why the council refused you planning permission for an extension, or your appalling experience with BA/Virgin Airways, or the impudent behaviour of the ticket-inspector on the 4.30 from Paddington to Oxford, or the exasperating way in which John Lewis/Peter Jones laid your new drawing-room carpet. Having trouble getting your washing-machine repaired? Forget it – so is everyone else. I suppose if you are really seriously mugged, it might just be worth a mention. But nobody, except your local police – who have no alternative – wants to hear your blow-by-blow account. Your fog story, your airport delay story, your story of being swindled/overcharged/cheeked/abused, etc by the insurance/British Gas/ the check-out girl at Safeways/the Inland Revenue are – I stress the point – of absolutely no interest whatever. That is what your family is for, to listen to them, just as you are there to listen to theirs. The reader has nothing to do with it. Mark well: you are not doing him/her a favour – he is paying you, to be entertained. So he does not want to be told that the nurses at St Mary's, where you went for a hip-replacement, were absolutely splendid and it has quite changed your opinion about the NHS, etc. Nor will she be spellbound if you tell her about going to Buckingham Palace to receive your OBE, and what a surprisingly beautiful skin the Queen has got, and how efficiently the car-parking arrangements are managed. Be your age: no one is interested in the fact that you are a minor – probably very minor – celebrity, except yourself. So do not write about your dog, except perhaps twice a year, or your children (once) or your wife (ever).

All the same, be yourself. An impersonal column is a contradiction in terms, like a discreet diary. For your column to be a success, the reader must like you, and in order to like you he must know you. So peep out from your puppet-box from time to time. People who regularly pay good money for newspapers and magazines positively want to develop personal relationships with them – love-hate ones, mostly, punctuated by grumbling, exasperation and actual violence. I have seen even Rupert Murdoch pick up a copy of one of his own newspapers, the *Sunday Times* – and *my* copy as it happened – recoil from it with fury, scrumple it up and hurl it with impressive force into the fireplace. This emotional relationship between paper and reader is at its most intense when the columnists are under scrutiny. So if you write a column, you are in the front line, less that a stone's-throw from the reader's trenches. Put your tin hat on a stick and wave it – let him know you are there.

One last point. Life is sad for most people. It is doubtless sad for you too. But, like Pagliacci, you must not let it show: on with the motley! By all means use your column to criticise the great, and right abuses and shake governments and bring low the proud. But make the point, from time to time, that we live in an infinitely beautiful world, surprisingly full of fascinating people, and heart-warming happenings, and laughter, and that God is in his heaven.

Is your journey really necessary, professor?

More and more young people are trying to get into universities. The trend is hailed with approval as though, in an ideal world, every boy and girl in the country ought to have a university education. The Government appears to share this delusion, since it is feverishly trying to divert funds from more worthwhile objects, or the still more desirable aim of reducing taxation, in order to provide extra 'places'. So I was glad to see one academic, Geoffrey Strickland of Reading, launch a fierce attack, in the *Sunday Telegraph*, on university expansion plans. He would prefer to see the money spent on retaining famous old regiments, believing they provide a better form of training for those aged 18 and over. Having been subjected to both forms, I agree with Strickland, provided enlistment remains voluntary.

Universities are the most overrated institutions of our age. Of all the calamities which have befallen the 20th century, apart from the two world wars, the expansion of higher education, in the 1950s and 1960s, was the most enduring. It is a myth that universities are nurseries of reason. They are hothouses for every kind of extremism, irrationality, intolerance and prejudice, where intellectual and social snobbery is almost purposefully instilled and where dons attempt to pass on to their students their own sins of pride. The wonder is that so many people emerge from these dens still employable, though a significant minority, as we have learned to our cost, go forth well equipped for a lifetime of public mischief-making.

I remember the days when the new University of the West Midlands was designed to contribute to the reinvigoration of our car industry; instead it provided the kiss of death, by churning out Trot shop-stewards a good deal more destructive than their supposedly uneducated working-class predecessors. It is no accident that Ontario, Canada's richest province, is now being wrecked by a socialist government led by a fanatical 1960s' Rhodes Scholar. The new form of totalitarianism, Political Correctness, is entirely a university invention, and the virulent outbreak of black anti-Semitism, which has Brooklyn in violent uproar, was bred on campus in the fraudulent

'Afro-American Studies' departments. At the very moment when these evils – and others – are spreading rapidly to Britain, a Conservative government plans to expose yet more of our children to them, at public expense.

Even if you can prevent universities from doing positive harm, it is not clear what positive good they are supposed to do. They have expanded haphazardly from medieval institutions designed to train theologians and geared to the ecclesiastical year. No one has ever thought out, from scratch, the best way to provide advanced training in a secular world. We have just grafted new notions on to the same old decaying corpse. The most sensible collegiate bodies today are the expanded business schools now spreading rapidly in Latin-America – I lectured at several of them this spring, and found them admirable – but even they have been unable to cast off completely the university heritage. The fact that universities are popular with young people is neither here nor there. They still have a social value, more's the pity, and of course, during a severe recession, it makes sense for school-leavers to postpone, by three years or more, their launch into an uncertain job-market. But a visitor from another planet, unfamiliar with the history of the institution, would think it odd that our ablest boys and girls, at a time when their mental and physical powers are at their highest, are withdrawn from the service of society and kept in comparative idleness at the expense of the rest of the community, which is denied such a privilege. To those who object to this by pointing to the cultural blessings a university education confers, I reply: don't think in abstractions, turn to the real, living products. For an archetype university graduate, recipient of these inestimable advances, you need look no further than Neil Kinnock. He and the way he thinks, talks and acts, are what the system is all about.

The space-visitor might question other aspects of universities we take for granted. Ought not doctors to be trained in clinics and surgeries and hospitals? And lawyers in courts? And engineers in factories, mines and on construction sites? And teachers in schools? And civil servants in government offices? Why take them away from the background of their work and concentrate them in an academic pressure-cooker? Again, he might look at many of the university courses and decide they make no sense at all. Last week's *Times Literary Supplement* revived the old, ferocious battle about compulsory Anglo-Saxon in the Oxford English degree. A don from Corpus had no difficulty in showing that, on its own merits, 'doing' Anglo-Saxon was ridiculous. But it was made compulsory because old-fashioned academics thought taking a degree in English was a soft option anyway – which it is – and should be stiffened by forcing the undergraduates to do something hard. Take away Anglo-Saxon and there is nothing left but idleness and an increasing clutter of nonsense, such as deconstruction, post-deconstruction and the like, all expressed in hideous jargon. The contempt of the Oxford English faculty for the rational world beyond has just been exhibited by the appointment of an unrepentant Marxist to one of it chairs. By all means drop Anglo-Saxon. But if English is taught at all as a degree subject, students should be expected to show a proficiency in at least two European languages and a familiarity with their literature, as well as our own. At some stage they should be obliged to take tough papers in grammar, syntax and spelling. Good handwriting should be required too. They should be asked to produce competent verse in a wide variety of strict metres, under examination conditions. Above all, they should be expected to write clear, concise, purposeful and pleasing prose, putting arguments with logic, sense and succinctness, and without recourse to jargon.

At present they are taught few if any of these things, and examined in none. What they get, instead, is ideology, polysyllabic constipation, and a certain diabolic skill in turning works of literature into texts for preaching class hatred. English faculties at many, indeed most, universities illustrate perfectly what is wrong with the university idea and why it has no long-term future.

7 September 1991

Lend me your moisturiser, old girl

'Perfume for men has arrived', states an ad in the current issue of *Tatler*. A poll taken by Fabergé suggests that men are spending longer in the bathroom each morning and making increasing use of cosmetics to improve their appearance. Hair-gel, mousse, moisturiser, hand and cold cream, even scent – often borrowed from their wives – are being furtively but daily applied to male skins. No doubt the poll is self-serving but it confirms the evidence of my own nose and eyes. At a lunch party not long ago, I noticed at least two men who had been using make-up. Like most trends, it started in America. If, in a big city like Chicago or San Francisco, you travel down in a hotel lift around 7.30 in the morning with a phalanx of male executives heading for key breakfast appointments, the stench of toiletries is overpowering.

Are we witnessing the start of one of those great historical shifts in relations between the sexes? Until the 1820s, in most Western societies, men and women competed shamelessly to spend time, money and trouble on their personal appearance. They made equal use of glittering fabrics, strong or delicate colours, jewellery and gilt, wigs, creams and powders, and both whalebone and padding. If you look at the paintings of say, Nicholas Hilliard or Van Dyck, it is, on the whole, the men who dazzle. Puritan interludes, as during the Commonwealth of the 1650s, affected women no less than men, thus keeping the battle of the sexes equal, and they did not last long. By 1663, that old curmudgeon Anthony Wood was complaining that men were spending more on their appearance than women, and making use of scent and cosmetics, including face-patches. He said that the officers of Charles II's Life Guards were among the worst offenders. The attempts of the sexes to outdazzle each other continued throughout the 18th century.

Jane Austen, as always, was quick to scent the wind of change. In *Persuasion* (written 1815–16), she contrasted the plain, masculine naval officers she admired (two of her brothers rose to be admirals) with the silly, scented Regency buck, Sir Walter Elliot. Sir Walter regarded himself as an authority on beauty, male and female, and the means to enhance it. He was devoted to Mrs Vincent Gowland's skin-creams. When his daughter Anne arrives in Bath, he compliments her on her improved appearance. 'Had she been using anything in particular?' 'No, nothing'. 'Merely Gowland', he supposed. 'No, nothing at all'. 'Ha! He was surprised at that', adding that he recommended 'the constant use of Gowland during the spring months'. Sir Walter, who liked to lounge around Bath, on the lookout for handsome men as well as women, arm-in-arm with his friend Colonel Wallis ('Fine military figure, though sandy-haired'), was particularly hard on the appearance of naval officers. There was poor Admiral Baldwin, only 40, but 'his face the colour of mahogany, rough and rugged to the last degree, all lines and wrinkles, nine grey hairs of a side, and nothing but a dab of powder at top'. By contrast, Admiral Croft, who rents Sir Walter's house, complains to Anne that her father seemed 'rather a dressy sort of fellow for his time of life'.

He had to get his wife Sophy to help him shift all 'the large looking-glasses' from his dressing-room.

But, *pace* Sir Walter, even Admirals took a lot of trouble with their appearance. The daughter of Sir Edward Codrington, victor of Navarino, left a description of watching her father put on his powder, while she would sit 'reading to him one of Miss Edgeworth's charming little stories', her father correcting her punctuation as she did so: 'There was the white powdering cloth spread out on the carpet, the powder-puff which seemed to me to be a fairy's work, the matter-of-fact powder-knife which cleared off the fairy's work from forehead and temples.' This was the last period during which men could scrutinise the physical beauty of their own sex without being accused of homosexuality. The artist-diarist Farrington records a large, all-male breakfast at which 'Gregson the Pugilist' was displayed in the front drawing-room, stripped naked, to be admired 'on account of the fineness of his form'. Farrington also went with Sir Thomas Lawrence, the portrait-painter, to inspect a 'handsome black man' who turned out to have 'the finest figure they had ever seen'. Ladies could comment on a man's shoulders, waist and legs without seeming bold. Legs, particularly calves, were much scrutinised at dances. The Wordsworths were mortally offended when Thomas de Quincey, whom they had befriended, wrote a magazine article criticising the poet's legs, and said he ought to have two pairs, one for walking and 'another for evening dress parties, when no boots lend their friendly aid to mask our imperfections from female rigorists'.

All this began to go when the revolution in male dress introduced by Brummel got a grip. True, he introduced the strap over the instep which stretched trousers tight (and caused Pope Pius VII to ban them as obscene), but in general he hated colours, favoured black, white and grey for men, and stressed the importance of cleanliness, daily baths, frequent changes of linen, and diet. He vetoed scents, unguents, grease and hair-oil, and thus prepared the way for the ultra-masculine male who took over in Victorian times. When I was a young man, only homosexuals used cosmetics. Once, up in London from Oxford for a dance, I found myself having to share a room with a queen of 25 or so. He behaved impeccably but I was fascinated to watch him make up in the morning: it took him half an hour, about par for a girl-model today.

This phase in human history, when ordinary males put up with presenting their beauty unaided, has lasted about 150 years and was bound to end. Television has played a potent part in the change.

Since politicians and other celebrities discovered the improvement make-up could bring to their appearance, they have been tempted to make discreet use of it even off the box. It is spreading rapidly, in my observation, along with the more obvious use of bright colours, glitter and jewellery among young males. It is only a matter of time before traditional male evening dress goes for good, and we are back among the silks and satins. And, when mousse and moisturiser march for men, can wigs be far behind?

21 September 1991

'Sleek and shining creatures of the chase'

Recently I sat in a canvas chair in the village street of Stogursey doing a watercolour drawing of its magnificent church of St Andrew. Originally a Benedictine foundation, c.1100, it has an odd, intriguing shape for an English parish church, and the play of light and shade on its white walls is tempting to the artist. I have painted it twice before, but on this occasion there was a silvery sky and pale sunlight which added a note of great subtlety. I was getting along splendidly and had almost finished when, suddenly, the entire foreground was filled with life. A scarlet-clad huntsman, on a noble chestnut horse, was taking a full pack of hounds out for their exercise. The sheer beauty of the dogs in shades of grey, white and yellowy-brown, almost took my breath away. I possess just enough talent, as a draughtsman, to feel intense frustration that I do not have a good deal more: how I longed in this instant, for the facility of a Stubbs or a Ben Marshall or a Munnings, to add this group to my drawing in the brief seconds before they passed out of sight!

My second thought was more sombre: if Labour has its way, this kind of scene will pass out of English village life for ever. All the villagers had come out to watch the hounds go through: their simple pleasure, like mine, would be denied. But I think we might lose more than that. My house is only a few miles away from Stogursey, up the slopes of the Quantock hills. A hundred yards from it is a copse, whose trees sway above a tangled mass of bushes growing out of a small, ancient stone quarry, abandoned perhaps hundreds of years ago. It is a haunt of foxes, whose comings and goings I watch from our terrace, sometimes with field-glasses, often with the naked eye, for they hunt rabbits right to the bottom of our garden and sometimes inside it. There are five at present, presided over by a vixen-matriarch of lithe beauty, with a white tip to her huge tail.

Will such creatures survive the banning of hunting? I do not know. There are countless foxes in the district and many packs of hounds. The hounds kill large numbers, but it is a contest of skill, which the clever foxes survive. There was a big, old dog-fox, with a bright orange coat, who also lived in the copse. He had plainly been hunted many times, and laughed at his pursuers. He disappeared two years ago, out of season, dying in his lair, no doubt, full of years and wickedness. The vixen too, will die of old age, I predict – she is too clever by half for the hounds – but I am not sure about her almost-grown cubs. One strikes me as particularly stupid. The hunt will probably get him this winter. Of course the cleverer the fox, the more kills he or she will make, of young lambs or chickens or ducks. The farmers put up with a system of control which continually improves the intelligence of the foxes because most of them hunt and are passionately devoted to the sport. But if the hunt is banned they will reach for their guns, and the gun is the great equaliser, against which intelligence is no defence. I could have shot the old orange fox many times over and, this summer, wiped out the five who live in the copse, with no difficulty, and without straying from the terrace.

I have never hunted, and it is many decades since I shot any kind of animal. Indeed nowadays I am reluctant to kill even an annoying housefly – such a miracle of God and nature is its complex, super-efficient body, when studied closely – and I give it three public warnings, as in all-in wrestling. So blood sports as such do not interest me. But, as a historian, I can accept the paradox that carefully-controlled hunting, and the survival of species, go together. If we want foxes, to observe and delight in, we must have hunting.

The same paradox applies to the red deer, the pride and beauty of the Quantocks. They are admirable creatures, noticeably bigger than the ones I see in the Highlands. The living is easier, the winter far less severe. All the same, they have only survived because Somerset and Devon are the one part of England where stag-hunting has always taken place. Like fox-hunting, it has the same effect of uniting the farming community behind a single system of control, one of whose purposes is to improve the herd. A recent survey has shown that our Quantock deer are in a fine state of health, and that their numbers are growing: there are now, it is calculated, about 800 on our little range of hills. I see them constantly, especially in the autumn and winter. There is no more dramatic sight than a long line of red deer silhouetted against the horizon on a bleak December morning. If hunting goes, some foxes will remain, but I fear we will lose our deer. They are monstrously destructive. Deer-fences are not particularly effective and cost a lot of money: many farmers are close to bankruptcy as it is. So they will shoot the deer as pests. Moreover, once the hunts are disbanded, and the watchful eyes of this system of communal control removed, the poachers from the cities will move in: they are already active.

No issue separates town and country more sharply than hunting. Recently a pop singer, who has made himself a multi-millionaire by filling the air with what are, to me and many others, hideous sounds, bought a tract of land in our part of the world, paying a high price for it, in order to impede stag-hunting. His wife is said to keep deer as pets. But in Devon and Somerset, the red deer are not pets: they are wild animals, living the life of freedom and danger for which nature designed them, as they have done for countless thousands of years. For many centuries now, their survival has been intimately linked with the lives of the farmer-huntsmen who share with them our superb hills, moors and woods. Into this network of history and custom, as delicate as gossamer in some ways, the urban ideologues thrust themselves, with their ignorance, arrogance and money. Yes: and their impudent tone of moral superiority. About the last person on earth I would listen to on moral issues is a pop singer, to me the symbol of metropolitan barbarism. Indeed, if there were a pack for hunting them, I might be inclined to subscribe. As it is, I doubt if such individuals, however rich, can destroy the local hunt: it is too deeply rooted in the community. But an urban-based Labour government, with all the power of a parliamentary statute behind it, is a different matter.

28 September 1991

It's always Christmas in the supermarket

Sociology magazines like to scrutinise supermarkets to unearth left-wing points. I read an article in one of them recently which claimed that the average income of customers declines steadily from the 9 a.m. opening onwards. The rich can 'choose their time' to shop, so go early, 'missing the crowds' and 'getting the freshest produce'. The poor shop late, are hustled and hassled, get battered fruit and veg, sometimes at reduced prices. The theory is insular and collapses completely once you go to America. When I spent a year in Washington, the hypermarket I used on M Street was open 24 hours a day, 365 days a year, and the only correlation I noticed between customer and time was that, during the small hours, even more lunatics than usual were at large.

The theory doesn't work here either, to judge by my regular visits to Sainsbury's with my wife Marigold. We go as soon as it opens and the people there are of every age, sex, colour and class. The one thing they have in common is scruffiness and, still more, impatience. If the staff are a bit late opening up, an angry crowd collects, usually led by a male shopper of the type the police describe as a 'loner', and who features in serial-rape/murder cases. There are some testy, short-fused female shoppers too, beefy ladies, not necessarily members of the Jackie Onassis Fan Club, who grip the handles of their trolleys fiercely and look as though they would like to use them to batter the doors down. I call this phenomenon Trolley Rage.

There is no question that supermarkets are a boon. The pair of us can collect a month's supplies in less than an hour. But I miss the old-style grocers' shops I visited as a small boy with my mother: the pungent smells, the enormous white aprons worn by the oleaginous assistants, the dazzling skill with which they cut cheese and bacon, and tied up the neat parcels they lovingly wrapped, while my mother sat near the counter on a tall stool studying her list. Most of all, the dramatic climax when the money and bill were put in an aerial railway and whizzed up to the lady in the high cash-box, then came crashing back with the change, bells ringing furiously. Children today get none of these pleasures, though it's true they enjoy riding on the trolleys.

My other complaint is that the taxonomy of our supermarket is eccentric, rather like the arrangement of books in the London Library, and seems to follow the workings of a woman's mind, rather than mine. I find myself hunting in vain for Bovril among Sauces and Condiments, where it logically ought to be. Instead it is to be found under Meat. Well, you may say, it is a meat product. So it is, but then what is Marmite doing there too, and that fearsome Australian favourite, Vegemite? I also have trouble with starch, which is not as you might expect under Washing Materials but jostling the hair-sprays. But I can see why a female, even say Baroness Blackstone, would lump them together.

Needless to say, Marigold's list has all the interesting items on it, as they require expertise. I get Detergents, Dishwasher Salt and other dull things. It is not so easy as one might suppose either, as she is most particular and explicit. No use getting Fresh Care Automatic Non-Biological, when what she wants is Non-Biological Persil Original. I am sometimes bewildered by the variety. I find it hard going when I am told to get 'loo-paper', or what I would call bumf. Should it be Bio-degradable Nature, or Low-Grade-Waste Greencare, or Recycled Environment-Friendly Revive, or Non-Chloric Bleached Nouvelle, or just old-fashioned Luxury Supersoft?

There are times indeed when, as I anxiously scrutinise the shelves, all their regiments of clamorous products congeal into a shiny mist. Here, for instance, are the multitudes of punchy-named cleansing-fluids: Vax, Vim, Jif, Oz, Bif, Bam, Bash, Flash, Ajax, Wham, Fresh and Bim, not forgetting Shiny Smiles and Lime Light. But what I have to get, when and if I can identify it, is Mr Muscle Spray Trigger-Top, and none other. What is more, Mr Muscle, discovered at last, turns out to have his own family, all different. Well might Captain Cuttle say, 'When found, make a note of.' Dizzy and dazzled by it all, I lean against the shelves, my mind wanders and I am liable to go off with someone else's trolley, often with an indignant toddler in it.

The mind-boggling fecundity of capitalism, in short, has its drawbacks. There is almost too much choice. I used to feel this even more strongly in Washington, especially when I visited the up-market hyper-deli in Georgetown, which has 150 different kinds of bread and over 200 cheeses. It is not surprising that Russians, on their first visit, can't believe it's real. When, some time back, a Soviet pilot absconded to the West with a new-model Mig, and was in due course taken round a Californian supermarket, he thought it had all been put on specially for him, like a Potemkin village. The idea that it was everyday stuff for 250 million Americans was impossible for him to grasp.

Supermarkets sometimes astonish me too. I only discovered last week that the magic eye at the check-out can differentiate between orange, green and red peppers, and mark them up accordingly. But, as always, the real surprises are the human ones. This gaunt, hungry-looking fellow, just checking out in front of me, what has he got in his trolley? Why, nothing but six Harpic Red-Tops, three dozen tins of Kleenoff Drain-Opener, a large yule-log cake and 12 Mars Bars. He's a loner too, or perhaps a visiting member of the Addams family. Has he carved up his wife, and is he about to dispose of the pieces, followed by a rich celebratory feast? The girl at the desk tots up the bizarre contents of his argosy without batting one false eyelash, and he pays with a £50-note. Outside, it is freezing, and an ancient, crumbling figure, wearing a crushed top-hat and straight out of Gissing, is playing 'White Christmas' on a hurdy-gurdy. The Kleenoff man gives him a pound coin before loading his purchases into a smart new Volvo. A supermarket makes me feel like a character in Pirandello, unable to distinguish between illusion and fact: does the real world lie within the glittering shop, or on the cold pavement outside? And will there be spiritual supermarkets in Heaven?

21 December 1991

For correctness doth make cowards of us all

There is a deep, ineradicable human need to be shocked by words or images, and therefore a corresponding urge to censor. I never believe people when they say they support total freedom of expression. They all have reservations in certain areas, which of course vary according to their cultural posture. A novelist or playwright who stuffs his work with four-letter words or 'full-frontals' would be outraged if he heard someone refer to a 'nigger' instead of a 'black'. Conversely, many people who would like to abolish the Race Relations Act would welcome tougher obscenity laws and a revival of the powers of the Lord Chamberlain. The desire to suppress is permanent in all our hearts; only the object changes. In due course, I dare say, 'black' may become censorable among the Politically Correct, and 'negro' restored to favour. Political Correctness itself is a modern variant of the old American Puritan tradition, once directed against witches, fallen women, the poems of Walt Whitman and burlesque shows. The woman academic at Penn State who recently objected to a print of Goya's 'Naked Maja', and obliged the university to remove it, speaks for this tradition. A hundred years ago she would also have objected, but on religious grounds: the Maja's nakedness would then have been an affront to 'decency', an insult to the 'purity of women'.

Now she uses the cant term of the 1990s: it is a case of 'sexual harassment'.

A hundred years ago, one need hardly say, the print would not have been displayed in the first place. It would be instructive to know when it was first acquired and put up by the university authorities. I suspect towards the end of the 1960s, reflecting an earlier archae-ological layer of progressive correctitude, when the need to 'abolish taboos' was paramount. For the painting is, and was intended to be, an affront to the prudish. Indeed, it is disturbing in all sorts of ways. Like nearly all the great reclining nudes, including those by Titian, Velazquez and Manet, it reflects the almost insoluble difficulties painters find in displaying the whole of a woman's nakedness and, at the same time, suggesting repose. The girl's body is not sunk in the cushions, as it ought to be; it is as though she is holding herself rigid to present the maximum display. Her legs are particularly awkward and her feet unnaturally placed. Her arms are stiff and do not support her head. Indeed, the head looks as though it belongs to another body and was simply stuck on, omitting the neck. I find it uncomfortable to look at this painting, for reasons which have nothing to do with sex.

Nevertheless, it is also potent sexually, as its history suggests. When it came to London, together with its pendant, the 'Clothed Maja', in May 1990, the National Gallery published a little pamphlet, *Goya's Majas*, by Enriqueta Harris and Duncan Bull, setting out what is known – not much, alas – about the pair, and I recommend it to anyone interested in this controversy. Until recently, Spain had always been a prudish country and it was rare for a painting of a naked woman to be displayed, even in private. Velazquez's 'Toilet of Venus' was an exception. Goya's Majas are particularly provocative, and the naked one even reveals pubic hair, perhaps for the first time in European art. Goya seems to have painted them for, or given them to, the all-powerful and lascivious minister, Manuel Godoy, who built up an enormous art collection at the turn of the 18th century. Most of it was for public display, but he also had a secret apartment or 'inner cabinet', described by a visitor in 1800 as hung with 'pictures of various Venuses'. An inventory of 1808 says it contained not only 'Goya: Nude gypsy/clothed gypsy, both reclining', but also Velazquez's 'famous Venus', given to Godoy by the rich and emancipated Duchess of Alba, no doubt in return for a political favour.

The Duchess, who was a friend, patron and possibly lover of Goya, is often said to have provided the body, though not the head, for the two Majas. In 1945, the current Duke of Alba actually had his forebear exhumed, hoping by measuring her dimensions to disprove the tale, which has nonetheless persisted. Goya was 50 when he spent several months, in 1797, at the Andalucian villa of the Duchess, then a widow of 34. He not only painted a standing figure of her, pointing to two words on the ground, 'Solo Goya', but filled a sketch-book with suggestive drawings of ladies. One of them is certainly the Duchess, showing her legs and backside bare, the rest clothed, and is possibly a joke allusion to the two Majas. Even amid the turmoil of French revolutionary Europe, there was something pretty shocking about Goya's artistic relations with the lady.

Goya was not only daring, even reckless, but a great survivor. He kept afloat throughout all the tempests which engulfed Spain in the early 19th century. The restorations of the Bourbons, however, involved the return of the Inquisition, and on 16 March 1815, when he was 68, he was summoned to appear before its Tribunal, under Section II of the Rules of Expurgation, to 'inspect' the two Majas, which the Tribunal was apparently holding, 'and declare if they are his works and why he made them, to whose order and to what purpose'. But no response from Goya has survived and there is no record of the proceedings, if any occurred. In March 1815, of course, Europe was suddenly plunged in uproar again by Bonaparte's escape from Elba, and in the uncertainty the case against Goya may have been dropped. Or he got one of his innumerable powerful friends to intervene. At all events, Goya went unpunished and the two paintings survived, to shock and intrigue future generations.

The print to which the woman objected, on the other hand, was promptly taken down. Every American university, it appears, has a special body which listens to complaints from those who feel them-selves 'oppressed' or 'harassed', and there is an interstate enforcement agency which keeps them up to the mark. They both acted quickly in this case and the 'Naked Maja' was consigned to outer darkness. It is a significant comment on our times to compare the two attempts to censor the little wanton. In the year of Waterloo, the Inquisition, symbol of reaction, in the name of traditional morality, failed to get its way. In 1991, the forces of progress, in the name of Political Correctness, succeeded without difficulty. It seems to me that, in our supposedly enlightened age, there is a lot of prudery, intolerance and censorship about – and a good deal of cowardice too.

30 November 1991

Paris is still worth a Mass, just

A short trip to Paris to see the Géricault exhibition at the Grand Palais. No one ever painted horses better, and the show was crowded with tweedy provincial ladies, up from Anjou and Normandy, chattering about *les coupes* and *les écourtées* (Géricault was particularly good at doing rumps and tails). Deluging rain all the time, and it was annoying to discover that they had not bothered to move the artist's masterpiece. 'The Raft of the Medusa', to the Palais, so we had to tramp to the Louvre to see it, further irritated by the sententious remark in the catalogue, 'The walk will be good for your health'. President Mitterrand's monstrous glass pyramid outside the Louvre never fails to enrage, especially when seen in the wet. Like the pharaohs, he built two small, ancillary pyramids by the side of his own, principal one. The first is for Madame la Présidente, no doubt. But the second? Perhaps for Edith Cresson, the *tricoteuse* Mrs Thatcher.

The French socialist régime, having abandoned Marxism, and forgotten the working class completely, is fiercely nationalistic. The atmosphere inside the Louvre is one of French cultural triumphalism, echoed in the Metro station below, which is superbly decorated. Not all these Metro face-lifts come off: the Bastille has a vulgar historical mural, badly drawn, garishly coloured, inaccurate; and above it, of course, is the new opera house, another eyesore built to Mitterrand's ego. But there are compensations. The big mid-19th century church of the Trinity, one of my favourites, is being completely restored, not before time. They have also just finished rebuilding and modernising the immense 1862 organ of St Sulpice, and we went to the inaugural concert there.

There are 250 major church organs in Paris, 24 classified as historical monuments, and this one, built by the great Cavaillé-Coll, must be the loudest, having inspired Widor's tremendous organ symphonies. Widor was one of many famous composers (another was François Couperin) who were organists at St Sulpice. He held the job for 63 years, retiring only when he was 90. Most of the programme thus consisted of 'local' works, including one by César

Franck, who often played on this magnificent instrument. St Sulpice is the only church in Paris, apart from Notre Dame, which will seat over 5,000 people, and it was packed: hierarchs, ministers, *le gratin*, two choirs, one of over 200 voices, the vast, rapt audience huddled together in glistening raincoats, umbrellas dripping; the darkness in the cavernous old church almost total except for a spotlight or two, huge waves of sound rolling over our heads and shaking the massive pillars of Caen limestone – quite an occasion.

Afterwards we went to Le Balzar, now said to be the smartest place to eat on the Left Bank, but it was after ten, full, and I was not prepared to wait in the bar for a table. There was another reason. In these fashionable joints, they push the tables close together and this means that, just as you are about to tuck in, the people on either side of you light up their Caporals and think nothing of puffing smoke right in your face. In this respect the French are totally unreconstructed: they are all nicotine addicts still and their smoking-manners are frightful. Draconian anti-smoking laws have now been proposed by the socialists. As in Britain, they proclaim that the nation's health is their prime concern. But Messrs Kinnock and Co. might note that rows between the government and health service employees are much fiercer in socialist France than over here. Only last week, they did not hesitate to use water-guns and tear-gas against protesting nurses, one of whom had her eardrums per-manently damaged by the high-pressure hoses.

While socialist ministers gun down ill-paid nurses, they have high-spending lifestyles which would make even Tarzan Heseltine raise his eyebrows. Women ministers, in particular, were kitting-up at the fashion collections, which were raging last week. Martine Aubrey (Employment) goes to the top Japanese designer, Kenzo; her pretty young colleague at Sport, Fréddie Bredin, patronises Yves St Laurent, as does Elisabeth Guigou (Europe), while Cresson herself favours Dior. The mind boggles at what these women must spend on their clothes.

Marigold and I visited some of the boutiques on the Place des Victoires which is now, under the disapproving gaze of Louis XIV on horseback, a hub of the fashion industry, though by no means the most expensive one. The prices were astronomical. Outfits are £1,000 up. When Cresson took office, her prime ministerial trousseau, I calculate, must have cost at least £20,000. Nobody seems to mind. But I recalled that, only a generation ago, the French socialist party was run almost entirely by small-town schoolteachers. Now it attracts the hard-faced go-getters, the ultra-ambitious, the grabbers and the successful. In Britain, the radical rich patronise socialism. In France they run the show.

Nor do they scruple to have their outriders push ordinary commuters off the road to make way for ministerial cortèges in the rush-hour. Paris is now a ritzy, poshed-up city, kept beautifully clean, which puts London's dingy streets to shame; but its traffic jams are horrible. Everyone keeps a car in central Paris, and uses it, all the time. They park their cars, with apparent impunity, right across the pavement so pedestrians have to walk in the roadway at their extreme peril. The jams into and out of the city are much worse than in London or New York. Arriving at De Gaulle airport, we took the best part of two hours by taxi to reach the Rue Cambon. Going back, we did a 50-mile detour to avoid the Saturday night foul-up in the west of the city. The plane was full of well-behaved, middle-class rugger fans, some of them clutching very small union jacks. 'We beat the froggies', they said quietly. Well, so I should think. Not much else for the British to rejoice in at present.

26 October 1991

A good old literary row

There is nothing I enjoy more than a literary row, and for this reason alone I applaud Nicholas Mosley's marching out of the Booker Prize jury, pursued by angry letters from Jeremey Treglowan and other luminaries. I also agree with him on the substance of his protest, that the kind of people who dominate these juries tend to short-list gimmicky novels, which have to be read backwards, upside down etc. I find it hard to think of anything, even the Arts Council, which has done more harm to English literature than the Booker Prize. Some time ago I criticised it strongly in this journal and, as a result, the chairman of Booker-McConnell, which provides the money, came to see me to ask how I thought it could be improved. I told him the prize should be awarded not by those who belong to the literary world, but by a jury of people outside it – schoolteachers, librarians, ordinary readers. He was aghast: 'Oh dear, I was thinking rather of some fine-tuning.' One has to remember that one of the attractions to businessmen who endow such awards is the opportunity to hobnob with literary celebrities ('As Salman was saying to me the other day ...'). They are less keen on meeting librarians. Moreover, a jury of ordinary readers might be in serious danger of picking the best novel but would certainly not generate the publicity which Booker squabbles invariably provide.

At a publisher's lunch last month we were talking about the propensity of writers, supposedly a sedentary lot, to engage in fights. I suggested an anthology, *The Oxford Book of Literary Rows*, and the publisher's eyes immediately lit up: 'That *would* sell!' Was not Christopher Marlowe actually killed in one of these tiffs? (By one Ingram Frizer, I believe; no doubt a theatre critic.) Not so long ago a bad review could lead to a duel. That was how poor John Scott, the brilliant editor of the *London Magazine*, who published the best of Lamb and Hazlitt, met his end. A friend, given a lift by Byron in his carriage, recorded that he 'kept his pistols beside him and continued silent for hours with the most ferocious expression possible on his countenance'. Another hasty review, I dare say. Byron nearly fought a duel with Tom Moore, and swore he would challenge Southey, then Poet Laureate, for saying he and Shelley formed 'a league of incest'. But nothing came of it. Hazlitt, a notoriously savage reviewer, went in mortal fear of a challenge, though the only violence to which he was actually subjected occurred when Charles Lamb's brother, John, knocked him down, 'following an argument about the colours of Holbein and Van Dyke'. It always amazes me that W.S. Landor, the most argumentative writer who ever lived – he figures as Boythorne in *Bleak House* – avoided a fatal encounter. Of course by the time Dickens had his famous Garrick Club row over his side-kick Edmund Yates, who had written a hostile profile of Thackeray, duelling was out.

Acts of violence I would like to have witnessed include the episode which led to the expulsion of Evelyn Waugh from the Beefsteak, described as 'fighting with the servants', or an even more bizarre row which brought about his departure from the Savile Club: unable to find the porter, who had the key to a large glass case containing cigars, which stood in the hall, he simply smashed it open with his Malacca cane. But I was fortunately present, outside the Savile – we had all just debouched from a taxi – when Maurice Richardson spread-eagled Henry Fairlie on the pavement ('Take that, you impudent whippersnapper!') for saying be 'belonged to the older generation'. The taxi-driver, evidently a sneaky fellow, reported the incident to the police, saying that 'an 'orrible fight' had broken out outside the

Savile Club. Happily the police, by a natural association of ideas, charged off to the Savage.

Maurice had been, at one time in a wandering life, a professional boxer, with a broken nose to prove it. John Davenport, by contrast, had not fought professionally but was even stronger and much more aggressive. The most desperate battle he engaged in was in the company of the novelist Gerald Hanley, author of *The Consul at Sunset*. They found themselves, one St Patrick's night, in a rather disreputable pub (since disappeared) near the Royal Court Theatre in Sloane Square. It was much frequented by the Irish and, following an unwise remark by John, casting aspersions on the morals of the Virgin Mary, the two men had to fight shoulder to shoulder to repel what Davenport called 'hordes of enraged Republicans'. But that, strictly speaking, was not a literary row.

Davenport's most famous act of aggression was to seize the diminutive Lord Maugham, then Lord Chancellor, and put him on the Savile's mantelpiece. Maugham ceased to be Chancellor in September 1939, so the business must have occurred before the war, when Davenport was the English master at Stowe, laying the foundations of the prose styles of, among others, Colin Welch and Peregrine Worsthorne. What the row was about I do not know, for it is not recorded in R.F.V. Heuton's *Lives of the Lord Chancellors, 1885–1940*. It probably had to do with the writings of Maugham's brother Somerset, of which (I recall) John did not approve. He had terrifyingly broad shoulders, powerful biceps and a barrel-chest, from which issued, oddly enough, a high, piping voice. His favourite term of abuse was 'short-arsed', and one has to imagine the scene when the outraged legal grandee ('Put me down at once, I say') was hoisted up to the shelf, accompanied by the immortal words, 'Sit there where we can all see you, you short-arsed little pipsqueak!' John, alas, sometimes hit less deserving targets. John Raymond once remarked, with some complacency, 'I always say everyone gets the Davenport he deserves.' Alas, not long afterwards, he fell foul of the monster and received what he ruefully described as 'a severe biff on the boko'.

By a curious coincidence, immediately after the lunch at which we discussed such matters, two of those present, a novelist and a journalist, were talking about this and that on the pavement outside. The journalist's wife arrived to pick up her husband and spotted the novelist, with whom she had an unresolved little disagreement, concerning a *roman à clef*. The upshot was that our budding Tolstoy got his devastating come-uppance there and then. I was not an eyewitness, so the account may be exaggerated. But one thing's for sure: it won't be the last literary row, thank God.

12 October 1991

Waiting for a few Delphic utterances

Last week's special number of the *Times Literary Supplement* on philosophy left me, as usual, wondering, what is philosophy for? I would say to A.J. Ayer, 'Freddie, teach me something useful.' To which he would reply, 'That is a foolish request. Indeed, as your formulate it, a meaningless one.' The philosophers I feel most indebted to have helped me in non-philosophical ways. Karl Popper taught me the scientific approach to truth-discovery, the most important thing I have ever learned. E.H. Gombrich, one of the few writers on aesthetics worth reading, made me aware of the physical basis of seeing art. Michael Oakshott gave me an intuitive glimpse – I would put it no higher – into political wisdom. Karl Rahner explained to me the reason why God not only exists but must exist. But these are not matters which much interest academic philosophers, the sort of people who write in the *TLS*.

They can teach you a new word or two, however: something I am always in the market for. Thus Derek Parfit, debating 'Why Does the Universe Exist?' comes up with 'axiarchy'. The word is not in the *Shorter Oxford*, so I worked it out for myself: rule by self-evident truth. The Declaration of Independence is, as it were, a celebration of axiarchy. Martha Nussbaum, writing on virtue, used 'eudaemonist', that is, one who supports an ethical system whose moral standard is the tendency of actions to promote happiness. I do not envisage using either term often but into the word bank they go. Sir Peter Strawson, on 'Echoes of Kant', is more serviceable because, like many academics, he teaches you how not to write. Consider this sentence, which made my sub-editorial pencil itch: 'Finally, while it is true that without a very high degree of causal regularity we should lack the very concepts of those relatively persisting objects which sustain the spatio-temporal unity of the world, the argument for the universal reign of natural causality – for absolute determinism – remains inconclusive.' First, I take out the 'finally', since there are still eight paragraphs, most of them long ones, to come; then the two 'verys', rarely necessary except for humorous purposes. 'Spatio-temporal' is otiose. But these preliminary elisions do not get one far: the sentence remains obscure and ought to be rewritten *ab initio*. What he means is: the laws of physics are useful but may not always work.

I used to argue with a tall, elegant lady philosopher, co-panellist on a television programme, who often rebuked me for loose reasoning. 'My thinking is muddled only according to the arbitrary rules of your particular academic jargon, to which I do not subscribe. Your "philosophy", as you like to call it, is no more than a don's parlour game.' 'Nonsense,' she would reply. 'We philosophers use exactly the same language as everyone else, the only difference being that we take more care and employ more precision.' 'In that case, since the object of language is communication, why is it often so difficult to understand what your lot are trying to say?' 'That is a failing, it is not invalidation.' And so on. Bertrand Russell was the only philosopher I have come across who always conveyed his meaning clearly and, because he did, you could debate the merits of his conclusions; and they were usually wrong. Even when he said something which was true, brief research into his *oeuvre* immediately revealed that he had also asserted the opposite, usually a short time before. Nobody disputed Russell had a powerful brain. But equally, no one in his or her senses would go to him for advice on anything that mattered.

And after all, isn't that what a philosopher ought to be – a person to whom you turn in search of wisdom, an oracle? Recently I heard John Major say that he wished Adam Smith were still alive so that he could ask his opinion. It is painfully apparent that Messrs Major and Lamont do not know what they ought to do about the British economy, any more than President Bush knows what to do about America's. If they all joined forces and held a synod of economists from Harvard, Oxford, Yale and Cambridge, they would be none the wiser but certainly deafened by the babel of conflicting voices. If, like me, they believe that economic policy is more a philosophical matter than a technical one, and turned to Quine and Strawson, Rawls, Dworkin, Dummett and, in desperation, Baroness Warnock, they would still be wasting their time. (Though a transcript of the answers, ruthlessly subbed, would make an amusing Sunday newspaper article.)

In India, even today, holy men squat on their haunches at shrines, waiting for folks to glean their wisdom. In the black quarters of Washington DC, you see notices in the windows of houses saying

'Counselling'; but that means astrology. The latest big city fashion is for local authorities to employ 'counsellors'; but this is presumably a dodge to get on the payroll left-wing activists who are otherwise unemployable. The genuine guru is now an endangered species, at least in the West. People travelled hundreds of miles to Weimar to consult Goethe or to Thomas Jefferson in Monticello or Carlyle in Chelsea or Ruskin on Coniston Lake or to pop questions to Edison on his front porch; not so long ago they went to I Tatti to look up Berenson or to Rapallo to tap Max Beerbohm. They still flock to Harold Acton at La Pietra. But no one in the whole world would dream of crossing the street to consult a modern philosophy don.

So what is philosophy for, then? I recall, in the late 1940s, leaning against the iron fence at Magdalen, watching the deer in the park. Similarly engaged was the formidable Gilbert Ryle, then editor of *Mind*. A dapper figure passed in view hurrying across the lawns. 'Do you know who that is?' asked Ryle. 'No.' 'It is A.J. Ayer. Might have been a great philosopher. Ruined by sex.' The figure disappeared, at speed, as though to a much anticipated assignation. Years later, I called at Ayer's house in London, on a journalistic assignment. The door opened to reveal a voluptuous young lady, in tight sweater and trousers, most unusual in those days. Taken aback by this apparition, I asked fatuously, 'Am I addressing Mrs Ayer?' She replied with a smile, 'I wish you were.' So Freddie, at any rate, knew what philosophy – or a reputation as a great philosopher – was for, and one doctrine he never subscribed to was Platonic love. Doubtless philosophy has other uses too. What it seems unable to do, in our day, is to tell us how to live, or die.

18 July 1992

Sinister serpents of old Nile

A photograph published this week shows Japanese tourists braving a blizzard to visit the Acropolis. It has been snowing in Jordan too. The eastern Mediterranean, and adjacent parts, have had one of the coldest winters on record. Earlier this month a great wind swept over Cairo, killing people and raising an immense dust-storm. We felt the effect many miles up the Nile, where we were cruising, witnessing crimson sunsets of unusual intensity. The wind was cold too, but that I did not mind, disliking heat more. Travelling slowly by boat up the Nile is still one of the most voluptuous of human pleasures, and I enjoy sitting, well muffled up, on deck, making endless watercolour sketches as the banks slip by, with their egrets, camels, donkeys and minarets, and peasants gorgeously attired in lilac and heliotrope, tangerine and sanguine.

Discount tales that the low level of the Nile makes cruising it impossible. Nor is it true, as a *Times* leader put it, that 'mass marketing of exotic travel has turned the Nile into something as cheaply nasty as the traffic jam at Boulter's Lock'. Of course there are difficulties, and firms which run these cruises should come clean with travellers in advance. But the Nile has always posed problems, as Kitchener and others discovered. The British built barrages, and even shallow-draught boats find negotiating their locks tricky, sometimes imposs-ible, when there is not enough water. Our boat had a tremendous tussle with the lock at Nag' Hammadi and at one point appeared truly stuck, but we got through in the end to a tremendous huzzah. In Egypt, as in Ireland, suspenseful activities always attract a lot of idlers, who generously provide unsolicited advice. I had time to paint a group of these experts as they stood or squatted on the lockside.

Egypt is, or ought to be, the paramount symbol of continuity, since in some ways things have not changed much since the 4th mil-lennium BC, when our detailed knowledge begins. The country rejects the unsympathetic innovator. When the young pharaoh Amenhotep IV changed his name to Akhenaton and carried through a religious revolution, he found the Theban establishment frostily uncooperative. So he removed himself and his followers to a horrific sun-trap down river at a place now called Amarna, and there they all lived in a kind of concentration camp. I imagine Akhenaton as a pseudo-intellectual, his head full of half-formulated notions, rather like Prince Charles, but with more willpower.

While he lived, his leading sculptor, Tuthmosis, did a good trade, for it was doubtless the thing for a member of the Amarna ruling class to have the king's head prominently displayed in his villa, just as today images of President Mubarak are found in countless humble homes. When Akhenaton died, the régime collapsed, Tuthmosis disappeared and men with hammers disfigured his images of the king, which were found in the rubbish of his studio thousands of years later, alongside unsaleable model heads of Amarna dignitaries. A model of Queen Nefertiti's head was left, literally, on the shelf. The shelf collapsed, centuries later, and the head fell safely onto a soft pile of mud rubble from the walls, and so was preserved, minus one eye. It is now in Berlin, a reminder of the fate of those who try to change Egypt.

The present troubles of the Nile are due in part to another heedless revolutionary, Gamal Abdel Nasser. He was that most dangerous political type: the man who is good at public relations and nothing else. The British had treated the Nile with respect. Their barrages, which did not essentially change its annual flooding system, culminated at Aswan in a dam, built in 1898–1902, and thereafter twice heightened.

Nasser was not content with this but, soon after he came to power, announced he would build an enormous new dam which would harness the river and transform the country. When the British and the Americans declined to finance it, Nasser nationalised the Suez Canal and brought down on his people a ruinous war. So it was the Russians who built and paid for the High Dam. As we are now learning, they have a long and disastrous record of trying to improve on nature by vainglorious schemes.

Harnessing the Nile in this brutal manner plainly brings some advantages. It supplies large quantities of electricity and, in theory at least, water wherever and whenever it is wanted. About 2 million acres, it is said, have been reclaimed or perennially irrigated. On the other hand, the High Dam has created a huge, straggly expanse called Lake Nasser, which has increased not only the rainfall but, more importantly, the humidity of southern Egypt, making the summer unbearable. The lake offers warm hospitality to malaria-carrying mosquitos and the snails which spread that curse of Egypt, bilharzia. The rich sediment which the annual Nile flood once spread over all its fertile banks and was the key to the country's prosperity for most of its history – as Herodotus noted, the Egyptian peasant had an easy time – now settles on the bottom of the lake, and there has been a sinister increase in salinity. Deprived of natural fertiliser, the farmers use expensive chemical ones which, among other noxious side-effects, have produced a dramatic growth of weeds which disfigure the river.

Damming has forced the authorities to remove, at immense cost, some of the monuments of ancient Egypt, notably Rameses II's spectacular temple at Abu Simbel. But others are covered by the waters and will never be seen again. Moreover, water leaks from the lake and pops up in unwanted places, undermining and destroying yet more precious relics of the past. The unforeseen consequences of Nasser's hubris seem unending and there may well be other nasty shocks in store.

Far from being deterred by stories of boats getting stuck, people who have never seen the Nile and its matchless treasures should go as soon as possible, while they're all still there.

29 February 1992

Valkyries riding over Jerusalem?

It is easy to sympathise with those Israelis who do not want Wagner's music to be played in their country. Wagner was an exceptionally unpleasant man and not the least of his nastier characteristics was his venomous anti-Semitism. It was not just the commonplace anti-Semitism of the day and age either; it was deep-rooted, ideological and intertwined with Wagner's whole approach to music, especially his own. It was also coloured by the fear, now known to be unfounded, that he himself was Jewish. During his radical period Wagner, like Marx (five years his junior), was much influenced by the young Hegelians, such as Bruno Bauer, who held the Jews responsible for many of the ills of the world. Marx produced his anti-Semitic tract, *On the Jewish Question*, in 1843–4, and five years later Wagner followed with his essay *Jewishness in Music*, arguing that Jews were poisoning musical culture just as Marx maintained they were poisoning society as a whole. Wagner concluded that only by renouncing their Jewishness could the Jews (and music) be redeemed, echoing Marx's conclusion: 'The social emancipation of the Jews is the emancipation of society from Judaism.'

These two evil men thought that by exposing the Jewish basis of bourgeois society they could bring about radical change. Marx expanded his anti-Semitic theory into his general theory of capitalism, a process largely complete by 1848 when he published his *Communist Manifesto*. The following January, Wagner began to work on a five-act scenario for an opera, *Jesus von Nazareth*, which portrayed Jesus as a social revolutionary, preaching that property is a crime against nature, and thus posing a threat to the rich Jewish priestly aristocracy, who had him destroyed. Nothing came of this project and in time Wagner moved away from radicalism, but his anti-Semitism, if anything, became more intense. In 1869, as if in protest at Bismarck's final emancipation of the Prussian Jews, Wagner republished his essay on Jews and music. A decade later, in an essay entitled *Modern*, he broadened his charge to assert that Jews were now dominating German culture as a whole and stealing the national heritage, including the language. This and other writings of Wagner were important in shaping 20th-century German opinion, especially under the Weimar Republic, where the alleged 'theft' and 'poisoning' of the race-*Kultur* of Germany was potent in converting middle-class Germans to apocalyptic forms of anti-Semitism and so to Hitlerism. Wagner charged: 'I regard the Jewish race as the born enemy of pure humanity and everything that is noble in it; it is certain we Germans will go down before them, and perhaps I am the last German who knows how to stand up as an art-loving man against the Judaism which is already getting control of everything.' This was very much Hitler's message: to some extent, indeed, inspired it, for Hitler was profoundly influenced by Wagner's music and thought.

Oddly enough, though Wagner's anti-Semitism was universally known – it pervaded his whole life – a number of distinguished Jewish musicians were associated with him. They included Joseph Rubinstein, Carl Tausig, Heinrich Porges and, above all, Hermann Levi, who conducted the first performance of Wagner's great 'Christian' opera, *Parsifal*. Such men abased themselves before the little tyrant and he exploited them, especially Levi, ruthlessly. But then he exploited everyone. Even more surprising, and perhaps less well known, is that Theodor Herzl, the founder of modern Zionism and thus the progenitor of Israel, was a passionate admirer of Wagner's music. Indeed he frequently heard Wagner at the opera house while writing his great work, *Der Judenstaat*, and claimed it inspired him: 'Only on the nights when Wagner was not performed did I have doubts about the correctness of my idea.' Herzl was a bit of a showman and made elaborate plans for the gorgeous ceremonies which were to accompany the actual founding of the Zionist state, including the 'coronation' of its elected ruler or 'doge', who would be a Rothschild. Wagner's music was to play a big part in these events.

Herzl, it seems to me, had the right approach; to treat Wagner's anti-Semitism as the expression of the base, the unredeemed part of the man's nature, and his music as something quite apart: an example of the way divine providence endows even the wicked with genius which transcends them. I have argued, in my book *Intellectuals*, that you cannot entirely separate the private life and the public works of writers, especially those who put forward proposals to transform the whole nature and condition of mankind: weaknesses in conduct tend to be reflected in weaknesses of argument – Marx being an outstanding example. You occasionally find the same thing in a painter: there is, for example, a visible streak of cruelty in some of the works of Ribera, to which his violent and ruffianly life provides a clue. But as a rule a painter and his canvases can be separated, and in music, which is so abstract an art, it seems to be possible to divorce completely the human personality from the composer. The meannesses, smallness of mind, lying and cheating of Beethoven find no echo in his music. In Wagner, despite all the intense German-ness of his thematic material, the anti-Semitic side makes no appearance. It is sometimes argued that one or two of his villains are anti-Semitic archetypes. Maybe they are, but not to the point where such a gloss cannot be removed entirely in production.

It is, too, significant, that anti-Semitism makes no appearance in that most sacramental of his works, *Parsifal*. It is almost as though, when Wagner's genius is at its fiercest, his anti-Semitism is, by that very fact, buried. Or so I would argue. Wagner's music can inspire all kinds of different emotions, often contradictory ones. It can doubtless deprave and corrupt, like other great works of art. But it can also ennoble, and at its best that is, in the end, its salient characteristic. In short, we might call Wagner a high-risk composer. But then taking risks is a necessary element in maintaining civilisation. Israel itself is a huge risk, a great adventure, embarked upon by men and women who put their ideals, their vision, above their comfort and safety, and so far the risk has proved abundantly worth it. Playing Wagner is a further, tiny hazard that Israel and its brave people ought to be able to take in their stride.

4 January 1992

Let's not be slaves to humbug

The *Sunday Times* reports a growing movement in Africa to put pressure on Britain and other advanced white nations to pay 'reparations' for slavery by writing off sub-Saharan Africa's debts of $163 billion. There may be all kinds of good reasons to write off debts which African states have acquired since independence, but the issue should not be mixed up with slavery. Slavery, and the slave-trade, were not institutions created by white capitalism. They are as old as human society. So far as can be discovered, slavery had always existed in black Africa. It was the usual method of recruiting labour for gold-mines, iron-works and large farms. Skilled labourers, such as blacksmiths, tended to be slaves. Slaves were also used to transport goods in long-distance trade and as a form of universally negotiable currency in commercial transactions. When Europeans arrived to create the transatlantic slave-trade, they were welcomed by most African chiefs, for whom exporting slaves was a bonus on top of other rewarding aspects of the slave system. They benefited hugely from it, especially in acquiring firearms, and when in due course Britain led the international campaign against the slave-trade, the chiefs were most reluctant to give it up. When Britain and the United States set up colonies of free slaves repatriated from the Americas – Sierra Leone in 1808 and Liberia in 1819 – they had to be defended by cannon and stockades from the local rulers, who rightly saw them as a threat to their profits. Descendants of these slaving chiefs are still prominent in African politics.

The truth is, if the misdeeds of ancestors can be passed on to their progeny, like Original Sin, all societies have a legacy of guilt over slavery. But Britain's ought to be lighter than most because of its redemptive record. It is true that British appetites and interests were important in building up international slavery as a huge commercial force. In the 18th century, our per capita consumption of sugar was the highest in the world and successful West Indian estate-owners, who possessed thousands of slaves, were the richest people in Britain. Our ships carried a large proportion of the 11.5 million blacks transported across the Atlantic, and the rise and prosperity of Liverpool was due, in large part, to the profits of the slave-trade.

On the other hand, it is arguable that, without Britain, institutionalised slavery would still exist in most parts of the world. Though the French Revolutionary government was the first to condemn slavery, root and branch, and to proclaim universal rights irrespective of race, the French did little to put their ideas into practice and later reneged on them; the British achieved a great deal more in promoting these objectives. The great humanitarian Thomas Clarkson (1760–1846), who was as influential as Wilberforce in making the slave-trade unlawful, gives in his history of the abolitionist movement a substantial list of British writers who argued against slavery, ranging from Aphra Behn, through Defoe, Pope, Shenstone, Savage, to James Thomson and Dr Johnson. Johnson, in particular, never missed an opportunity to condemn slavery and shocked the dons at an Oxford high table by toasting 'success to the next revolt of the Negroes in the West Indies'.

By the 1790s, indeed, boycotting products produced by slave labour was a favourite activity of the English chattering classes. In 1797, when Coleridge was with Wordsworth and his sister Dorothy in West Somerset, all three used conscientiously to sweeten their tea or coffee with honey, which was Politically Correct, rather than sugar, which was not. But some chatterers denied the political correctness of tea and coffee too. Cobbett begged readers of his *Examiner* to use roasted wheat as a form of *ersatz* coffee. The *Black Dwarf* urged the public to make tea from hay, and coffee from a mixture of roasted peas and mustard. By then, of course, slavery was already unlawful in Britain. 22 June 1772 was a important date in world history, when, in the Somerset case, Lord Chief Justice Mansfield ruled that slavery was inadmissible under the Common Law since it was 'so odious that nothing can be suffered to support it but positive law'. That judgment covered Wales and Ireland as well as England, and the Scots followed suit in 1778.

We were not the first country to outlaw the slave-trade – that honour goes to Denmark, which banned it in 1802, five years before Wilberforce got his abolition bill on to the Statute Book – but we were the first and for many years the only nation to enforce it with severe penalties and vigorous international action. We had to bribe such countries as Spain and Portugal, and bully others, like France, Brazil and the Netherlands, into following us in making the trade unlawful. Lining up a reluctant international community behind us on this issue was a primary aim of Castlereagh's foreign policy, because by this time the anti-slavery campaign had become the cause of the entire British people. As he put it, 'The nation is bent upon this object. I believe that there is hardly a village which has not met and petitioned on it.' The actual suppression of the trade was very largely the work of the Royal Navy. Generations of British seamen, who felt passionately on the subject, risked their lives to arrest the slavers who kept the trade going. Ending the slave-trade was the greatest and most enduring of all the triumphs of Britain's 'gunboat diplomacy'.

The role of Britain, significantly enough, was acknowledged at the time by the first black supremacist, the Haitian patriot Pompée

Valentin de Vastey. Writing in the early 19th century, he argued that cultural history had been taught with a white bias, and that Africa was the real 'cradle of the sciences and the arts'. Sooner or later, 'five hundred million men, black, yellow and brown' would reclaim 'the rights and privileges which they have received from the author of nature'. But he admitted that 'noble and generous England' had been 'the principal power in Europe that took a lively interest in our fate', and blacks would be 'most ungrateful and injust were we ever deficient in gratitude to the people and government of England'. Vastey also foresaw that Britain had a 'civilising mission' in Africa, under an enlightened colonial policy. What he did not foresee was that we would abandon that mission too soon, and hand over the peoples of Africa to a generation of professional black politicians and soldiers, who have robbed and exploited them as ruthlessly as ever the old slaving-chiefs did. These are the men who have reduced most of black Africa to beggary and insecurity, in the process borrowing billions which they have stolen or wasted. To blame the West, and above all the British, for the ills of Africa is humbug.

11 January 1992

When the champagne started to go flat

It is simple and convenient, almost everyone likes it, and there is no other drink which gets things humming so quickly and surely. So we always serve champagne at our parties. But it is expensive and seems to have become sharply more so in the last year or two. Why this is I do not know but even the standard non-vintage house champagne we get in the local supermarket now costs over £13 a bottle. At the same time, I find that perfectly acceptable champagne (perhaps for legal reasons it is called something else) is made in at least half a dozen other countries: the United States, for instance, Australia, South Africa, Chile, Spain and Italy. The Italian champagne is particularly good. I do not say that other countries can produce wine of the quality of vintage champagne from Krug or Bollinger or Veuve-Clicquot. What I do say is that a good bottle of the Italian stuff is at least as good as its equivalent from France, and from a third to less than half the price. So that is what I am going to get in future.

There is another reason. I like the Italians and I do not like the French. That is, I have nothing against the French as a people. What I object to is the way their leaders behave towards this country. I know that France is not in any meaningful sense a democracy, that its parliament is a puppet one and its politics incorrigibly corrupt. Nevertheless, it does have elections and a constitution, and its president and other bigshots are in various ways accountable. If the French really don't like them they can always have another of their revolutions. Hence the French as a whole must, to some extent, take responsibility for the actions of their masters.

And what actions! They really seem to hate us. François Mitterrand always behaves as if the British prime minister, whoever he or she is, were a personal enemy. Edith Cresson spits anglophobia every time she opens her cruel little mouth. Jacques Delors appears to spend a great deal of his time, as the supposedly impartial and supranational president of the EEC Council of Ministers, not so much pushing French national interests – of course, he does that too – as doing everything in his considerable power to damage British ones. What is the source of his anti-British venom I do not understand. He has spent his life in academia, banking, bureaucracy and socialism, all separately conducive to a sour, malignant view of life, and in combination devastating; maybe that explains it. At all events, he is a bitter enemy of this country and since he took over his present job in 1985 he has done his best to turn the EEC into an anti-British institution.

But why the British in particular? The French have much stronger reasons to hate the Germans, who have conquered and pillaged them within living memory; or the Italians, for that matter, who turned on them like a jackal in 1940. Why us, then? I think the reason is – humiliation. We have witnessed their shame too often; we have responded with generosity and, as is sadly true, no good deed goes unpunished. A long succession of French leaders, over the past two centuries, chased out of their own country by their own angry subjects, have sought refuge and asylum on our shores and been granted it.

The first to arrive was the future Louis XVIII and his kid brother Charles. Louis was enormously greedy and fat, and grew greedier and fatter here at Hartwell, Bucks. The Duke of Wellington, dining *en famille* with him and his royal ladies, noticed a large dish of early strawberries brought in: 'The King very deliberately turned [it] into his own plate, even to the last spoonful, and ate [it] with a large quantity of sugar and cream, without offering any to the ladies.' That even beats Waugh and the bananas. The Duke also recorded that, when he had to tie the Garter ribbon round Louis' vast calf, 'it was like putting your hands round a young man's waist'. But at least he showed some gratitude. When we restored him to his throne in 1814, he said to the Prince Regent on his way back to Paris, 'It is ... to this glorious country, and to the steadfastness of its inhabitants, that I attribute, after the Will of Providence, the re-establishment of my house on the throne of its ancestors.' Louis had the wit to die on it but the brother, Charles X, was soon kicked out and by August 1830 was back in Britain, penniless, with his ridiculous Commander-in-Chief, Marmont.

Charles's successor, the Orleanist 'King of the French', Louis-Philippe, was also greedy, though more for money than food. In shape he looked like a pear. The French put up with him for 18 years, then gave him the boot. He was smuggled across the Channel by the British consul in Le Havre, who had to shave him, strip off his wig, dress him in goggles and a cap, and present him as his uncle, 'Mr Smith'. Palmerston arranged for £1,000 to be supplied to the destitute king and his family from secret service funds. He died at Claremont on the royal estate in 1850. Twenty years later, another bumptious French ruler, Napoleon III, rejected by his subjects like his uncle Napoleon I (who, be it remembered, surrendered to HMS *Bellerophon* to save his skin), took refuge here, ending up in Chislehurst. The long line of refugee embodiments of France was completed in 1940 by General de Gaulle, who was received with warmth and responded by giving us all a hard time. But, as Churchill remarked, 'The Almighty, in His infinite wisdom, did not see fit to create Frenchmen in the image of Englishmen.'

I have omitted the many French writers and artists who followed in the wake of their rulers: Victor Hugo, who took refuge in the Channel Isles, for instance, or Emile Zola, who spent a year here fleeing from the police during the Dreyfus case, or Camille Pissarro, who found asylum in Norwood, of all places. Nor, when I say de Gaulle 'completed' the list, am I sure the last name has been added. The Fifth Republic, which had done well until recent years, now looks a mighty fragile edifice. I doubt if the Paris mob has become any less bloodthirsty over the years, and hot-footing it across the Channel is still the safest move for an absconding French politician. We may yet have to accord a polite welcome to Mitterrand, Delors and Cresson, the last no doubt with hardly a single Saint-Laurent to her back, and I dare say we will find some suitable accommodation for this gruesome trio. But in the meantime, bring on the Italian fizz.

8 February 1992

Carriage folk and chauffeur persons

For over two centuries, the great dividing-line between those who were really well off and the rest was whether you kept your carriage. You were either 'carriage folk' or you were not. Moving into the carriage-keeping minority was the most obvious sign that you had arrived. There is a neatly contrived moment in Jane Austen's detective-story, *Emma*, when Frank Churchill, who has been secretly corresponding with Jane Fairfax, inadvertently lets slip the news that Mr Perry, the well-to-do apothecary of Highbury, is about to 'set up his carriage' – an important social event for Perry and his neighbours and an item of information Churchill, the second he is aware of his slip, is at a loss to explain how he came by: 'It must have been a dream.'

We are not told what kind of carriage Perry sets up. A barouche, let alone a barouche-landau, as owned by Mrs Elton's rich sister, would have been too grand. Phaetons, gigs and especially curricles were for fast young men, or sporty gents like Admiral Croft, who did not mind the odd smash or two. It might have been a sociable, with two seats facing each other. More likely it was a chaise, the standard family carriage, which held three (the post-chaise was a faster version, carrying only two). The important thing about owning your own carriage, however, was not the cost of the vehicle. It might indeed be enormous, if you had a big barouche built by a smart London coachmaker to your own specifications, with a travelling library, table, collapsible bed and a close-stool. On the other hand, you could buy one second-hand cheap and have it repainted.

The real expense was running it. A sizeable carriage needed two horses, and four for long journeys (you 'went post' after the first stage, meaning you hired horses from inns; if you hung onto your own, they had to be rested every two or three days, which slowed you down). So to begin with you required a sizeable stable, with spare horses, as well as a coach-house. That meant a groom, possibly two. Then again no gentleman, let alone a lady, drove his own coach, so you needed a coachman. He was a dignified sort of fellow, an 'upper servant', and correspondingly expensive, in vittles and livery as well as cash, and of course he was much too grand to do the work of the grooms or stable lads. In town, too, you had to have a footman (the very rich had two), who mounted up behind, elegantly swaying from foot to foot as the carriage drove round corners. His job was to jump down when the carriage stopped, dash round and lower the outside steps, then open its door with a flourish (a proper coach had no inside handles as the gentry were not accustomed to opening doors for themselves). If the lady inside were going shopping, obviously at an establishment which catered to 'the carriage trade', its proprietor would already be outside on the pavement, bowing a welcome. If, on the other hand, the lady was 'calling', the footman's job was to run up the steps of the private house and deliver a sharp 'rat-a-tat-tat' with the knocker. Everyone could recognise the footman's knock, and knew what to expect. Hence, being carriage folk brought deference. But it was endlessly expensive. And having to 'lay up' your carriage or, worse, sell it, was an unmistakable sign of diminished means, if not outright failure. Everyone knew.

The distinction today between the rich and the rest of us is more subtle, though it still has a great deal to do with transport. I am not talking about the tycoon class (in the 18th century their carriages were drawn by six horses mounted by outriders, and they had an escort of equerries). A typical tycoonish movement was executed by Robert Maxwell on his fatal last journey. He took his private lift to the pad above his flat in Maxwell House, got into his helicopter which buzzed him to Heathrow, and slipped into his jet which flew him to Gibraltar; then straight onto his waiting yacht. The joy of it all for Maxwell was that it didn't cost him a penny; everything was stolen.

No, the category which has replaced the old carriage folk is not the helicopter-jet owners: it is the chauffeur folk, those who never have to touch a steering-wheel. Owning a car is nothing. Many working-class families can muster three or even more. They command more horse-power than the richest duke ever did in the days of clinking harness and hoofbeats. The real distinction is between those who have to wriggle their car through the traffic, find a parking-space (or not), feed meters, argue with policemen, car-park attendants, meter-maids, doorkeepers, garage mechanics and all other enemies of the self-respecting private motorist, and those who simply get out at their destination and say, 'Thanks, Freddy. Be back at 2.30 sharp.'

How many people fall into the class of 'chauffeur folk'? Ten thousand, perhaps. They include company chairmen and chief executives, and others high enough up the business pecking-order to warrant their firm spending about £30,000 a year on setting them up with a car and driver. Then there are government ministers, recognisable by the red dispatch-box beside them on the back seat. Judges, generals and the like, *ex officio*; a few rich lawyers, a very few rich doctors; television executives and newspaper editors, advertising bigshots and showbiz. It isn't the make or cost of the vehicle which matters; it's having the faithful Jehu in front to do for you all the hard and tiresome things which take the pleasure out of car travel. There, indeed, is our new privileged class.

But of course none of it is paid for out of anyone's private pocket. It is all on the firm, part of the 'service contract', a perk. That is the delightful part of it, but also the danger. What comes with one turn of fortune's wheel can go with the next. Malcolm Muggeridge once gave me some wise advice: 'As you get older, dear boy, try and make do with less. Learn to do without pleasures and comforts before they are taken away from you. Oh, and never take a job with a car and driver – when you lose it, that's what you'll miss most.' Sound counsel, which I have followed. Outside the big hotels you see the long line of large, dark cars lining up, bored drivers at the wheel, waiting for the lunch-hour to draw to a close. But those who are sauntering out, buttoning coats, tossing away a cigar, are not necessarily the same as last year's crop, or the next. Firms come unstuck, jobs are lost, governments fall, there's blood all over the boardroom walls and, suddenly, Jehu is no longer waiting, and the tube beckons. Even more inexorably looms retirement and the bus-pass. All things considered, better to stick to taxis.

15 February 1992

Lexicographer, spare those minor clerics

In what work do these terminal sentences appear? 'He died of erysipelas in the head, contracted by attending a political meeting.' 'He was always eccentric; and his behaviour one night at dinner was so strange that a guest intervened. He was placed under restraint at

Northwood, in Surrey, and died without issue.' 'After vainly travelling abroad in hope of relief he died unmarried.' Yes; quite right. The tone is unmistakable: the *Dictionary of National Biography*. It was that modern antiquary Geoffrey Madan, a perpetual browser in its tomes, who spotted these gems. Madan, like all scholars, would have been delighted by the news that the *DNB* is to be revised; and equally, like me, apprehensive that some quaint babies will be thrown out with the antique bathwater.

I have lived with the *DNB* for half a century. I used it at school and of course at Oxford. Aged 20 or so, I bought, cheap, the 63 brown volumes of the original edition, 1882–1900. Later and richer, I acquired the 22 blue volumes of the 1908–9 recension. Later still, I disposed of them, in favour of the two-volume compact, to save shelf space, though I have kept and added all the supplementary volumes. The compact is invaluable but it has its limitations. Consulting it for any length of time gives one a headache and it is impossible to read it for pleasure. But the real defects of the *DNB* are more fundamental. Women are treated badly. Mary Wollstonecraft is condescendingly dismissed as 'Miscellaneous writer (see Godwin, Mrs Mary Wollstonecraft)'. Even many great men are simply not there: Gerard Manley Hopkins, for instance, or George Cayley, the aeronautical pioneer, or Jonathan Otley, the founder of meteorology. There are countless inaccuracies, pitfalls for the unwary. In 1966, a Boston firm put out a 200-page volume, *Corrections and Additions to the DNB*, which reprinted material from the *Bulletin of Historical Research, 1923–63*. I find this useful but only if I am aware that an entry is wrong or incomplete.

Hence the case for a radical overhaul is overwhelming and I have often urged it. But I beg those in charge of the project, the British Academy and the Oxford University Press, to bear some points in mind before they get started. First, history is too important to be left to academics. It is vital the new *DNB* should not be run by a dons' trade union. All great reference books, such as the famous 11th edition of the *Encyclopaedia Britannica* (1910–11), have featured outstanding writers who not only present the facts but bring them to life. Second, the stress should be on inclusion rather than on selection based on merit. There are, I agree, almost insuperable problems here. The *DNB* must accord exhaustive treatment to the very great, like Shakespeare or Darwin or Churchill. But the real value of the work is its information on people not even of the second but of the third and fourth rank, who will never merit a biography or even a learned article. I am thinking not so much of politicians, say, who can be found in the marvellous *History of Parliament* or the *Complete Peerage*, or physicians, who have *Munk's Roll*, but of those who do not fit into well provided professional categories. I have known interesting writers, for instance, who never even got into *Who's Who*, let alone the *Oxford Companion to English Literature*, who are now dead and the most elementary facts about their lives and works in danger of passing into an oubliette.

Then there are the innumerable people who do not fit into any category at all but are simply worth recording. I was disturbed to read, in the *Daily Telegraph*, that the British Academy president, Dr Kenny, thinks more 'scientists and engineers' should be included and 'fewer minor clerics'. More boffins by all means, but spare those clerical gents: they are often the salt which gives the *DNB* its savour. I am thinking, for instance, of James Gatliff, 1766–1831, Perpetual Curate of Gorton and a minor cleric if ever there was one. He published a four-volume theological work 'which involved him in pecuniary difficulties with his publisher' and led to his imprisonment for debt. Released, he put out a vindication, called 'A Firm Attempt at Investigation; or, the Twinkling Effects of a Falling Star to Relieve the Cheshire Full Moon', believed to be a scurrilous reference to the Bishop of Chester. Or there was Henry Aldrich, 1647–1710, Dean of Christ Church and designer of Peckwater Quad, who translated 'Tinker, Tailor, Soldier, Sailor' into Latin, was a fanatical smoker and wrote a song 'to be sung by Four Men smoking their Pipes, not more difficult to sing than diverting to hear'. (Well: dons had even less to do then than now.) Or Scott's friend, the Revd John Marriott, doughty hymn-writer until, without warning, 'he was seized by ossification of the brain'. Or even the less minor Charles Lloyd, 1784–1829, tutor to Sir Robert Peel, who got him made Bishop of Oxford. In return, Lloyd changed his mind over Catholic Emancipation and supported Peel 'by an impressive speech in the House of Lords'. Alas, 'for some time Lloyd had taken insufficient exercise, and his health was further weakened by the censure of the newspapers and the cold treatment of his friends. A chill which he caught at the Royal Academy Dinner hastened his end.'

Nor are minor clerics the only characters we must hang onto. Let us not annihilate Elizabeth Bland, *fl.* 1681–1712, one of the first women to write Hebrew and compose phylacteries, who taught the language to her son and daughter, sole survivors of her six children. I vote, too, to retain Anthony Addington, father of the Prime Minister, who kept a mad-house, was empiric doctor to Chatham, and cured his son William Pitt the Younger of a childhood complaint by prescribing large quantities of port. And John Henderson, the 'eccentric student', the most brilliant linguist of his day, 1757–88, who 'believed in the possibility of holding correspondence with the dead', and killed himself by sleeping in a damp bed. We must find space also for T.H. Bayly, 1797–1839, author of 'I'd Be a Butterfly', 'She Wore a Wreath of Roses' and 'Oh, No, We Never Mention Her'. He would have written other songs but he invested his wife's dowry in coal-mines, 'which proved unproductive' and 'made him melancholy'; and he was inflicted in addition by brain fever 'and other and more painful diseases, dropsy succeeded to confirmed jaundice'; so he 'expired'. There are scores of such people, odd, vivid, gifted and creative in their fashion, egregious spear-carriers in the great march past of our forebears, whose ranks must not be thinned.

14 March 1992

Everybody needs to own something

On Saturday, reflecting that there was now a real risk the socialists would come in, I decided to spend some money before they got a chance to confiscate it. So I bought a painting. It would not have occurred to me to buy anything else. In most respects I am the archetypal anti-consumer. If the majority were like me, the entire economy would seize up. Scanning the ads in a colour-supplement, my eyes glaze over. There is absolutely nothing they display which I want. If I walk down Oxford Street or Knightsbridge, I have not the smallest temptation to go into any of the shops. I have never bought a car in my life. Clothes do not interest me. Expensive restaurants merely try my patience. As my work takes me to distant places anyway, I never take holidays as such. All the things for which Rosemary Aberdour lusted, which drove her to steal £3 million from hospitals and landed her in gaol last week, I not only can do without, they actively disgust me. Hell is being trapped in a night-club with 'the beautiful people' and forced to live in a 'luxury penthouse flat'. I would be happier in a monastery, even a charterhouse.

But I could not do without paintings and books. And, when I have money, I buy them. The itch to own books is a disease, which in my case is chronic and incurable. There is no reason to it. As a young man I led a wandering life and, three times, was forced to sell my books before moving on. I argued that I didn't actually need them, that libraries were always available. But it was agony nonetheless, and once settled in a new place, the accretions began again. When we moved from our house in Iver, back to London, I sold two or three thousand books – massy historical sets, encyclopaedias, bound runs of magazines, that sort of thing. I have never ceased to pine for those volumes. In any case, vast quantities of other books have since been acquired so I now have more than before the Great Purge, revealed retrospectively as pointless. Handymen are constantly summoned to make more shelves, but still the rows of books insinuate themselves, like serpents, creeping upstairs and into bedrooms, slithering along walls and into cupboards, piling themselves in corners, standing reproachfully in piles on tables, even under sofas. I buy them in Foyles or Waterstones, in grand Mayfair rare-book emporia, in dark junk-shops in back streets, even in those cut-price joints which spring up like mushrooms whenever a shop space falls vacant. These last are not to be despised: last week I got in one of them, for virtually nothing, the *Travels* of Prince Pückler-Muskau, which (oddly enough) I did not possess, and a life of that wayward, mad genius Gilbert Cannan, described to me vividly years ago by old Martin Secker, who first published him.

Anyway, one way or another the books continue to arrive, sometimes dozens in a week. So, more rarely, do the paintings and drawings. When I bought the latest, a magnificent rendering in oils of that favourite 19th-century white-water scene, 'The Falls of Clyde', by Thomas Spinks ('fl. 1872–1880', according to Christopher Wood's *Dictionary of Victorian Painters*), my wife said, 'Yes, but where will you hang it?' It is true there is no room. I occasionally give a picture away, but never sell one, *pietas* obliging me to follow my father's maxim: 'Never try to make money out of a poor, dead painter, who probably starved.' So they accumulate, and the fresh arrivals have to fight for wall-space. But it is my superstitious belief that good, self-respecting paintings hanging in a room recognise a newcomer of quality, and contract themselves to make way for him.

Besides, I feel a continuing sense of loss about the pictures I should have bought and couldn't, or didn't. There was the beautiful little Constable watercolour I was offered for £18, at a time when I simply did not possess such a princely sum and had no means of borrowing it. There was a more poignant moment, just after we were married (so it must have been 1957). I had just bought, for a few pounds, a superb oil by Albert Moore, then held in little esteem. I was offered two more, smaller ones but a pair, for £45. As it happened, I had the money. But we did not then possess a refrigerator, and £45 was exactly the price of the new one we needed. So Mary had to yield to Martha, art to utility. There were other similar instances over the years, so that I feel there are a number of works *missing* from my collection, gaps to be filled, even though the walls are replete. That, at least, is my metaphysical rationale for buying more. But the truth is I am just acquisitive when it comes to books and paintings, if nothing else. I want to own. When I look around them in my house, neatly arranged on the shelves, well-lit on the walls, I feel emotions not unlike Archdeacon Grantley's when he shows his recalcitrant son, who wants to marry a penniless beauty, around the family woods and fields, in *The Last Chronicle of Barset*.

It is my view that such feelings, in moderation, are not only entirely proper but are a permanent, ineradicable response of the human spirit to the beauty, variety and richness of the world around us. The desire to own, like the urge to create, is God-given; indeed the two instincts are complementary: one cannot long exist without the other. The belief that acquisitiveness is intrinsically and always wrong, taught by heretic theologians and orthodox socialists, is false and, if pressed, wicked. It is a great destroyer of happiness. Think of the narrowness of life for the millions who lived in communist Europe, denied for so long – four decades in the satellites, seven in Russia – the simple satisfaction of owning things, like gardens and fields and homes or little businesses, of making collections, of commissioning a craftsman or an artist to make a particular, treasured object. Think of the beauty lost in consequence. And all because an arrogant, aggressive minority felt they had the right to try to transform human nature according to their gruesome secular faith. We do not exactly face the threat of such deprivation here, I hope. Nevertheless, I dread the prospect of Neil Kinnock, ignorant, unreflective, almost unread, and just behind him a *camarilla* of would-be cultural commissars, TV *littérateurs* and showbiz riffraff, giving us orders and imposing on us their repellent notions of moral, civil and artistic conduct. The worst of all occupations by aliens is a cultural one.

4 April 1992

A danger of tales left untold

One of life's most agreeable pleasures, now in danger of disappearing, is reading a skilfully turned-out, highly professional short story. It is an art form in itself and mastering the short story form is, for a writer, a wonderful education in plotting, character-sketching and, most of all, economy in the use of words. When I was teaching myself to write, round about 1950, it was the short story I practised most. I must have written scores of them. Hardly any were published but I felt I was learning and making progress. Moreover, just the act of writing them was a keen pleasure.

Sixty or seventy years ago, great writers were still producing magical tales, varying from 1,500 words to six or seven thousand. There was Kipling, for instance, the master of them all, cunningly serving up a mixture of comic dialogue and the bleakly sinister. The young Hemingway was just getting into his stride. Then there was Somerset Maugham, for my money the most consistently entertaining, if a little heartless. Has anyone ever written a neater tale than 'The Colonel's Lady'? G.K. Chesterton could be relied upon for ingenuity and cerebral surprise, James Thurber for maniacal comedy: nothing has ever made me laugh so much as 'The Night the Bed Fell on Father'. The range of tales available was prodigious, from Raymond Chandler's powerful crime stories, originally written for the pulp trade, to the dockside tales of W.W. Jacobs. I picked up an old anthology of Jacobs the other day and was deeply impressed by his fertility of invention and the scampering pace at which he keeps the plot bowling along. There were dozens of second-rank professionals like him, turning out reliable stuff to order, keeping us entertained.

What made me try my hand at the stories was, of course, rumours of the fabulous sums to be earned in the magazine market, especially in the United States. There was the *Saturday Evening Post* and *Collier's* and the *Lady's Home Journal*, with a constant demand for 5,000-word stories. These magazines had huge sales and would pay a dollar a word, sometimes more. They were mighty choosy, though, and could take their pick of the best writers. Somewhat more up-market, and even choosier, was the *New Yorker*, happily still publishing high-quality short fiction even today. Britain was much less well provided, the *Strand*, the greatest story magazine of them all, being on its last legs (it closed in 1950). But there were still plenty of outlets, including the women's weeklies, which also had huge sales in those days and actually published rather higher-quality stories and serials than their critics would allow. There were, too, quirky little papers like *Lilliput*, which was both discerning and generous, as well as the highbrow publications, *Penguin New Writing* and *Horizon* (that, too, folded in 1950). Even newspaper editors would occasionally run short stories: the old London *Evening News* had, I seem to recall, one every weekday: very short – 1,000 words or less – but often beautifully contrived.

As these markets contracted or disappeared, fiction writers ceased to be able to make a living from short-story writing alone. That is what happened to Angus Wilson, the most gifted man in the genre since Maugham, whose *The Wrong Set* (1949) is one of the most scintillating collections of tales ever published. He had to turn to novels, in which he never shone to the same degree. Some writers continued to practise the craft, come what might. V.S. Pritchett, for instance, produced an annual quota of high-quality tales until quite recently. I have read, too, outstanding collections by such highly professional women writers as Elizabeth Taylor, Olivia Manning, Doris Lessing and Edna O'Brien. When I was an editor, I usually ran a short story or two at Christmas-time, often provided by Graham Greene, who loved writing them. But it is significant that a top writer of fiction like Evelyn Waugh, who produced some splendid tales in the 1930s, wrote very few in the last third of his life.

The case for the short story is twofold. From the reader's point of view, there is much to be said for a tale of between 5,000 and 10,000 words, which will happily while away a train journey or a lazy weekend afternoon. A magazine fits more easily than a novel into a briefcase. More important, however, there are many first-class fictional ideas which come off beautifully when briefly told but cannot be expanded into novel length. Hemingway's 'The Short and Happy Life of Francis Macomber', told with superb economy of means and tensile strength, is the perfect tale but would be a frightful bore – indeed, would simply not work at all – as the plot of a 75,000-word novel. Kipling was a natural short-story writer who was not at ease with the novel form and length: *The Light That Failed* is powerfully conceived but there is something wrong with it. Somerset Maugham wrote some highly successful novels but his stories are in an altogether higher range of art: indeed the best of his novels, *Cakes and Ale*, might be described as a very long short story.

I suppose writers will always produce tales, but the skills honed so carefully and zealously in the century 1850–1950 will simply not be there, and the rich feasts we enjoyed will not be available, if publishers and editors fail to provide regular, remunerative markets. I believe the demand is still there, and the expertise to supply it will still be available for a few more years yet, but it will gradually disappear unless some of those who wield power in publishing make a conscious effort to keep the art alive. Why don't the colour magazines publish short stories? Why do we so rarely get the chance to read them in the up-market broadsheets? I would like to see regular fiction in the middle range, too: the *Daily Mail*, the *Sunday Express*, the *Mail on Sunday*. It might be an excellent idea for editors who care about our literature to set aside, each year, a sum of money for the commissioning of high-grade short fiction. It would be an investment for the future – in the Kiplings, Hemingways and Maughams of the 21st century.

18 April 1992

Counting our blessings in the May time

The television pictures coming from Afghanistan are heart-breaking. The fierce, bearded men, running into Kabul on their bare feet, rockets slung across their backs like thick spears, shouting Allah is Great, may look and sound jolly, but their injured wives and sisters and children, lying frightened and agonised in hospitals which have few doctors and little equipment or drugs, tell the other side of a dreadful story. And the wretched Bosnians, exposed in their battered cities to the heavy guns and tanks of the Serbian army, with nowhere to go but their barren hills, excite deep but helpless pity. After the huge relief of the end of the Cold War and the destruction of the most evil empire the world has ever known, it is as though providence were reminding us that man remains a permanently flawed creature, endlessly capable of inflicting misery on himself and others. The End of History, indeed! That will only come when time has a stop, the present world is wound up, and the mysterious next one begins.

In the meantime, how fortunate we are to live in dear England, with all its faults, especially now that spring is come. And what a spring! As I look out of my window, I see the fallen cherry-blossom in great pink and white heaps on the front gardens and pavement: seldom do I recall such profusion. Across the street there is a white lilac of spectacular richness and beauty. Wherever I look, there are trees and shrubs coming into leaf and blossom, an amazing variety considering we have less than a score of houses. A horse-chestnut shoots out its candles. A giant clematis, making an early appearance, climbs and riots all over its supporting cherry. There are tall, neatly trimmed privets, too, concealing as it were secret delights.

From my study, from which I write this, I look down into the rear garden, where our handsome stone copy of Donatello's David stands guard, Goliath's severed head firmly under foot. He grasps only the hilt of his sword, the blade is missing, but no matter: with his exquisite naked grace and woman's flower-strewn straw hat on his long-haired head, he is an amazing figure. Yet another coloured cherry, its blossoms still almost intact, taps its branches against the window. From where I sit, I can count a dozen different shades of leaf and verdure. We have had much welcome rain lately and the greens are intense: the lawn might have come straight from West Cork.

Here we are truly *rus in urbe*. The quiet is intense, underlined by the occasional faint sound. Yet only a hundred yards away is the bustle of Westbourne Grove with its Chinese, Indian, Greek, Lebanese, Turkish, Spanish, Italian, Thai, Sudanese restaurants, aromas from all Europe, Africa and Asia, its shops which stay open till midnight all the days of the year, its endless procession of neighbours, strangers, eccentrics, rich and poor, drunks and beggars, all colours and ages and mysterious categories and genders, which in its own Bayswater fashion reminds me of the Chandni Chowk in Delhi. Charles Lamb, who revered the kaleidoscope of London, would have savoured and relished it all.

Our houses were put up within a few years of his death in 1834, when the farms, market-gardens and gravel pits finally yielded to bricks and mortar. They were built, as part of a major estate development, in pairs of semi-detached villas. Quite modest in size, they were designed for what was then termed 'superior servants', who worked on the estates or in neighbouring grand houses: butlers and housekeepers, agents, coachmen, *chefs de cuisine*. Many, like ours, have been added to since, at various periods, with all kinds of bits and pieces and floors, rather like a miniature version of an old English country house, the whole covered and harmonised by white stucco. But some are virtually intact, and very elegant they look: a strong reminder of a period when Victoria had been only three years on the throne but a growing number of people were conscious of rising incomes, better prospects, 'peace, retrenchment and reform' – the beginnings of Liberal England, the Age of Improvement.

It may be that another age of improvement can open, now that the spectre of Marxist socialism has been banished and we can set about solving difficulties and ending abuses in practical ways without the poison of ideology and class warfare. Around where we live, the improvements have long since got going. The great Gavin Stamp, who is right about so many things, complains of the degradation of London in recent years, as though all is destruction and waste. He is wrong for once. In dozens of streets near us, through which I walk every day on my way to church in the morning or to Kensington Gardens in the afternoon, there has been continuous change for the better since we came to live here. The old barbarism of knocking down groups of terraced houses and replacing them with incongruous modern blocks, like those steel teeth they inset in Russian mouths, has long since ended. I could count, in our neighbourhood alone, hundreds of Victorian houses, from the Eighteen-Fifties, Sixties, Seventies and Eighties, which have been lovingly, or at any rate efficiently, gutted and modernised, their façades kept intact, repainted and restored to their pristine sturdy beauty.

There is a corner house in particular I have watched, over recent months, with growing pleasure as it emerged from its scaffolding and canvas. At one time work stopped, and I thought the recession had made another kill. But no: it was resumed, and the whole is now complete down to its original fenestration and cornice and Ionic portico, gleaming and ready to be occupied. I congratulated a workman who was putting the finishing touches to the steps, and he said: 'Yes, better than this modern stuff – there is more satisfaction in it.' Do you hear that, down below, Monsieur Le Corbusier? There are in truth many quiet reasons for rejoicing in London this spring, and as we look at the world beyond our safe shores, let us count our blessings.

9 May 1992

Learning to be an old entertainer

It has just occurred to me that, for the first time, the holders of all the four great offices of state, Prime Minister, Home and Foreign Secretaries, and Chancellor of the Exchequer, are younger than me. Three of the four, indeed, are so young that such phrases as 'Can I do you now, Sir?' and 'Don't forget the Diver' mean nothing to them. All of which suggests that I must think about growing old. I mean, not just older but old. 'The thing about growing old, dear boy,' Malcolm Muggeridge used to say, 'is that you must decide, well in advance, how you are going to play it.' As he pointed out, some people avoided the problem because youth or even middle age had eluded them anyway. There was, for instance, an Archbishop of Canterbury called Ramsay who had looked and talked like an old man since his mid-20s. And C.P. Snow was always an ancient, an absolute Nestor, though he was only 50 when I first met him.

In any event, better to play it old than young. There is nothing more off-putting than the jaunty step and glittering eye of a well-preserved old man. Evelyn Waugh started his superannuated act in his mid-40s, quickly adding props, good for on-stage business, such as an ear-trumpet, Lord Curzon used a footstool: the arrival of a servant with this antique piece of furniture was always a signal to his cabinet colleagues that 'the Marquis is on his way'. J.B. Priestley, who had thought a lot about the histrionics of age (he died on the eve of his 90th birthday), awarded the palm to Harold Macmillan: 'He gets over the problem of being old by pretending he's very, *very* old.' It was true: sitting at the head of the table at the Beefsteak Club, or facing the largely hostile younger generations at the Tory Philosophy Group, he engaged in elaborate quavering and doddering, scarcely able to lift a glass of Dom Perignon to his withered lips, which made his flashes of wit, penetration and pure, undisguised venom all the more effective. By the time he died in 1986, aged 92, he had been doing the centenarian for a decade, giving the impression his pockets were stuffed with telegrams from the Queen.

Seriously, though, the real problem of age is how to make the most benevolent use of that other form of constantly accumulating capital you can't take with you: memory. Unlike money, you can't bequeath it. It vanishes in the instant of death. So the old distribute it lavishly, while there's still time, and not just once but repeatedly. 'Old men forget,' wrote Shakespeare. That is just the trouble. They do not forget. They remember only too well, and are eager to press their vintage treasures into your hands, or rather ears. Compton Mackenzie was a minatory example. He had lived a long, varied and interesting life, every second of which he remembered with breathtaking clarity. He was a superb teller of true stories, in his soft, Highlander's lilt, and the first half-hour of his company was pure magic. The second half-hour you edged away, more and more desperately. A weakness of age is a reluctance to recognise that, in conversation, it is more blessed to receive than to give, accompanied by a growing irritation at *anecdotus interruptus*. Recently I have noticed that Kingsley Amis has perfected an impressive new version of his goggled-eyed-serial-murderer-raving-lunatic face, accompanied by a testy 'Would you mind allowing me to finish my story?'

The way to solve this surplus memory problem, I believe, is to be like the Sibyl and wait to be asked. The publisher Martin Secker, who lived well into his 90s, and at whose house I used to listen to Mackenzie, one of his first authors, had exactly the right reticence. His personal knowledge of literary men and women went right back to the first decade of the century. He was not diffident about sharing it but he always waited to be asked. 'Martin, what was Arthur Ransome like before he discovered *Swallows and Amazons?*' 'Is it true Norman Douglas was caught *in flagrante delicto* in the V&A?' 'Did D.H. Lawrence have a Notts accent?' You would then get the answers, in accurate detail. I admired a similar self-restraint in Lady Violet Bonham-Carter. She had been endowed, like Mackenzie, with total recall but she did not exercise it at your expense. If, however, you inquired of her what it was like to take a hansom cab up to Hampstead at the height of the Commons row with the House of Lords over Lloyd George's budget, she would tell you, down to the last clip-clop. She would even tell you which member of her father's cabinet was most likely to take advantage of a shared hansom-cab rug to put his hand on a girl's knee. The glint in LG's roving eye, the whiff of FE's cigars and his brandy-breath, Lord Beaverbrook's taste in chintzes, the way Mrs Gladstone dressed and Mrs Greville undressed – impossible to better the meticulous bravura with which this eloquent old woman recalled *ante-bellum* London society. Harold Nicolson was good too: his account of delivering the declaration of war to the German

Embassy on the night of 4 August 1914 was electrifying. But, like most of his tales, it was a bit too rounded; it smacked of midnight oil. Nor did he wait to be asked before telling it.

The conclusion, then, is that the secret of a popular old age – as of any age, come to think of it – is the curbing of self-indulgence. The old should not broadcast their memories, like pop-music in a horrid pub, but wait, like books on the shelves of a library, to be consulted. Even better than waiting for the young to ask questions, is to put them yourself. The most successful handler of old age I know is Lord Longford. One reason for this may be that he always greets you with a query. 'Are you still suffering withdrawal symptoms at having to give up Mrs Thatcher?' 'What do you think of Joan Collins?' 'Written any good books lately?' Though he is now 86 and recently had a bruising struggle with a grandfather clock, I heard him last week 'set the table on a roar' at a glittering Park Lane banquet. Afterwards, he asked me: 'My new gag – "The good news is that I have mislaid my speech and will have to improvise; the bad news is that I've mislaid my watch too" – did it make you laugh? Did it work?' The art of being an old entertainer is to consult the audience.

27 June 1992

There's no short cuts on t'fells

It is exactly 50 years since I first visited the Lake District and discovered the delights of walking on the high hills. We lived in north-east Staffordshire, on the Derbyshire borders, and tramped a lot on the moors. But hills of over 3,000 feet – real mountains! – were quite new to me. I shall never forget the excitement of first seeing the great range, spread out in the early summer sunshine, in subtle shades of azure, sapphire, lapis lazuli and indigo, from the platform of Oxenholme Junction where we changed from the main line. We travelled in the maroon livery of the old LMS, 'our' railway. People had much stronger loyalties then; we thought the LMS the world's best, exactly right, as opposed to the LNER, regarded as common, or the GWR, smug and stuck-up, or the Southern, just plain boring. Our buses were brown but the rattletrap which took us from Windermere slowly up Langdale was painted yellow, in itself a fascinating novelty, though less so than the grim precipices which soon crowded around us. We walked the last half-mile to the little cluster of whitewashed buildings right at the head of the dale, the farm where we stayed.

For six shillings each a day, my sister and I had full board at this ancient, stone-flagged, fortress-walled, primitive but spotlessly clean homestead. Though it was wartime, we tucked into huge plates of bacon and eggs at breakfast, and roasts of beef and mutton in the evenings; and to take with us on our walks we had delicious sandwiches, lovingly wrapped in neat packets of greaseproof paper. To drink we had a choice between Tizer and Dandelion and Burdock, both much esteemed in the North. These were the only items in our diet not produced on the farm, which abounded in fresh cream, salted butter, crusty bread, blackberry pies, and Eccles and Goosnagh cakes.

Being a 13-year-old, I had a narrow little bed in a room I shared with Jack, described by the farmer's wife as 'a serious walking gentleman'. I owe him a great deal because he taught me how to love the fells and respect them by learning their lore and dangers. He took me up Dungeon Ghyl and Pavey Ark, the immense cliff above Langdale, showing me how to scramble safely. Together we saw the Lord's Rake on Scafell, and the famous Nape's Needle on Great Gable. At night and early in the morning, for the sun woke us at six, he regaled me with irresistible horror-stories of his rope-climbing days: how Herbert Arkwright had been 'near killed' on Middlefell Buttress, and how they'd brought down the body of poor Stanley Hardcastle, lost on Crickle Crags, by taking the door off a barn and using it as a stretcher. His lugubrious northern nature abounded in gloomy advice. 'Ne'r stick thy foot on Gimmer Crag, lad, and if tha must, avoid Amen Corner, I beg thee.' 'Take no notice of Hell's Ghyll, there's nowt in there but trouble.' 'Watch out for t'screes on backside of Bow Fell, lads 'ave vanished there without trayce.' He told me a gruesome tale of how a young man and girl, 'being shameless like', bathed naked in Angle Tarn, and had been sucked down into its icy depths by an outraged deity. Jack liked a good shudder, and would then compose himself for sleep by reading a chapter of the Bible.

The simplicity of those days seems far away now. The work on the farm was back-breaking and endless, and none toiled harder than Mary, the kindly, red-cheeked daughter of the house, in her starched white apron, glittering fresh each morning. She had been looking forward to her annual treat, a dance at Chapel Stile, to which she proposed to walk five miles there and five back. But at the last minute a sick cow kept her at home and up most of the night. She was philosophical about it, telling me: 'Well, at least they won't find out I can't do slow foxtrot, nor samba neither.' Daughter of a statesman, as Lakeland freehold farmers are called, she could doubtless expect to make a suitable union, in due course, with a statesman's son, when he came back from soldiering. But there was not much romance in her life, punctuated by the changing but always harsh rhythms of the year. She had once been out 15 hours, she said, rescuing sheep from drifts in a heavy January snowfall.

Wordsworth had been dead 90 years then, but the dales had probably changed less from his time than they have since. There was a taxi in Ambleside but few cars in Langdale and less petrol. The old walked, the young biked. Some remembered the coaches, and having to get out, to spare the horses, going up Dunmail Raise or Honister Pass. Unlike the commercial crossbreeds of today, which can't be left untended on the fells, all the sheep were the old Herdwick line, bravest and cleverest of their species, and sweetest to eat though small and yielding little wool. There were still old-style shepherds. On High White Stones, back of beyond behind the Langdale Pikes, I met one with an impressive white beard, who said he was 80; he had his great-grandson with him. At Sawrey, in the next dale, Beatrix Potter was still alive and president of the Herdwick Association. All kinds of old trades carried on. Gnarled men built dry-stone walls for ten shillings per seven yards. In the Furness Woods, there were charcoal-burners, leading a primitive, nomadic life in makeshift huts. Savage-looking creatures worked little copper mines near Coniston. You could watch the slaters, squatting on the ground, their trousers tied with cord just below the knee, splitting the slates with astounding speed and accuracy. There were many more locals than 'offcomes' in those days. You might see one or two climbers on top of Scafell or Gable, but otherwise the hills were as empty as when Coleridge risked his neck scrambling into Borrowdale.

Coleridge picked his own reckless route, straight down the rocks, and left a hair-raising account of it. Jack took a censorious view of such southern folly: 'There's not much sense below the Trent,' as he put it. He warned me: 'Always take map and compass, torch and whistle, and an extra jumper.' He taught me how to distinguish between a genuine path and a meandering sheep-trail, and added: 'Thou must stick to the path. Remember, on t'fells *there's no such thing as a short cut.*' True, and in a much wider sense, too. Looking back on the past half-century, it strikes me that we would have been spared much misery if ideologues, millenarians and *exaltés* of all political persuasions had not forced humanity to learn the hard way that there are not short cuts to anything.

30 May 1992

Filthy foreigners going up in smoke

Few people combine knowledge, elegance and common sense as effortlessly as Drusilla Beyfus, and it is no surprise that her new book on etiquette, *Modern Manners* (Hamlyn) is a model of practical wisdom. Of course one can argue with some of her rulings. She is not tough enough, in my view, on adulterers and homosexuals, especially the latter. Why should a hostess make special provision for 'gays' who come to stay bringing their 'friends', or indeed invite them in the first place? After all, other guests may not like living in the same house with people who could have Aids. On the other hand, she deals with the smoking issue judiciously. She rules that even 'considerate hosts' may 'draw the line at smoking'. Well, so I should think. Some people still light up in your drawing-room without permission or apology, or puff smoke at you from the next table in a restaurant just as you are beginning your meal. But opinion is moving fast against smokers in both America and Britain: on this issue the Atlantic is narrower than the Channel. Dr Johnson observed in 1778: 'The French are a gross, ill-bred, untaught people: a lady there will spit on the floor and rub it with her foot.' In his day, courtiers would urinate in the stairwells at Versailles but they did not dare smoke in the salons. Today, he would be forced to notice, even members of the Académie Française will smoke all through dinner in a three-star restaurant without the smallest consideration for their neighbours. Italians are just as bad, the Spanish still worse; even the Scandinavians have not yet got the point. Differences over smoking are resurrecting all the old distinctions between Anglo-Saxons and filthy foreigners.

What neither the smokers themselves, nor cowardly people who put up with them, will admit is that smoking, by its nature, is an outdoor activity, like playing football or walking a dog. It crept indoors only for a comparatively brief period. James I, in his *Counterblaste to*

Tobacco (1604), thought it unconscionable that anyone should smoke in a house. Most men, he argued, only took up smoking because they saw others doing it, and as for women, he blamed the wicked smoking husband who may 'reduce thereby his delicate, wholesome and clean-complexioned wife to that extremity that either she must also corrupt her sweet breath therewith, or else resolve to live in a perpetual stinking torment'. Most opinion agreed with him. Even many ale-houses forced smokers to sit on a bench outside. Houses were sacrosanct. As late as 1855, Bishop Murray of Rochester wrote to a correspondent: 'Yes, it is true that I have appointed Mr — to Would-ham. But oh! *If I had only known* ... that when he came here the other day to be instituted he actually smoked in the bedroom! He *never* would have had that living!' A perfect gentleman did not do such a thing or at least puffed the smoke straight up his bedroom chimney. If he smoked on the house steps or terrace, which was allowed, he took care 'not to allow the faintest whiff of smoke to penetrate into the hall'.

In the view of one historian, Jill Franklin (*The Gentleman's Country House and its Plan, 1835–1914*), the rot indeed set in with a filthy foreigner, in the shape of the Prince Consort. Osborne, which he designed and had built in the 1840s, was perhaps the earliest house in England with a smoking room. At first these places were deliberately made remote, at the end of Stygian corridors or up towers: to get to the 'summer smoking room' in the castle William Burges designed for Lord Bute at Cardiff in 1868, you had to climb 101 steps, no easy matter if, as was likely, you were already suffering from emphysema. Disaster really struck when the smoking room was put next to the billiard room, thus bringing together two bad habits – not for nothing did the great Herbert Spencer lay down: 'A proficiency in billiards is a sure sign of a misspent youth.' According to Miss Franklin, fast women had made forays into the billiard room as early as the 1840s. They invaded it *en masse* in the 1860s. In the 1870s, they stepped through the communicating door into the smoking room, and there whipped those nasty little mother-of-pearl cigarette cases out of their velvet reticules and lit up shamelessly.

Once women were party to the indoor smoking conspiracy the rules began to break down completely. Men now smoked openly in front of ladies and in any part of the house. On the eve of the first world war, the stiffer element was fighting a losing battle and, in the general slaughter, the anti-smoking barriers went down everywhere. By the 1920s, Bright Young Things were smoking even in dining-rooms. The climate of opinion in the inter-war age was such that advertising campaigns were run to persuade flappers to take up smoking for the sake of their health, as an alternative to fattening chocolates. In the 1950s, people, led by women, were beginning to smoke between courses and by the 1960s they thought nothing of dropping cigarette stubs on carpets during parties.

In short, indoor smoking has lasted only a century, is a matter of cumulative small encroachments, and is marked by an accompanying rise in gross and disgusting behaviour. What we need to do is put the clock back equally persistently and firmly. I am no enemy of the right to smoke. Last week's US Supreme Court ruling that printing health warnings on cigarette packets is no defence against suits for damages, which will set off an avalanche of vexatious litigation by cancer victims or their heirs against tobacco companies, is a disastrous denial of the fundamental moral doctrine of personal responsibility. Our own domestic restrictions on cigarette advertising are a form of censorship and the European Community proposals of the gruesome Madame Papandreou are absolutely outrageous. While approving EEC subsidies of £600 million a year to the Greek tobacco industry, she is simultaneously waging a campaign against Anglo-American advertising agencies and wants to force old-fashioned tobacconists to take down charming metal signs which have been part of our streetscapes for 150 years. All this fanaticism, especially when it is self-interested, must be fought by tolerant, fair-minded people, smokers and non-smokers alike. But let us bring the habit where it belongs, out into the open.

4 July 1992

Sailing from Monte in the wake
of the bouncing Czech

Maxwell's enormous yacht, up for sale at about £10 million, and costing another million a year to run, has been sold for a 'satisfactory' price, according to the agents Camper & Nicholsons. So the recession is not hitting everyone hard. The idea of anyone having that much money to spend on fripperies strikes many people as wicked – 'obscene' is the cant word. Others, such as General de Gaulle, regard owning a luxury yacht as vulgar, something to which only giant tanker-owners and other moral outcasts would stoop. Hence his contemptuous remark, after studying Jackie Kennedy at the president's funeral, '*Elle finira sur le bâteau d'un armateur.*'

Lord Beaverbrook, too, was critical of yachts, or 'yats' as he called them, though for different reasons. He had had an unfortunate experience taking delivery of a 'steam yat' on the American East Coast, which hit an obstruction after it had cruised less than a dozen miles. He was on the bridge, standing next to the captain at the time. 'What was that noise, Captain Brogan?' 'I don't know, my Lord. I will find out.' 'Well, it sounded like a twenty-thousand bucks noise to me.' 'And so,' he added, 'it proved. Everything which goes wrong with a yat costs you twenty thousand bucks, at least.' This cautionary tale concluded with a warning: 'My advice to you, young man, is not to be in a hurry, when the time comes, to buy yourself an expensive steam yat.'

So far I have found no difficulty in following Beaverbrook's advice. Yet I must admit that, of all the glittering baubles vast wealth can buy, the only one which tempts me in the least is a yacht. Why? It is the sense of freedom – the idea that you can get on a boat you call home, with your family and friends, and tell the man on the bridge to take you anywhere in the world. Size and luxury, and therefore expense, are essential. There is no surer formula for a holiday disaster than embarking on a small yacht. It brings instantly to mind Dr Johnson's condemnation of the sailor's life: 'Like being in a prison, with the chance of being drowned too.'

Close quarters on a reeking boat where all is uncongenial work, greasy meals and buffeting by the elements is a solvent of friendship and an aggravator of any family discord going. The disadvantages are well conveyed in the Somerville and Ross story, *The House of Fahy*, in which Bernard Shute, to entertain his friends, hires a gruesome schooner called the *Eileen Oge*, and comes a cropper. Come to think of it, the two authors tell an even more off-putting tale about Lord Derryclare's unfortunate pleasure vessel, *Sheila*, with its 'narrow, hog-backed deck' and 'strong whiff of pollack', which contrives to foul its anchor in the bay at Eyries, 'a collection of dismal, slated cabins, grouped around a public house, like a company of shabby little hens round a bedraggled cock'.

Spaciousness, then, is of the essence, the swift and faultless service which belongs to a well-found ship, a first-class chef, stabilisers, air-conditioning, a big pool, phones, television, faxes, and, not least, the pop of champagne corks as the waves lap softly against the stern and cast intricate light-patterns against the awning above. Maxwell's *Lady Ghislaine* has a gymnasium and a discotheque. I would turn the gym into a library and the disco into a gallery for paintings. Associations with Cap'n Bob would not bother me; quite the contrary – a little bit of notoriety is part of the fun of owning one of these exotic toys. I'd enjoy telling guests: 'We've had the guard-rail mended but this is the place where the previous owner walked the plank.' Nor would I mind a touch of haunting. If the high seas can accommodate the Flying Dutchman, why not the ghostly Czech too, condemned to bounce for ever across the billows? But the name of the boat would have to go. I'd be inclined to substitute the *Lady Maggie*.

The trouble with owning such a yacht now is that much of the romance disappeared along with the brass-and-mahogany fittings, the barefoot sailors pumicing the gleaming white decks, the flap of canvas, even the smuts of coal-smoke. The 19th century was the classic period, beginning with Byron's *Bolivar*, built in Genoa to the designs of an English naval architect – the same who conceived Shelley's ill-fated *Don Juan*. The *Bolivar* was built for speed, and his lordship would sit on the poop-deck penning *Sardanapalus* or *Marino Faliero* while the Ligurian coast slipped by. Even more notable was Lord Cardigan's magnificent *Dryad*, which accompanied him to the Crimean War and, anchored off Balaclava, served as his regimental headquarters. After leading the Charge of the Light Brigade and reporting to a furious Lord Raglan, the C-in-C, he returned to the *Dryad*, had a bath, drank a bottle of champagne, ate dinner prepared by his French chef, and went to bed in his state-room. The *Dryad* was also the setting for Cardigan's second honeymoon, when the death of Lady Cardigan ('My dear, the old bitch is dead, let's get married at once!') allowed him to make an honest woman of his mistress, Miss Horsey de Horsey.

In those days and for long after, the Admiralty ran a succession of big steam yachts, the perk of the First Lord. In the golden, elegiac summers before the Great War, letters and memoirs tell of unforgettable cruises in HMS *Enchantress*, with Churchill as host, and such luminaries as 'Squiff', 'Margot', 'LG' and 'FE' enjoying the Mediterranean sunshine, with a 'greyhound of the sea' in attendance. But that was the Indian summer of romantic yachting. After the first world war there was not quite the same sense of easeful certitude. Edward VIII brought the Mediterranean cruise into disrepute in 1936 by his disastrous expedition with Mrs Simpson, and in the post-1945 world a succession of grotesques – King Farouk, Lady Docker, Aristotle Onassis – used their yachts to plumb Stygian depths of vulgarity. So what? If the romance has gone, there is still a lot to be said for joining one's vessel at Monte, just as the sun goes down over the Massif des Maures. 'Evening, Captain, how soon can we sail?' 'Half an hour, Sir.' 'Right. We should make Ajaccio by dawn. After that, we shall see. Positano, perhaps. Or Amalfi.' 'Aye, aye, Sir.' There's nothing like an expensive yat for bringing out the Walter Mitty.

15 August 1992

The strange case of thirty thousand spouses

When I arrived in Korea last week, for a brief visit, I found Kimpo airport at Seoul teeming with an enormous number of young men. They appeared to come from all over the East and, as most of them were foreigners, long queues stretched in front of the immigration desks. This annoyed me but it did not seem to disturb the young men, who were laughing and chattering. They were clearly pleased with life. When I finally got through, I remarked on the phenomenon of the young men to the people who met me. 'Oh,' they said, 'if you had been here earlier in the day you would have found the airport crammed with young women.' The fact is I had stumbled upon the ingathering of what was described as '30,000 pure young men and women from 120 countries' who had come to Seoul to be married in a giant wedding ceremony in the Olympic Stadium.

This event had been organised by the Reverend Sun Myung Moon, and he conducted the ceremony which took place on Tuesday. I received an invitation to it in exquisite Korean script and I regret I could not be there. The Revd Sun Moon is a strenuous campaigner for world peace, and one way he believes it can be furthered is by encouraging young people to marry across national, racial and colour divides. This is a radical attitude anywhere but more so in the East than in the West, for many oriental societies are still endogamous. Neighbouring peoples, such as Koreans and Japanese for instance, are highly suspicious of each other, what we would call 'racist'. So encouraging them to intermarry may well be a step in the right direction. However, I don't intend to argue the point either way. What aroused my interest was being told that many of the 30,000 brides and grooms had never actually met, though they had corresponded and exchanged photographs. They had been matched up, as it were, by the Revd Sun Moon personally or by his organisation.

Most people in the West find this outrageous but we are in a minority, if a growing one. The *Far Eastern Economic Review* tells us, in its current issue, that when the population peak is reached, the population of China will be 1,890 million, India 1,875 million, Pakistan 520 million, Bangladesh 295 million, Indonesia 370 million and Vietnam 165 million. That is 5,115 million from just six countries, making all our western societies together look puny. And the likelihood is that most of the marriages generated by this huge mass will be arranged by parents or families in one way or another, as they always have been. But parents and families are often motivated by unworthy considerations, usually financial. So it may be that matching by a disinterested outsider, concerned only with decorum and compatibility (and, in Mr Moon's case, internationalism) would be an improvement. That, interestingly enough, was Dr Johnson's view. Even in England, he thought, 'Marriages would in general be as happy, and often more so, if they were all made by the Lord Chancellor.'

His own marriage with a widow, Tetty, entered into from love, was far from happy; a failure indeed. Surveying the multitude of his friends and acquaintances, he saw that unions produced by mutual choice often worked badly. The notion that a man can find bliss only with one special woman, still widely held today, he thought rubbish. When Boswell asked him: 'Pray, Sir, do you not suppose that there are fifty women in the world, with any of whom a man may be as happy as with any woman in particular?', Johnson replied, 'Ay, Sir, fifty thousand.' This is a harsh, shocking doctrine to us. We find it hard to credit that the 4th Duke of Norfolk, who lost his head for conspiring to marry Mary Queen of Scots, had no contact with her except by letter. 'For other eyeliking hath not passed between them', as Walsingham put it. We are brought up on the romantic notion of a *coup de foudre*, a flash of recognition of mutual need, which only personal contact can produce. Yet Hollywood, the place where the ideology of romance is pursued most relentlessly both in theory and in practice, is notorious for the multiplicity of its failed marriages. Henry VIII, the unhappy prototype of the much-married man, as Antonia Fraser's new book reminds us, made the disastrous error of mixing reasons of state, which were naturally predominant, with personal romance. He wanted male heirs and supposed a girl with flashing eyes more likely to produce them. If anyone ever did, he illustrated Johnson's maxim that to marry again is 'the triumph of hope over experience'.

It seems to me that our present royal family has now tested the theory of romantic marriage to destruction. Traditionally, most royal unions had been arranged. When Princess Margaret fell in love with Group-Captain Townsend, she was argued out of her desire to marry him. But that was the turning-point. Thereafter, the Palace, egged on by the media and with the approval of public opinion, foolishly scrapped its prohibitions and allowed its young people to marry anyone within reason whom they fancied. The result has been a series of much publicised disasters, with possibly more to come. Having failed to stick to its principles, the monarchy now finds itself in real trouble, with the media in full cry and public opinion increasingly following. It should ignore both and go back to the well-tried old methods, risking being called stuffy. But it is probably too late for that.

Meanwhile, young people, who study royal behaviour carefully, are in danger of drawing the wrong conclusions from the breakdowns and scandals. Instead of reacting in favour of more prudential marriages, putting sense before sensibility, they are turning against formal marriages altogether. It matters not that informal arrangements, such as that between Mia Farrow and Woody Allen, are still more likely to end in anguish and recrimination, as a growing body of evidence proves. To many emancipated young women – and it is the women who decide, in most cases, whether marriages occur or not – it now seems a shrewder bet not to marry at all. That is the road to misery and economic disaster, both for individuals and society. So I am glad that someone, albeit in distant Korea, is trying out another alternative, and I shall look with interest to see whether the statistics confirm the wisdom of these new-style arranged unions. The Lord Chancellor, a canny Scot doubtless anxious for fresh business, ought to keep an eye on them too.

29 August 1992

Why do Italian opera-goers behave like beasts?

Recently I attended the last performance of four of Verdi's *Otello* at Covent Garden. I felt privileged. It was without doubt the finest operatic production I have ever seen or heard in my life. Singing, orchestral playing, conducting, sets, were all superb. Sir Georg Solti, by careful coaching, at which he is so gifted, managed to get from the young man who played Iago a performance of astonishing mastery. Placido Domingo was in fine voice, as was Kiri Te Kanawa. There were magnificent sets, based I think on Veronese; and the costumes of the men bore a marked resemblance to those worn in Velazquez's *Surrender of Breda*, an inspired idea. The end of the first part, in which Otello surrenders to Iago's insinuations, resolved for me a problem which has worried me all my life: was Verdi a greater composer than Wagner? The answer is yes, because Wagner, with all his gifts, did not write music of this quality. I want to pay tribute to Jeremy Isaacs, who is head of Covent Garden, for giving music-lovers such a treat, which I at least will remember all my life. I do not know to what degree Isaacs was responsible for this production, but as he always gets blamed when things go wrong, it is only fair that he should get the credit when things go supremely right, as on this occasion.

What made me angry was that a week or so later Pavarotti, an even greater artist than Domingo, was booed by the thugs who sit in the upper circles of La Scala in Milan. He was singing Don Carlos, a role he had never played before; a severe trial. He sang a wrong note because he made a mistake in breathing. This is very easy to do, as I learned at the age of 13, when I was singing the treble solo in Hummel's wonderful *Benedictus*. Father Rogers, our choirmaster, was angry with me, but he was generous enough to admit that we can all make such mistakes. The claque at La Scala, some of the most villainous persons who have ever been permitted to enter an opera house, continued to barrack and abuse Pavarotti, who is a man – considering his genius – of astounding modesty, for the rest of the performance. Instead of resenting this, he said, 'I did make a mistake, and will try to do better next time.' There spoke the true artist, humble and contrite in his willingness to admit he sometimes falls short of the standards he sets himself.

It is not the first time that the public at La Scala has insulted great musicians. Indeed, considering that the Milanese on the whole are civilised people – they buy, for instance, in great numbers, the best newspaper in Italy, *Il Giornale* – it is amazing how badly they behave when they get into their magnificent opera house. Consider, for instance, the case of Puccini's *Madame Butterfly*, which had its première at La Scala on 17 February 1904, with the wonderful soprano Rosina Storchio in the title role. Puccini had worked on this opera for nearly four years and had taken immense pains to combine all that was best in Orientalism with the highest standards of Italian lyric writing of his day. The result has been loved by millions of opera-goers ever since. The sense of drama, the pathos and tragedy, the musical line, the orchestration and the sheer beauty of this wonderful opera have seldom been equalled. Mozart himself would have been proud to have written it. Puccini, his librettist Giacosa, and Illica, the producer, as well as a superb cast, went to enormous trouble to ensure that the première was as perfect as it could be.

But what happened? The work was booed from start to finish. Puccini himself called it 'a lynching'. Puccini was ill, the result of an early car crash, which he had experienced a year before. Even this was turned against him by a hostile newspaper, which ran a headline the following day: 'Butterfly, a Diabetic Opera, Result of an Automobile Accident.'

The first night itself was pandemonium. Much of La Scala was packed with anti-Puccini fanatics. As Puccini put it, 'Those cannibals did not listen to a single note – it was a terrible orgy of mad-men drunk with hatred!' Another eye-witness wrote: 'Little could be heard above the devil's chorus of growls, shouts, groans, laughter and giggling.' When Butterfly endured her all-night vigil, waiting for Pinkerton, and Puccini had bird noises put into the orchestral sound to mark the dawn, they were greeted by men making noises like the braying of asses, the mewing of cats and the barking of dogs.

Why do the Italians do these things? As a rule, they are polite and civilised people. I have painted all over the world, setting up stool and easel, with my box of water-colours and brushes in Venice and Brescia, in Padua and Naples, in Rome and Genoa. In France and Germany I have often been met by rudeness, hostile comments, and the most annoying thing of all – young men deliberately standing between me and the subject I am plainly painting.

Such behaviour is, in my experience, totally unknown in Italy. Quite the contrary. Ordinary Italians, whatever their class or income or profession, make sympathetic noises, encouraging comments – often well-informed ones, too – and generally give good, positive advice. And, when they like what I have done, they are warm and generous in their praise. I have found this in every part of Italy. The Italians love art, even amateur stuff of my quality – one reason why they are so good at it themselves.

So why do they boo a superb artist like Pavarotti? Why, when they enter an opera house, do these sensitive and civilised people becomes fiends in human form? It is an extraordinary mystery to which I do not know the answer. Moreover, the disease is catching. I understand that last Friday some people at Covent Garden booed a woman conductor. What a disgrace to a great opera house.

19 December 1992

Heavy trouble in Sweden

The striking blonde in the next seat to me on the plane to Stockholm turned out to be an investment banker. 'Unfortunately,' she said to me, putting down her financial paper, 'we Swedes are now in heavy trouble.' Then followed a discussion about interest rates. 'Ours will have to go up again,' she pronounced. It is a measure of the new coming-together of Europe that all of us, even the rich, stately Swedes – they had the world's highest living standards in 1959 – are now chained to the usurer's galley, with the whip-cracking Germans calling the stroke-rate. It's new to the Swedes and they don't like it, though they keep ruefully calm

But, being engaged in launching the Swedish edition of my latest book, I had other things on my mind. So had the man who met me at Arlanda airport and drove me to Stockholm: meter-maids. They are blonde, too, but somewhat beefier and very strict. I love Stockholm, which has the prettiest city-centre in Europe, with masses of sea, ships and stone and the excellent Grand Hotel plonked right in the midst of it, but it isn't a place to break the law and there are a lot of laws in Sweden. Even the cars tick you off, with flat electronic voices, if you do something wrong. We drove straight to my publishers, and I was closeted with photographers, first on the editorial floor, then in the attics. I was made to stick my chin out 'to catch our sensitive northern light' and the result made me look like Musso holding forth from the Palazzo Venezia. Then I was interviewed at length by a nice, bearded, serious man called Ake Lundqvist from *Dagens Nyheter*; and so on to the Institute of International Affairs, to give a lecture and answer questions. I had been there before: a delicious, tile-and-terracotta interior of what had been a 19th-century bank. They said I had a bigger turnout than Yeltsin, but that was no doubt Swedish politeness. There were some worried questions: was Sweden right to seek to join the EEC? Were the Germans marching again?

Then another interview and off by car to Uppsala. On the radio we heard the early evening news: bank-rate to go up to 75 per cent 'The Finns are in even worse trouble,' said my driver with gloomy satisfaction. The dinner, served in the wan evening sunlight, was superb: the Swedes do more varied things in the way of poaching, pickling, smoking and salting fish than any other people. The professors wagged their heads: 'Thank God we got rid of the Social Democrats in time!' At the university I gave the history dons and students a lecture, interrupted by the chiming of many bells. More worried questions. It was dark when we emerged: a quiet, underlit, old-style university town, with no high jinks and the red lights of students' bicycles winking in the street. I gave a lift in my taxi, which took me back to Stockholm, to Bo Lundqvist, the brilliant artist who does my Swedish dust-jackets, and a delightful blonde undergraduate who can't find a flat in Uppsala and so commutes from the capital: the taxi saved her a 90-minute train-trip. The Swedes work hard, whatever people say.

Then onto the night-sleeper to Gothenburg. Everything spotless, stainless steel, ingeniously contrived shower-room, soft, comfy bed, warm towels. What I thought was a box of Kleenex turned out to contain a large scrumptious ham-and-cheese sandwich, so I ate that and then settled down for the night with William Shawcross's life of Murdoch. We bumped and glided through the dark forests. At eight in the morning I was met on the platform by Per Dahl, also from my publishers, a young man who has an encyclopaedic knowledge of Baltic politics and gave me the lowdown on recent events. How, for instance, Königsberg had restored all the pre-war street-names so they once more had a Goeringalle and a Rosenbergstrasse. Much talk of the collapse of Finland's Russia-oriented economy as Moscow can't pay for anything. Dahl is also an accomplished craftsman and typographer and he presented me with a copy of my book sumptuously bound in reindeer skin. We had breakfast at the Europa Hotel, and he suddenly realised his credit-card was from a Swedish bank which had just gone bust and been 'lifeboated'. Another sign of the times.

At the Gothenburg Book Fair, however, they assured me books were still selling merrily. I signed copies, shook hands, chatted to other publishers, booksellers. A bearded Englishman, who runs one of the biggest bookshops in Stockholm, said he loved it: 'Best place in the world to live and work.' We walked around the stands, and I saw familiar faces. Margaret Drabble was there, Julian Barnes, the exotic and delicious Shusha Guppy. Talk of options, royalties, deals, Rushdie. A smiling Boris Pankin, former Soviet foreign minister, gave me a signed copy of his book. My publishers were exultant that my interview and Musso chin were splashed all over the front page of the arts section of the biggest Swedish daily. We lunched luxuriously on the panorama floor of a new skyscraper with a group of literary and arts editors. Gothenburg spread out before us, once known as 'Little London', Sweden's window to the West. 'Most provincial, as you can see,' said a Stockholm editor loftily. We had some good laughs, unusual in lunchtime Sweden. They liked my joke about Mendelssohn and Hegel.

Finally to the new auditorium, a state-of-the-art building open for the first time that day. At the touch of a button, massed rows of seats appeared from nowhere, and the main hall divided into four segments, each seating 500 people. But the sound-proofing of the electronically worked partitions left something to be desired. My lecture on 'The Writing of History' was hilariously punctuated by sounds from the next segment where the author of *A Guide to Swedish Folk Music* was giving a talk with illustrations from the piano-accordion, chorus and foot-stamping. There was also a kerfuffle at the entrance to my segment, where a group uniting extremist leftists and rightists, who have recently put out a Swedish edition of *Mein Kampf*, were distributing leaflets attacking me as a tool of the Confederation of Swedish Industry. No wonder the bank-rate was 75 per cent! What this had to do with the early 19th century, the subject of my book, was not explained, but they referred to me as a *tivolijournalist*, a new Swedish term of abuse. Pondering this, I was swept by taxi to the airport and so home. I think I rather like being a *tivolijournalist*.

19 September 1992

When the kissing had to start

One of the ways in which the Western style of life is being imposed on the entire world is in the far from minor matter of kissing. The outstanding example is Japan, the ultra-modern-archaic society *par excellence*. Some peoples, of course, do not kiss at all, preferring to rub noses or make other points of intimate contact. The Japanese do kiss, but until comparatively recently it was always in private. Looking through the magnificent three-volume *Japanese Prints and Drawings from the Vever Collection* by Jack Hillier and distributed by Sotheby's, I can find only one example of lovers actually kissing, though occasionally they are doing what are to us rather more indelicate things.

The failure of the Japanese to kiss in public angered the Americans when they took over in 1945. Hollywood had made an art form out of the kiss, since in those days the Hays Office permitted little else, and all over the world GIs were imitating Clark Gable's prolonged close-up osculations. So kissing was democratic, almost by definition, and the Japanese, by refusing to do it, were demonstrating their obstinate attachment to authoritarianism. This could not be tolerated. Word went down, not perhaps from General MacArthur himself, who was not a great one for kissing, but certainly from senior aides, that the kissing had to start. Kyoko Hirano, who has made a study of one aspect of the American cultural impact, *Japanese Cinema under the American Occupation 1945–52*, published by the Smithsonian in Washington, says that Japanese film-makers were positively ordered to include kissing scenes in their movies. As their subject matter tended to be ferocious hand-to-hand combat, kissing looked a bit incongruous; and some of the cast declined to be filmed doing it, rather as a few actresses in the West still hold out against nude scenes. But in general the *diktat* was observed.

It is not clear what is the present line on kissing in the White House. Bill Clinton appears to be a great kisser, not always in public either. But it may be, now he has actually won, he will renege on this, as on other election promises or hints on the grounds that compulsory kissing is Politically Incorrect. All the same, the march of democracy and kissing continues relentlessly. Certainly, there is much more of what used to be called bussing. When I was a young man, in the second half of the Forties, very few men and women greeted each other by kissing cheeks. That was a custom practised by royalty, along with their trades union habit of calling each other 'cousin'. Debs also kissed each other when they met (not their partners). Others kissed only as a mark of specific affection rather than social gesture.

It is true that if a French politician or general awarded you a medal, he gave you not just a buss but a positive smacker on each cheek: a fairly disgusting experience, we thought, from which you would emerge reeking of garlic and possibly covered in lipstick. But then the French were very forward in kissing. On an early visit to Paris I remember being shocked by the flamboyant way in which young lovers embraced in the métro, other Parisians paying not the slightest attention. But was not that just another example of French decadence, also then symbolised by the Olympia Press? Years before, a pious nun had told me that all indelicate words and indecent jokes were ultimately manufactured by the Devil in the *vieux quartier* of Marseilles.

Today, men and women greet each other with a kiss all the time. It is one of the few post-war examples of an upper-class habit filtering downwards (the use of 'loo' is another). As a rule it is the other way round: even Tory grandees now refer to voters as 'punters', and to judge by their behaviour half the Cabinet is composed of yobbos. But cheek-kissing, or what I call the double-buss greeting, which should be accompanied, on the male's part, by an appreciative *mmmmm* noise, as though one were enjoying a juicy steak, has spread steadily to encompass most of the middle class and is even (thanks to television) penetrating further. I would be very interested if someone could tell me when the decisive moment came. I first became conscious that the habit was established in the middle-Sixties, that decade of momentous innovation, when George Brown, then a senior minister, was criticised for kissing a female member of the royal family on both cheeks, at some government gathering, and then adding, 'And one in the middle too.' The fact that George, who boasted of having been born in Peabody Buildings, was taking advantage of the new custom was a sign of how far things had gone.

They have gone much further since, but it is still not quite clear what the rules are. When you come across a woman you vaguely know at a party, do you shake hands or buss? Mistakes are bound to occur. I sometimes have been kissed by a woman I have never set eyes on before; or, in my own confusion, find myself embracing a haughty matron I do not know. Not to kiss, in error or inadvertence, can cause offence, especially to ladies. 'Don't you like me any more then?' I received this ticking off from Edna O'Brien, whom I had failed to kiss at a crowded gathering last year. The room was dark, she had changed her hairstyle and, to be honest, I hesitated; and he who hesitates in bussing is lost. Shaken by this *faux pas*, I became a little disoriented, or buss-happy. The next morning, at a lunch, I kissed Margaret Thatcher, something I had not done all the years she was in power. I believe strongly that one should not kiss a prime minister, even if she is a woman, or perhaps especially if she is a woman: the dignity of the office must be considered. But a former prime minister is, I suppose, a different matter. Anyway, the deed was done and she did not seem to mind.

But there is a point about bussing which has received insufficient attention. Who ought to do the actual kissing, the man or the woman? Or does it depend on the way the two people feel about each other? The French, who naturally have thought deeply on such matters, have an old saying which applies more widely than to the embrace itself: '*Il y a toujours un qui embrasse et un qui tend la joue.*' Very true. Drusilla Beyfus, our leading authority on manners, tells me: 'There are no clear rules whether the man or the woman kisses, or whether it's first on the left cheek, then on the right, or vice versa, or only one, or both.' She thinks that, where there is special affection, one in the middle is quite OK too, though it doesn't exonerate the late Lord George Brown. She believes that the element of uncertainty 'adds to the fun'. So, come to think of it, do I.

23 January 1993

Darkness of Maastricht falls on Spain

Anyone who has any lingering doubts about whether Britain should accept the Maastricht federal system – and I am now convinced it is an unmitigated evil – should visit Spain. I have spent a lot of time there in the past month meeting a wide range of people, from MPs to businessmen. With hardly an exception, they regard Maastricht as an undemocratic monstrosity, forced on a suspicious and reluctant people, who are denied a referendum, by a corrupt and unrepresentative government backed by the main opposition parties. Because of the iniquitous PR-list system, MPs have to vote for the Treaty whether they like it or not, or risk political extinction.

The Spanish are an extraordinarily attractive people who are totally without vanity but have deep-rooted pride. They are fearful that they will become an economic and political colony of the Franco-German alliance. They see a strong analogy with the Napoleonic invasion of the early 19th century. Many liberals then began by supporting Joseph Bonaparte as king, introducing the 'modern' ideas of the French Revolution (just as some intellectuals still cling to the notion that the EEC is an enlightened concept). But once they were engulfed by the reality of the French occupation, with its systematic looting and murder, they rose as one man – and woman – and began the great war of resistance which, led eventually by the Duke of Wellington, threw the French ignominiously out of their country.

Many Spanish now see Felipe Gonzales, the socialist prime minister, as a performing poodle, dancing to orders from his socialist master in Paris, François Mitterrand. And, of course, Mitterrand himself is the elderly puppet of Chancellor Kohl, rather like the decrepit Marshal Pétain during the war, since the French currency is entirely dependent on underwriting by the Bundesbank. EEC subsidies have helped to provide Spain with a phoney economic boom, but the level of public debt is colossal, the economy is teetering on the brink of free-fall and many grandiose projects are coming to a chaotic halt as the money runs out. If the Spanish have to implement Maastricht and bring their budget into balance, they will either have to raise taxes enormously or virtually abolish their welfare state. How can either be done? They are looking for a saviour from abroad, another Duke of Wellington. Many see such a figure in Margaret Thatcher, who can talk over the heads of governments to the peoples, and raise the banner of resistance to Maastricht all over Europe. She was doing precisely that in Madrid at the Palace Hotel, where we were staying, and her popularity is such that her arrival brought the entire traffic of the city to a complete standstill.

The battle against Maastricht is a democratic struggle against the corruption of the élites, for the Brussels system, which will be hugely strengthened by the Treaty, is the perfect machinery for generating graft of every kind. The Spanish are increasingly outraged by the scandals rocking their socialist government. They are, to be sure, used to corruption. This month, I visited the ancient royal city of Valladolid, which I had not seen since 1950. It was then an unspoilt medieval town, full of spectacular palaces and ecclesiastical buildings. Now I discovered to my horror that 40 palaces and 15 monasteries have completely vanished, replaced by hideous redbrick offices and blocks of flats. This was brought about by planning permissions bought during the last phases of the Franco regime. But Spanish friends tell me the graft, after a decade of socialism, is now far worse, and this seems to follow a pattern of socialist corruption, reminiscent of what went on behind the Iron Curtain, which has been particularly noticeable in Greece, Italy and France. I dread to think of the British Labour Party, which seems hell-bent on being raped by Brussels, being infected with this fatal virus.

Spain when I first knew it, 40 years ago, was a poor, noble country, and it is now in the process of becoming a comfortable one. But it remains a baffling mixture of ancient belief and modern razzmatazz. At the little town of Medina de Rioseco, I was privileged to attend a service in which a young Carmelite nun took her final vows. This discalced, or barefoot, order is one of the most severe: totally enclosed, living mainly on vegetables and eggs, when they can get them; and the particular convent the girl had joined has no heating at all, though the winter climate is bitter. Under the law, a girl of less than 18 requires parental consent to join, and this was stoutly refused. But on her 18th birthday she was off, and now, five years later, she was taking her final, perpetual vows. The bishop asked her to swear them through a fearsome iron grille, covered in outward-pointing knives, and she answered in a firm, confident voice. Her parents were in the pew in front of us, weeping copious tears, and afterwards the bishop embraced them both tenderly, while a splendid local choir, accompanied on the organ by the town baker, sang the *Hallelujah Chorus*. We were then taken round by a side door to the visitors' grille, through which we could see this beautiful young nun, wearing a garland of white roses as a bride of Christ, smiling, her eyes lit with the joy of the true religious spirit.

At the other end of the spectrum, I stayed in a spectacular new hotel, just opened in Barcelona, which embraces all the miracles of modern high technology. The panel by my bedside alone contained no less than 15 special controls, none of which I began to understand, not having taken a degree in computing. What particularly mystified me was that every time I turned a light on it automatically turned itself off after 30 seconds, most disconcertingly. I did not discover, until I was just about to check out of the hotel, that I might have prevented this by pushing my entrance card into a special 'master-switch' slot. But how was I to know? Nor could I discover how to turn on the hot water, which was also governed by a complex electronic system. As a result, I had to take my bath that morning in icy cold water and in Stygian darkness. I might just as well have been a Carmelite nun.

31 October 1992

Personal reflections on being busted

No: I have not been caught by Customs, like Taki at Heathrow, with the stuff hanging out of my back-pocket. I have had my head cast in bronze. The sculptor, Gerald Laing, is one of those brave and gifted souls – they are more numerous than they were a few years ago, thanks be to God – who are trying to recover the beauties and techniques of European art from the ravages of 20th-century modernism, now at its last gasp. This new renaissance has not been easy. Many skills, passed on by example from generation to generation, and steadily improved until they reached their apogee in the late 19th century, had virtually ceased to be used and were certainly not taught in the schools. With one or two exceptions, modern textbooks prove useless. Gerald was lucky to find an old copy of *Modelling and Sculpting the Human Figure* by Edward Lanteri, who was Professor of Sculpture at the Royal College of Art a century ago, which taught him a lot.

He was luckier still to come across the Roman bronze-caster George Mancini, at the end of his working life, when he was at last ready to divulge the secrets of his art at his foundry in Fulham. Mancini was brought to London before the first world war by Lord Kitchener, to cast garden statuary. One of his last works in Rome was a giant equestrian statue of Garibaldi: Mancini, the sculptor and the architect of the base all had lunch in the belly of the horse before it was sealed up. He used exclusively traditional tools, such as bow drills, scorning modern welding and grinding techniques, which make corrections to the bronze possible, preferring instead to get a perfect cast. Thus

Gerald, by learning from him, became part of the grand tradition.

The process of being busted was absorbing from start to finish. Gerald came to our house to model my head, lifesize, in clay over a prepared armature (support), using wooden tools and measuring calipers. He astonished me by the speed at which he worked and the rapidity with which my head and neck took shape. After three sittings he had completed what seemed to me a stunning likeness. Then he took the clay head down into our garage and made a plaster of Paris mould of it in two parts. When the mould was opened, the clay was automatically destroyed.

Gerald took the mould back to his beautiful little castle on the Black Isle, in the Moray Firth, where he has his foundry. He cast the mould into a reinforced plaster positive image, identical to the original clay model. These casts can be easily handled and stored indefinitely. His next step was to make a flexible rubber mould of the cast (in two halves), reinforcing it with a plaster jacket. Then he removed the inside plaster model, and coated the interior of the rubber mould with a layer of melted wax, to the desired thickness of the bronze (about three-eights of an inch). The cold wax, hollow and the same shape that the bronze would be, was removed from the rubber, and four feeds (wax rods as thick as a finger) fixed to the bottom edge of the wax and joined together as a wax cup. Then he dipped the wax in a slurry and coated it with ceramic powder, leaving it to dry. This coating process was repeated ten times until he had a ceramic shield over the wax, inside and out, about a quarter-inch thick.

The climax started when the whole thing was placed, cup downwards, in a kiln, and heated rapidly to 750 degrees, being held at that level for 20 minutes; the wax melted and ran out, leaving the mould empty, dry, sterile and hot, in exactly the shape he wanted the bronze to be. Meanwhile he heated a crucible of bronze ingots in the furnace to a temperature of 1200 degrees. When this was hot enough he rushed the mould from the kiln to a pit in front of the furnace and inserted it into a bed of sand with the cup uppermost. The final move was to use tongs to lift the crucible from the furnace, clear any dross from the surface of the molten metal, and pour the rest into the mould through the cup. Once the metal cooled, he broke away the ceramic shell, cut off the feeds, cleaned the metal, drilled holes for the bolts to secure the bust to its base, and began the process of patination by using corrosive chemicals and heat. Once satisfied with the seaweed colour of the bronze, he was off to his next assignment, to do Pavarotti for Covent Garden.

The bust now reposes in a corner of our drawing-room. My wife thinks it is a bit stern, adding, 'But then you are like that, aren't you?' Gerald believes in total accuracy: no flattery. The impressionistic way he has done my hair reminds me of Alessandro Aligardi (1598–1654), especially in his marble heads of torchbearers, angels and so on; the face recalls the bravura of Louis-François Roubiliac (1702–62), notably in his terracotta bust of Pope in Birmingham's Barber Institute, or his marble bust of Swift in Trinity College, Dublin. So there is a touch of both the baroque and the rococo in the handling, and I am delighted with it all. I hope Pavarotti is equally pleased when his head emerges from the pit. What I can't decide is how to light it. Canova favoured wax candlelight, but then he was thinking in terms of marble, for which it is undoubtedly the best. But it is a bit impractical nowadays. I haven't yet solved this problem.

What prompted my sombre reflections was the thought of all the waste produced by modernism. We have lost two generations – half a century – of true sculpture in the pursuit of ugliness and, despite the efforts of Gerald Laing and a few other new masters, some skills have been lost, though I hope not for ever – in drawing and painting no less than in sculpture. We now have to make up for the time we have so profligately squandered in this century, by ensuring that our schools of art are properly run by people who have the requisite standards of technical expertise; only then can students rejoin the mainstream of European art, which has been flowing underground for so many decades. That is why I support the admirable efforts of this journal's art critic, Giles Auty, to bring about a counter-revolution in British art, which will topple the frauds and con-men from their innumerable positions of power, and expel the barbarians who have dominated our academies, galleries and cultural institutions for so long. If that means spilling a little blood, as well as melting wax, I for one will not shrink at the prospect.

30 January 1993

Chess: a game of violence

The end of the Cold War opens the age of the Chess Wars. There is something symbolic in the decision of Short and Kasparov to break with the sinister World Chess Federation, whose dictatorship was sustained by East-West tension and which was overdue for discreditation. A *Times* leader thinks the breakaway of the leading players should make the game safe for 'free enterprise, meritocracy and democracy'. I would not be so sure. If chess becomes a world craze, as now seems likely, we shall be hearing from powerful, ancestral voices which have not yet spoken. What of the 800 million who inhabit India, where the game in its prehistoric form, *chatarunga*, was invented? Or the billion Chinese, who also claim to have fathered chess, and who have a distinctive variant, *choke-choo-hong-kai*? Then there are the Japanese, who have been playing their version, *shogi*, for a millennium, and who will be taking a growing interest now that money has displaced politics as its dynamic, and control of the game is up for grabs. Nor should we underestimate the Americans: what if Disneyland, for instance, should decide chess is worth taking over? I have a nightmare of millions of kids being introduced to the game by gigantic Mickey-kings and Minnie-queens, with Goofy-knights, Donald-Duck-bishops and Snow-White-and-the-Seven-Dwarf-pawns, while the world champions battle it out in plastic Wagnerian castles.

Strictly speaking, chess ought to be the most innocuous of human pastimes, a game not of chance but of pure ratiocination, since there is no luck in it whatever other than the tiny advantage of white over black – and even that is evened out in a series. It is a feast of cerebral skill in which there is no urge to gamble, the quintessential intellectual's game from which sensuality, cupidity and animal instincts are banished, and *homo sapiens*, pure and undefiled, wins by brain power alone. Unfortunately, clever people are as prone to vanity, spitefulness and aggression as anyone else – more so, perhaps – and so chess is just as likely as any other pastime to end in tears and rage. If Mr Jorrocks could describe hunting as 'the image of war without its guilt, and only five-and-twenty per cent of its danger', then chess is entirely risk-free, but the bellicose imagery is ubiquitous. All chess games end in genocide or unconditional surrender, or after protracted trench-warfare attrition, peter out in an angry peace (or 'draw') which is mere preparation for further hostilities.

Great craftsmen from scores of races, working in ivory, silver, stone, porcelain, cast iron and wood, have exercised their inventiveness in chess sets, but the prevailing theme is confrontation and battle. It is true collectors can find sets of heavily glazed Doulton mice, or Meissen frogs, or foxes painted by the Nazarene Von Kaulbach, or locusts

made in glass blown in the Venetian lagoon, or Chinese ivory rats
with ruby and amber eyes. But no one ever played an actual game
with these off-putting things. The set I would most like to possess
was made in the late 18th century in ceramic by Wedgwood, with
designs by the sculptor John Flaxman, who used Mrs Siddons as his
model for the queens and her brother Charles Kemble for the kings.
But such treasures are cabinet pieces. The vast majority of sets stress
conflict and ceremonious annihilation. Long before the West arrived,
mandarins played with sets of Chinese and Mongolian soldiers.
Brahmins used Hindu and Mussulman warriors, then, when the East
India Company took over, switched to turbaned armies fighting an
array of 'Johns' in top hats.

The theme of antagonism in chess has been explored in countless
variations all over the world for many centuries. A thousand years
ago, Dark Age intellectuals were bidding craftsmen make pawns like
Viking invaders and Saxon house-carls, and only the other day I saw
in a Baker Street shop a set of constables dominated by Sherlock
Holmes, in white, and Professor Moriarty's gang in black. This
dualism of crime and its prevention is not so different from the
Flemish sets, made in the 16th century and after, featuring Virtue
and Vice, with the white king and queen reverently clasping bibles
and the pawns as cherubs, while the black king is Mephistopheles,
and his queen does a striptease to the delight of pawn imps. French
and German craftsmen produced some memorable battle scenes in
enamelled pieces: Gustavus Adolphus versus the House of Habsburg,
Catholics and Huguenots, Richelieu's red-crossed guards with His
Eminence as king, against musketeers led by Anne of Austria as
queen. I believe there is an 18th-century set of Wolfe and Montcalm,
and there are certainly many different Waterloo sets, both French-
and English-made, featuring Bonaparte and (quite anachronistically)
Josephine as queen, Wellington, Ney, Masséna, the Prince Regent
and his much-hated Caroline. The old Russian Imperial Porcelain
Factory, before it was nationalised, even produced a set of Communists
and Capitalists.

Antagonism, fury, instant slaughter, long-meditated revenge and
the lust to annihilate your opponent are thus natural to chess and
may help to explain why grandmasters so often hate each other –
their personal animosities, as in boxing, helping to increase the
saturnine appeal of the game. The symbolic violence of chess may
also explain why, until recently, the game had so little attraction for
women, who tend by nature to be eirenic. My awareness that women

were not keen on chess came at an early age, five or perhaps even less, when I watched my parents in the terminal stage of a game to which my mother had been reluctantly conscripted. *Father* (impatiently): 'No need to ponder any further. You have only two possible moves, this – and that.' *Mother*: 'I have only your word for it. Supposing I think of a third?' *Father*: 'No. I have worked them all out. You have two moves only.' *Mother*. 'You are wrong. There is a third.' *Father* (excitedly): 'I don't believe you – what is it?' *Mother*: 'This.' *Kicks table over and scatters pieces on the carpet.* That was the only time I heard my father swear, for which he was instantly rebuked, my mother thus ending with the moral advantage too.

However, things are changing. A 15-year-old Hungarian genius, Judit Polgar, has beaten Boris Spassky in a match and achieved grandmaster status (not, I notice, 'Grand Mistress' or even Grand Person – chess is a conservative game, as befits its antiquity). In addition to everything else, we are facing the rise of chess Amazons.

6 March 1993

Dennis Potter and the art of abuse

There is a silent Laurel-and-Hardy short called *Fight of the Century*, which develops into a large-scale and deeply satisfying pie-fight. The last few feet of the film are, alas, missing but even before that an entire street of people, including men in top hats and ladies with lorgnettes, are sloshing each other in the face with these splodgy missiles. I and my grandson, Tycho, watch this little movie over and over again with delight. Why should a 64-year-old and a three-year-old alike take such enormous pleasure in seeing men and women get their mugs covered in custard?

One reason, I think, is the speed with which the pompous and pretentious descend to the same mindless level of mutual aggression once their self-esteem is physically assaulted. We are cave-man bruisers under the skin. Thus we are all currently enjoying the brawl between Camille Paglia and Julie Burchill, two grotesquely overrated, overpaid and spectacularly aggressive and self-important women – an encounter which has been described by a third, Germaine Greer, as 'mud-wrestling with tits'. What the row is about is as much a mystery as the pie-fight. The point of it all is the abuse. Burchill threw the first pie by reviewing Miss Paglia's book in *The Spectator*, and asserting that Paglia 'couldn't think her way out of a wet paper bag', is 'crazy as a loon' and hands out 'crap'. Paglia throws back that Burchill's work is 'sloppy, dishonest and distorted', marked by 'clichéd locutions, braying rhetoric and meaningless incoherence'; she is a 'sheltered, pampered sultan of slick, snide wordplay'. Both claim victory like old-style boxing champs. Paglia: 'I went over her like a tank.' Burchill: 'I'm 10 years younger, two stone heavier, and nastier.'

The truth is, as these hoydens know well, that verbal pugilism is a highly salable commodity, the key element in a heady cocktail which boosts sales, circulations and ratings. Hence the conundrum: which is the winning mixture of abuse, sex and politics? The *Sun* newspaper? Or a Dennis Potter play? The answer is – both. Of course, there are differences, but they are essentially about markets, not morals. The *Sun* supplies erotica, potted views and vituperation to the blue-collars, shopgirls, typists and pensioners. Potter's brew is the tipple of the chattering classes. It's all a matter of business, innit?

To be fair, both the *Sun* and Potter also have a talent for verbal wit and a sense of pathos, carefully crafted for their respective audiences. When it comes to articulating rage, however, I think I give Potter the edge. He does not have quite the slashing scalpel of John Osborne, our maestro of polemic; after all, he is only a television dramatist, not a proper one. All the same, he can teach the *Sun* a thing or two, and I commend to Kelvin MacKenzie and his splash-subs Potter's latest philippic, originally delivered on Channel 4 and partly republished in the *Guardian*. But then it has doubtless already been, as the lawyers say, 'drawn to the attention' of MacKenzie, as he is dismissed therein as 'a sharp little oaf'. Rupert Murdoch, however, is the main target. He is compared to 'an enormous toad who croaks at all our doors and windows'. He and his employees are foul- and wet-mouthed, sewers, vandals wreaking vengeance and oozing ordure, guilty of cannibalism, fetishism, sadism – worse, Thatcherism – and sordid, money-grabbing, people-despising, voraciously nibbling rats. Just to open the *Sun*, Potter says, is to 'stain your soul' or risk having it 'emptied' from your 'blown-away body'. The solution is to have Murdoch strung up but 'cut down while still alive and left to croak out expletives'.

This tirade is not entirely aimless pie-throwing like the Burchill-Paglia exchange. Potter is incandescent because his latest offering,

Lipstick on Your Collar, has been taken apart by the tabloids for indecency, and to the uninstructed, Murdoch is the living symbol of tabloid journalism. I doubt if Murdoch has heard of Potter. Equally, I doubt if Potter has ever met Murdoch, so all his rage has been unleashed without a clear view of the target. Quite why Murdoch should attract such hatred is puzzling. So is his nickname. He is not at all my idea of a digger. He comes from the Australian gentry. His father, Sir Keith, was a Harmsworth protégé who figures in Tom Clark's rousing book, *My Northcliffe Diary*. He built up a nice little newspaper empire down under, though he never engrossed the equity. Murdoch's mother, the Dame, is a sort of antipodean Lady Bracknell. He had the usual education given to Australian boys of his class and, like many of them, came to Oxford for a final polishing. Considering he has spent his entire life in the media, he is reassuringly unscarred by it all, being courteous, soft-spoken, amusing, well-informed, a good listener and not particularly opinionated, at any rate by Australian standards. It is a pleasure to have him in one's house. I am not sure I would say the same about Potter, who sounds like the sort of person one would keep not just at arm's length but out of spittle range. If, however, he were confronted by the mild-mannered and inoffensive Murdoch, I suspect he would be at a loss how to proceed. A much more convincing symbolic personification of media capitalism would have been Potter's Channel 4 boss, the well-upholstered, gold-hand-shaking Michael Grade, whose chubby features are usually to be glimpsed, like his Uncle Lew's, at the sucking end of a colossal cigar. But Grade, being a patron of the chatterers, is exempt from criticism.

All these rows, in fact, are elaborate pantomimes, fought in public but according to hidden rules and secret alliances, and for opaque objectives of which ordinary people are unaware but which are transparent to the initiated. In the old days, historians used to distinguish between the Real Nation and the Political Nation, the latter being the ruling élite which determined things unless the people rose in irresistible fury. Now we have a third force, the Media Nation, the few thousand men and women who set the agenda and write the score on both sides of the Atlantic. Sometimes they have important issues to go on about. Most of the time they simply hurl pies. It may be childish and a waste of good verbal custard; but nothing which matters is at stake, no one is going to get hurt, and the Real Nation, like my grandson and myself, settles back and enjoys the fun.

3 April 1993

When a first night sparkles

As someone who, these days, goes to a first night only occasionally, I find the enjoyment much enhanced by its rarity. Indeed, there is nothing in the whole web of complexities which constitute our civilisation to beat a London first night for subtle variety and number of its pleasures – ten at least, by my count. First, there is the immediacy and uniqueness. In the last seconds before the curtain rises on a new play, you share the excitement of King James's court at Whitehall settling down to *King Lear* on Stephen's Day 1607, or, for that matter, the young bloods of the Inner Temple watching *Gorboduc* begin it all in 1562. And for a Tom Stoppard first night, as at last week's *Arcadia*, the intellectual electricity fizzles with incomparable urgency. The chattering classes know they are in for an evening of mental gymnastics and are tingling with anxiety about whether they can pass the test.

Second, there is the story. At a first night it is unexplored territory. Nobody has yet been able to spoil it for you. Stoppard delights in complex plotting, whizzing about in time, keeping you guessing and opening and shutting doors as often as in a Feydeau farce. Last week it was, as it were, *Occupe-toi de Milord Byron*. What had his Lordship been up to that dawn in 1809? Had he shot the minor poet? Would he, indeed, make a sensational appearance? Then, third, there are the things you learn, especially from Stoppard. The second law of thermodynamics I have known since it was drummed into my head by old C.P. Snow. But chaos theory is another matter. The fact that a 13-year-old, Lady Thomasina, could work it all out for herself before she even knew the meaning of the words 'carnal embrace' is a fascinating reversal of present-day standards. But not improbable: Byron's daughter was a teenage mathematical genius and later helped Charles Babbage to invent the first computer. The play is a testimony to early 19th-century education; not only John Patten but the fat man who runs the NUT should see it, and weep.

Fourth, there are the actors, nerve-wracked but also uniquely creative on a first night because they are giving birth to the characters whom the playwright has fathered. Last week I delighted to see

Harriet Walter present Stoppard's frisky Whig *grande dame* as a cross between Lady Ottoline Morrell and the Lady Lucy Lambton. It was fascinating, too, to watch Felicity Kendal demonstrate how a sexy, witty but above all beady-eyed, non-academic historian sets about demolishing a would-be fashionable don anxious to make a splash and appear on the *Breakfast Show* – and played here with enormous panache by Bill Nighy.

But, fifth, I am old-fashioned enough to go to the theatre hoping to be charmed by actresses' sensuous wiles. Last week I was rewarded by a bravura display from Emma Fielding as Thomasina, showing her as a glittering child skipping with excitement on the brink of intellectual and sexual awareness, then, as the 16-year-old, well over it and plunging ecstatically into the heady waters of ·adolescent romance. I could sense a number of gentlemen in the audience yearning for the exquisite creature on stage, and who can wonder? Not since the young Audrey Hepburn first launched herself have these alluring tricks been played with such assurance.

There are other physical pleasures too. A new play is, six, a visual experience, and one without a magnificent or at least striking set is at a huge disadvantage from the start. In *Arcadia*, Mark Thompson supplies a light-filled, classical-revival framework which both cunningly captures the time and mood of the play and gives the cast an ample space to strut, fret and argue. Even the misty, sunny, cloudy backcloth made a telling visual point: not quite Derbyshire and Chatsworth, perhaps, but certainly Sussex and Petworth. Nor, seven, did Stoppard forget the evocative sounds which, often as not, make a play cling to the memory more surely than the actors' voices. Here, towards the end, as events moved towards a climax, we had the unmistakable industrial music of Mr Newcomen's steam-engine softly supplying the horse-power to transform the landscape outside from classical order to romantic mystery.

An eighth pleasure, particularly keen on a first night, is the reassuring sense of a firm directional hand which makes all the other pleasures work smoothly, effortlessly, above all naturally. Trevor Nunn does this for *Arcadia* without a hint of intrusion, of director's ego. Of course he has a cast of great strength and quality. Even so, it was good to hear a text of such complexity (and length) delivered without a hint of fluffing or misapprehension. And Nunn had to contrive not merely to differentiate the movements and voices of Regency England and today, but finally to weave both sets of characters together into a seamless garment of stagecraft. When I first read the script last year I wondered how a director could possibly bring this off. Now I know.

Nine, the jokes. Few works of art are complete without some. That is why Shakespeare put excellent ones into *Hamlet*: he knew that nothing more surely binds an audience together into a receptive unity than shared laughter. Stoppard opens this play with a sparkling display of jokes which, like so many of his, spring from verbal confusion – in this case between flesh, as such, and what Catholic moral theologians disdainfully term its 'irregular motions' (i.e. sex). As the 13-year-old is the unwitting straightwoman in the dialogue, there is no doubt about the intrigued thoroughness with which the audience is ignited. That brings me to point number ten.

The final pleasure of a first night is being part of a collection of people – rich and smart, some of them even successful and celebrated, certainly more critical and easily jaded than most – and observing the process whereby playwright and cast win them over, or lose them. There is craft on the stage; a study of minds in the audience; an interactive contest between both. Last week at *Arcadia* the stage won clearly, a fact signalled to me after the curtain came down by an exchange between a neighbour in the stalls and his wife. 'I understood it all, darling, even if you didn't.' 'Beast! I followed every word.' 'That's my clever girlie!' So, I repeat: when a first night works, it beats all for sheer entertainment.

24 April 1993

A sudden outbreak of marriage

Recently, in our circle of friends and acquaintances, there has been a sudden outbreak of marriage. People coming up to 50, or already in their fifties or even sixties, confirmed bachelors, long-standing widows or widowers, divorcees, couples who have lived together without benefit of clergy for as long as anyone can remember – all, seemingly with one accord, have been trotting off to churches and register offices, or both, and plighting their troth. Who started this current trend, I am not quite sure. But I suspect it is catching. Indeed, I know it is. We were sitting around the kitchen table, discussing this and that, when my wife casually mentioned that Laurence and

Cecilia (or perhaps it was Ned and Josie), a couple who had been cohabiting since at least the end of the Vietnam war, had just told her that they were married the week before, without warning, fuss or explanation. 'Well, that does it!' said Kitty, slapping the table and jumping to her feet, the light of matronly battle in her eyes. 'I am going straight back to Edward to tell him he must come up to scratch.' So she did. And so did he.

Now the extraordinary thing about this revival of marriage is that it runs directly counter to the whole spirit of the age. All the resources and provisions of the welfare state, the injunctions of political correctness, the weight of academic opinion, the advice of tax accountants, the verdicts of the courts and the direction of new legislation – has anyone read the Children's Act 1989? – combine to suggest that marriage today is not merely unnecessary, expensive, evidence of heterosexual triumphalism and homophobia, old-fashioned, reactionary, Thatcherite and suburban, but legally perilous too.

One has only to glance at the marriage service in the Book of Common Prayer to realise how improper, indeed provocative, matrimony is in the 1990s. The text is full of forbidden words and undesirable expressions. It speaks of a 'miracle', a sure sign of religious fundamentalism. It refers to 'men's carnal lusts' instead of 'sexual orientation'. The very word 'men', used in isolation, is offensively patriarchal. There is an uncalled-for aside about 'brute beasts', evidence of blatant speciesism, and talk of 'servants', 'obeying', 'subjection' and 'weaker vessels', which suggests attachment to an outmoded class system or male supremacy or both. One passage has an insulting reference to wives as 'fruitful vines' and another flatly asserts that the purpose of sex is 'the procreation of children', which is strictly contrary to everything agreed at the Rio summit and taught by the Friends of the Earth, Greenpeace, Mr Jonathan Porritt, Mr Teddy Goldsmith, Madonna and other contemporary sages. There is even a sentence enjoining 'chaste conversation coupled with fear', which is nothing less than a call for the restoration of censorship. In short, this is not the kind of language which the Rt Hon Mrs Virginia Bottomley could recommend to the House of Commons or the Bishop of Durham to the Synod of the Church of England or Mr Andreas Whittam Smith to the readers of the *Independent*.

Yet oddly enough the news of this matrimonial recidivism, these *deuxièmes noces*, these triumphs of hope over experience, has been well received in our circle, has caused pleasurable flutters of good feeling among old married couples like ourselves, among newly-weds of the younger generation, and has been warmly welcomed by children and stepchildren. Even grandchildren, informed of what is going on, have made approving noises. The fact is, despite all the secularist propaganda, marriage continues to exert a strong appeal to our instincts for what is right for individuals and society. In this respect the human race, or the civilised part of it, has not changed in nearly 3,000 years. A passage in Homer's *Odyssey* conveys this feeling exactly. In the late Dr E.V. Rieu's translation it reads: 'There is nothing nobler or more admirable than when two people who see eye to eye keep house as man and wife, confounding their enemies and delighting their friends.' I like that word 'nobler'. It is apt. There is indeed something noble about marriage; and, in late middle age, it is even heroic.

But in addition to those permanent, instinctual feelings, I suspect there is a particular contemporary reason why quiet, sensible, mature people are suddenly rallying to the marriage standard. For the institution has taken some hard knocks recently. First, there has been that grotesque and hostile parody of marriage which has been enacted in a Manhattan courtroom, as Mia Farrow and Woody Allen, each flanked by platoons of lawyers, shrinks and counsellors, and watched by strings of wide-eyed, silent, reproachful children, both adopted and (as they say) biological, have hurled accusations of cruelty, incest, betrayal and madness at each other. The case has attracted huge interest even over here: men and women I know have taken sides, often quite violently. In a way all the modern age and its secularist, faithless, psychiatrist's values have been on trial in that courtroom, and a disgusted world has pronounced a unanimous verdict: 'Guilty!'

But we expect showbiz people to make a mockery of marriage. What has done more damage and seemed far more shocking is the collective assault on the institution recently carried out by the royal family. As Bagehot noted, 'A princely marriage is the brilliant edition of a universal fact, and as such it rivets mankind.' But a princely divorce, or separation, or row publicly carried on in the tabloids, is a grotesque edition of an increasingly universal fact, and as such depresses mankind no end. However worldly or sophisticated or cynical we may be, we feel let down, betrayed, grievously disappointed. We all need to be set a good example, to look up to someone. But who is there left? So, feeling the lack of such mentors, and by a kind of unconscious, therapeutic instinct, numbers of middle-class, middle-aged couples are suddenly joining the ranks of the respectably married, and thus signifying their approval of what the Prayer Book rightly calls 'this holy and honourable estate'.

15 May 1993

No time to be lost to sample gay Bulgaria

'Bulgaria ought to be much better known in the West,' said the parliamentary deputy to me in Sofia last week. 'Then tell me the three most important things it ought to be known for,' said I. 'First, there are unique characteristics to our folk-music, which were used by Béla Bartók. Second, we invented the Cyrillic alphabet and gave it to the Russians. Third, wall-paintings in our ancient churches show that Bulgaria formed a bridge between medieval iconography and the Renaissance.'

It is true that the Bulgarians love music. Some say they are the most musical people in the world. Near our hotel, I watched an exquisite little blonde girl, perhaps no more than ten, beg by playing on her violin the 'Ode to Joy' from Beethoven's last symphony. There were other musical beggars: a very old man with once ferocious mustachios piped folk-rhythms on a long, thin clarinet, accompanied by an even older man on a bowed lute. Down the road, you could see what was described as *'The Screw Spinnig Round* by Benjamin Britain'.

It is true about the alphabet too, though in Stalin's day the Russians denied it. The Bulgarians have an overwhelming passion for the printed word, and, despite an almost total lack of physical resources, they are now producing and reading books avidly. That was why I was there: the Sofia University Press had translated my book *Modern Times*, and had asked me to launch it and give a lecture at the university. The Marxist tyranny is over. The vainglorious Communist Party headquarters building, which dominates the centre of Sofia, has been taken over by a cinema and second-hand clothes-stalls. The gruesome giant tomb which housed the mummy of Dimitrov, the local quisling who communised the country on Stalin's orders, is still standing, covered in graffiti. But the mummy is gone, incinerated, its ashes buried in the wretched man's home village. Most Bulgarians I met do not like the present ruler, Zhelyn Zhelev, though they elected him president a year ago. But at least they can say so publicly. Sitting on the terrace of our hotel, we watched tens of thousands march past in an early-evening demo, shouting, 'Out with the traitor!' and 'No more red rubbish!' Their sad, careworn faces moved our hearts. They can read newspapers too. There are over 600 of them now, a riot of print. After my lecture, in a splendid but dingy marble hall, I was besieged by journalists with microphones and tape-recorders. What was going to happen to Bulgaria? How could it achieve democratic salvation? Would the horrors of communism return?

The deputy's third point, the proto-Renaissance, also has some validity. Sofia is dominated by the huge granite mass of Mount Vitosha. We drove up through its tree-covered lower slopes to the little village of Boyana, where a tiny pink-brick medieval church lies hidden in a bosky fold. In the year 1259, a great, unknown artist covered its interior with a dramatic series of realistic paintings, breaking away in one giant bound from the stiff formalism of Byzantium and anticipating Giotto. Whoever he was, he deserves a high place in the pantheon of the world's central artistic tradition. But I was selfishly glad his work is still largely unknown. My wife and I were the only visitors, and afterwards I could sit on a warm stone wall and paint a watercolour of the little church, undisturbed except by tiny songbirds and a young shepherd boy who was driving his sheep, their bells tinkling, down the lane. The balmy air, heavy with the scent of wild flowers, the absolute calm and quiet, the nearby presence of a great artistic spirit, induced a sense of total well-being.

'That's it,' I was told at one of the western embassies. 'Bulgaria is a kind of Garden of Eden. Life here, at any rate if you have hard currency, is perfection, and it's tempting to try and keep it a secret.' That is not difficult, for the moment. Package tours take some British, especially from the North, to high-risc blocks on the Black Sea coast, but the ancient towns and villages of its wild, mountainous countryside are virtually unvisited. A recent survey showed that the third least-borrowed volume in British public libraries was a Sixties tome called *Gay Bulgaria*. It's hard to decide quite why the country is so delectable. The food, except of the simplest kind, is dull. It is very cold in winter, very hot in summer. True, the wines are good and modestly priced – indeed, everything seems absurdly cheap. The ice-cream, too, is delicious. But it is the people who charm.

'We want a quiet life,' another deputy told me. 'No dramas, or adventures, or territorial ambitions. We leave that to the Serbs. They are the best at fighting. The Rumanians are the best at acquiring territory they have no right to. The Greeks are the cleverest. We Bulgarians have been in a lot of wars and we always pick the losing side. So no more wars for us. All we want to be is good, low-profile, well-behaved Europeans.' The Bulgarians have certainly been made to suffer. Half a millennium of vicious Turkish oppression, then four disastrous wars, followed by half a century of destructive communist economics. Rusty, deserted factories litter the fine countryside. Bare-backed peasants and their wives and daughters work with ancient ploughs, hoes, even their bare hands, in the hot June sun. Mules and donkeys are commoner than tractors. The people look vulnerable. The girls are remarkably slender, often beautiful in their shy way, with small, delicate bones. Even the soldiers, in their absurd, ugly, Russian-style uniforms, and the young policemen, seem lost, bewildered. But they all smile: they all want to love and be loved, be understood, helped to a decent life. I did not hear a harsh word while I was there. Even the demo lacked venom.

The Bulgarians have always appealed strongly to a certain kind of westerner. J.D. Bourchier, the famous correspondent who covered the Balkans for the *Times* between the 1870s and 1920, made his home there. He asked King Ferdinand for permission to be buried just outside the monastery of Rila, 6,000 feet up in the south-western mountains. His wish was granted and his simple granite tomb, outside the great entrance to the monastery, overlooks the tumultuous icy waters of the River Rilska. This is a fairy-tale spot, immense jagged peaks marking the skyline, their tops still snow-covered last week, dense pine and beech woods framing the monastery itself, with fortress walls surrounding its medieval tower and its polychrome church crowned with copper-green domes. Inside, there are vast wooden galleries opening into guest-rooms. Who would not be a pilgrim to this magic place? But hurry. Time's winged chariot, with its consumer economy, is on the way.

19 June 1993

Water buffaloes on the American campus

In New York I find people plunged in angry gloom about the Clinton presidency: 'Even worse than we'd expected.' One Bill Clinton decision which has aroused particular *frissons* is his nomination of Sheldon Hackney to run the National Endowment for the Humanities, a key post in American culture-formation. Hackney is a prime example of the high-placed liberal appeasers and stringalongs who are making it possible for Political Correctness to bulldoze the American education system into rubble. He is president of the University of Pennsylvania, the once great institution founded by Benjamin Franklin, now a hell-hole of PC and racial hatred.

The things that go on down there almost pass belief. Hackney cited the privileges of free speech to justify the appearance on campus of the violent black racist and anti-Semite Louis Farrakhan and the hard-core homosexual pornographer Robert Mapplethorpe, but in his book anyone who is not on the Left's culture-list of approved persons has no rights at all. Recently, blacks at his university destroyed an entire issue of a student newspaper because they objected to an article in it criticising positive discrimination in favour of themselves on the campus. Hackney refused to condemn their action on the grounds that 'there can be no ignoring the pain that expression [of views] may cause'.

With the authorities abdicating their responsibilities, militants swagger about the place rather like Nazi students on pre-war German campuses. Last January an 18-year-old Israeli student, Eden Jaco-bovitz, was hard at work on a theme paper at midnight when a group of black women students began shouting and singing and howling 'woo woo' underneath the window of his room. They said they were 'looking for a party'. After enduring the noise for 20 minutes, he shouted down at them to stow it and was greeted with the usual obscenities. Other disturbed students also shouted, but only Jacobovitz's words were recorded. According to the women, who immediately reported the matter to the campus police, he called them 'water buffalo'. This is an English translation of a Hebrew word *behayma*, described as 'a mild epithet to chide an uncouth person'.

The campus police, instead of taking action against the noisy women who had caused the incident, immediately began an elaborate prosecution of the Israeli student on the grounds that he had broken a university law which prohibits 'racial epithets' which 'inflict direct injury' on minority students.

The object at the University of Pennsylvania seems to be to create an atmosphere of terror in which whites will keep a low profile and cringe, while the black militants rule the roost. If that be the case, it seems to me that white students who simply want to get on with their degrees should boycott the place altogether and leave the blacks to carry on wrecking things. There are many good alternative universities in Pennsylvania. One of the riches of the United States, and one reason I am not despondent about the plight of the campus despite all the ravages of PC, is the sheer number and variety of places of higher education. There are about 3,500 universities and colleges, most of them highly competitive and capable of rapid change and improvement under a dynamic president and an ambitious board of trustees. Some famous Ivy League places like Princeton, Yale and Harvard have been badly bruised by PC and weak leadership, but none of them is indispensable and plenty of others are only too eager to appropriate their reputations by displaying first-class objective scholarship, tolerance and freedom of thought.

I was in America to spend a weekend at Adelphi University in Long Island, attend its annual Commencement and receive an honorary doctorate. These ceremonies are much more fun than similar functions here. They take place in the open in blazing sunshine in front of tens of thousands of people, who are addressed by all kinds of celebrities. The same day as we congregated at Adelphi, William and Mary celebrated its 300th anniversary with a speech from Bill Cosby the comedian, Spelman College was harangued by the talk-show hostess Oprah Winfrey, Hofstra University had the famous puppeteer and ventriloquist Cynthia Gregory, Penn State got the head of Merrill Lynch, Smith College the Pulitzer Prize-winning columnist Ellen Goodman, and the University of North Carolina produced Ted Turner, boss of the world television news network CNN. There is a great deal of cheering and irreverence. Many of the thousands of new graduates mark their appreciation of their parents' struggles to keep them in college by adorning their mortarboards with the slogan, 'Thanks, Mom and Dad.'

Adelphi will soon be celebrating its centenary, but in the last decade it has been totally transformed and rejuvenated by an out-

standing classical philosopher, Peter Diamandopoulos. He comes from
Crete where, as a 13-year-old in 1941, he defended his country
with a tommy-gun against invading Nazi paratroopers. Unlike most
university presidents these days, he is a scholar as well as an
administrator, which is one reason why he has been able to recruit
such an outstanding faculty. He is an entrepreneur, too, and scored
a big hit with his cheeky advertising slogan, 'Harvard, the Adelphi
of Massachusetts'.

The Clinton years are clearly going to be a tough time for American
scholarship and culture, and a disastrous one for American morals –
Washington is rapidly being transformed into Sodom-on-the-
Potomac – but they will also provide paradoxical opportunities for
up-and-coming universities like Adelphi to thrust themselves right
into the front rank by upholding the traditional high standards of
the academy. American parents, and the young people themselves,
are not fools. They know that a university which surrenders to
Political Correctness eventually wrecks the value of its degrees in the
market-place. And they are quite capable of shopping around for
institutions of higher education which stick to their principles and
keep the barbarians off their campuses. So, while the Hillary Clintons
and the Sheldon Hackneys perform their debased ideological caracoles,
universities which keep the faith are quietly consolidating their
positions in the hearts of the young.

29 May 1993

Dancing to damnation

Most people innocently assume we are gouging our way slowly out
of recession because that is what the media tells them. But a powerful
band of experts believes the world is about to plunge far more deeply
into it. Two of the richest men I know, Jimmy Goldsmith and George
Soros, have been buying gold. I also hear that Indian ladies are
stocking up on chunky anklets and bracelets, always a bad sign. Last
week I lunched at Boodle's with three City seers and the leading
authority on cycles, and all preached unmitigated woe.

I like a good gloomy conversation myself, just as I prefer funerals
to weddings, and I enjoyed fuelling their fears. And indeed there is

good statistical cause for dismay. The United States, the world's largest economy, has what now appears to be a permanent budget deficit and a structural trade imbalance, both of colossal proportions, and is run by an administration chiefly worried about skin pigmentation and gender. Britain has the biggest budget deficit in its history and an unbridgeable trading gap, with a bunch of demonstrably failed corner-boys in charge. The Japanese banks are technically insolvent, and as for Germany – but I won't go on. William Rees-Mogg has recently published a book giving hundreds of excellent reasons why we are about to experience a financial melt-down, and you can read all about it therein.

But while I relish probing the gloomy entrails, my own prognosis is cheerful, and for good reason. In the first place I have lived with these doom-sayings a long time. I first attended the annual conference held in New York by that admirable publication, the *Bank Credit Analyst*, which keeps a beady, independent eye on banklending, in the early 1970s. There I heard, from immensely learned persons, dire tales of reckless bankers and profligate spenders and a coming apocalypse. So these financial sandwich-board men, with their slogan 'The End Is Nigh!' have been parading for at least 20 years.

Then again, my approach to the future is always historical, and the first question I ask is: What did people do on previous occasions? And I have yet to come across a financial catastrophe which was preceded by widespread doom-mongering. Quite the contrary. Right up to the eve of the first international market crash, which began in December 1825, everyone was very cheerful indeed. The Chancellor of the Exchequer, a lachrymose booby, was known as 'Prosperity' Robinson. Charles Lamb rejoiced when he slashed liquor duties: 'Gin reduced four shilling in the gallon, wine two shilling in the quart. This comes home to men's minds and bosoms.' He called the government 'the best ministry we ever stumbled upon'. Mrs Arbuthnot, whose husband was a member of it, was furious with him for not allowing her, as a matter of propriety, to speculate in shares like everyone else. It's true her diary also records her friend the Iron Duke warning against 'the bubble'; but then he was also prophesying that the latest invention, the steam railway, 'would never answer'.

Everyone else was on the roller-coaster, Palmerston joining boards of gimcrack mining companies, Disraeli, not yet 21 but already a City shark, using the publisher Murray's fortune to set up a new

daily which would 'beat the *Times* hollow', recruiting Sir Walter Scott
as its patron and Lockhart as its editor. A few weeks later, all was
dust, but right up to the eve the carousing went on.

It was the same in 1929. Winston Churchill was touring Canada
and the United States just before the Wall Street débâcle. He had
recently spent five years as Chancellor, so he was neither innocent
nor ill-informed. He was speculating 'on margin' and wrote to his
wife a few weeks before the crash: 'Now my darling I must tell you
that vy gt & extraordinary good fortune has attended me lately in
finances.' He urged her to go ahead with her spending plans – 'you
shd be able to do the nursery wing all right' – and boasted that they
would all be 'well-mounted in London this autumn'. In America,
everyone was not only buying bigger and better cars – just before
the crash, Detroit had turned out 5.3 million and Ford had just sold
its millionth Model A – but enjoying mass air travel for the first
time. Posters insisted 'Air Mail Is Socially Correct'. That summer
Transcontinental Airlines flew the first regular coast-to-coast air
passenger service, and three weeks before the market broke Charles
Lindbergh took a Pan-Am plane to Panama with the inaugural cargo
of mail. Pilots were practising instrument-only flights and Universal
Air Lines were just beginning to treat passengers to regular in-flight
movies. All was innovation, optimism and action. Keynes's first
reaction to the crash was flippant: 'Wall Street *did* have a go
yesterday!' and he promptly dictated an article to the *New York
Evening Post* prophesying a rosy future for industrialists and farmers,
with low interest rates and high commodity prices.

Well. Things are very different today. Not everyone is as lugubrious
as my Boodle's friends, but not a soul I know is singing hallelujah
either. Most are psychologically prepared for bad news. No one is
splashing out. There are few shindigs. The Ascot attire was pawnshop
quality. London builders and decorators are on their best behaviour –
I have never seen anything like it – a sure sign of deep-rooted fear
among the mechanicals. Estate agents are humble. Smart restaurants
answer the phone. Cabbies are touchingly grateful for modest gra-
tuities. What does all this portend? If historical parallels are any
guide, then we are beginning a slow but sure recovery, happy days
will be here again by mid-decade and we shall enter the 21st century
with rip-roaring bravado.

People notice the violent swings of mood, the ups and downs of
the economic indicators, but only objective historians are fully aware
of the gradual but absolutely unswerving long-term trend upwards.

This has been a characteristic feature of the western economy since at least the 11th century (with a blip in the 14th), and there have been no recent developments to suggest that a trend now evident for almost a millennium is about to be inexplicably reversed.

Looking back, it is hard to think of any generation which, on balance, has been worse off than their parents. Of course divine providence may now be forming different ideas. Recently I heard a senior prelate (a papist, of course) warn and electrify a lunch party by stating, almost as a self-evident fact, that unless the outrageous depravities of the world were fundamentally reformed in this decade – something he judged unlikely – then he expected Almighty God to wind up the universe early in the next century. I rather agree with him. But that is a speculation in metaphysics. So far as the physical world is concerned, we will soon be dancing ourselves to damnation again.

26 June 1993

London, where the grass is greenest

There are times when I hug myself on my good fortune in being a Londoner. What – has Johnson finally gone mad? Not at all: let me make my case. This has been a wet May and June but the compensation is that, for the first time in some years, the grass of the parks looks genuinely green once more, and not just green but, seen in the shade against strong sunlight, almost blue in its luxuriance and riot. Riding gently down Constitution Hill in a taxi this week, I glimpsed again a sight which is to me quintessentially London: contrasting strips of blue-green shade and brilliant sunlit grass under the umbrageous canopy of great, ancient trees, while all around one is conscious of massive buildings and the vibrant, teeming life of a huge metropolis – the true *rus in urbe*.

No other capital city can provide these glimpses. Nor are they glimpses alone. A few minutes from my house in Bayswater, I can enter Kensington Gardens at Notting Hill Gate and walk across the grass all the way through Hyde Park, Green Park and St James's Park to Westminster while scarcely setting foot on a pavement – a grand, rustic perambulation through the heart of London, taking in not just endless sward and countless trees, but masses of splendid borders, ornamental lakes, bridges, fountains, pagodas and follies, not to speak of wildfowl both homely and spectacular.

Don't tell me you can do this in New York because Central Park, excellent though it is in its way, is rather a grim, grey place. One is conscious that it is built on impenetrable, heartless rock, because it breaks through the thin skin of earth in many places as if to remind you that, close to the surface, this is still the savage New World, not an ancient, long-domesticated haunt of civilised man. Indeed, when I walk in Central Park even in broad daylight, I am conscious of wild human beasts lurking in the undergrowth or hidden in the rocks – druggies, sex maniacs, black militants, aimless assassins, heavily armed beggars who will kill you for a dime and think nothing of it. The endless rim of skyscrapers always visible on high makes a gritty statement that Central Park is not *rus in urbe* but a rocky back garden in megalopolis. Anyway, by this time of year, when London is at its incomparable best, the Big Apple is already too hot and sweaty, going rotten, the ugly worms peering out in search of trouble.

Paris comes closer to the ideal, but, as even Nancy Mitford had to admit, there are no proper parks in the city of light. The Tuileries, the Elysée, the Luxembourg, Monceau and so on are dainty, artificial parterres, with altogether too much gravel, which becomes glaring white in the summer sun and gets into your shoes. These are gardens in which a *boulevardier* may stretch his legs a tiny bit, in the hope of picking up a *soubrette* (some hope, in my experience) or even a *grue*; floral tablecloths in which a *flâneur* may dawdle ornamentally, but not real parks for walking in. To be sure, such do exist, but right at the end of the Metro, so that just getting there involves an expedition through interminable jammed streets or the torrid bowels of the earth, and even when you reach Vincennes or the Bois de Boulogne you rediscover that the French have never been able to grow real grass.

The grass in Green Park is the best in London. Although this little Eden is only 36 acres, with its splendid trees and lack of artificial ornamentation it comes closest to the sylvan-meadow ideal of a great city park. We owe this glorious green oasis to Charles II who found it a mess – banks, ditches, barren earth – enclosed it behind a high red-brick wall and called it 'Upper St James's Park'. He put deer in it, built a snow-house and an ice-house, and took his daily walk up it, the route becoming known as Constitution Hill. Queen Caroline, long-suffering wife of George II, also loved this stretch and had William

Kent build her a little library there, reached by what is still known as the Queen's Walk.

Green Park was much used by the military to do those intricate evolutions in gleaming brass and pipeclay beloved of 18th-century sovereigns, so it was a natural venue for celebrations of victories. To mark the Peace of Aix-la-Chapelle in 1748, George II ordered a tremendous firework display there. Captain Thomas Desaguliers, described as Chief Fire-Master of His Majesty's Laboratory, had at his disposal 88 Catherine-wheels, 87 'air balloons', 21 'cascades', 71 fixed and 131 vertical suns and wheels, 12,200 sparklers, 10,650 skyrockets and numerous other *feux d'artifice*. A Temple of Peace, 400 feet long and 114 high, was designed and built, from which the King and other grandees could watch the display. It included a musical gallery, and in it a 96-piece orchestra, mainly of brass, wind and percussion, performed Handel's 'Music for the Royal Fireworks', specially written for the occasion and punctuated by discharges from 100 cannon. In all this demonstration of firepower, the Temple of Peace was ignited and burned down, the conflagration also consuming the Queen's Library.

No detonations in Green Park nowadays, thank God. I like to lie calmly in its herbaceous tranquillity, gazing up at the skyline of dwellings stretching from the Ritz to Spencer House, in which London's super-rich live. Lord Beaverbrook made his London home there, in Arlington House, from which he could take his morning constitutional, like Charles II. One day when Randolph Churchill called, the butler (who always referred to his master thus) told him, 'The Lord is walking,' to which Randolph replied hopefully, 'On the water?' Where the Beaver once growled out instructions to his editors, it is appropriate that Rupert Murdoch should now reside, on his brief touchdowns in London that is; and Jacob Rothschild can also be seen, at times, on the broad stone terrace of the town palace he has so magnificently restored and brought to glittering life. Indeed, when a royal garden party is on, as occasionally happens this time of year, the place really looks quite posh, and stable, especially when the strains of 'Pomp and Circumstance' come drifting over the walls from Buckingham Palace. Once again, there is nothing like this in New York and Paris. If London could only keep itself clean, and lock up its burglars and car-thieves, what a grand city it would be.

3 July 1993

A world where crime pays

The latest ploy used by Jehovah's Witnesses to get you into edifying conversation on your doorstep is to say, 'We've called to see if you're worried by the spate of burglaries.' I stand no nonsense from these people, needless to say, my usual riposte being, 'We're papists here, quite enough religion already, thank you, and there are at least six Bibles in the house' (slam door). However, I *am* worried by the spate of burglaries. Who isn't, except presumably the burglar classes, who seem to include multitudes of teenagers these days? The police say that even if you are in your house, in broad daylight, you are not safe from these pests, unless you double-lock your front door. Teenagers, black, white, Asian – it makes no difference – simply cut a section of plastic from a bottle of mineral water and, lo! a single lock, however sophisticated, is powerless to keep them out.

My wife and a friend were sitting in our London garden, three Sundays ago, about eight in the evening, with two grandchildren asleep upstairs, when one of these opportunists got in and whipped my portable computer from my study, then nipped upstairs and stole such of my wife's jewels as were not hidden away. They were welcome to my Tandy, obsolete and the property of Lord Rothermere anyway, but Marigold's little baubles were dear to her. Anyway, the idea of these footpads, many of them with expensive drug habits, creeping about one's home is disagreeable.

In 1883 the Russian historian Nicholas Karamzin, asked to characterise his country, pondered for a minute, then said, 'What goes on in Russia? Thieving.' That remains the chief Russian activity today, of course, the only difference being that it has spread to the rest of the world. Anything not nailed down, chained to the railings or ingeniously hidden is pinched. All classes steal, often things of little value they do not need. Last year the Ritz lost 300 tea-strainers, 3,000 facecloths, 6,000 ashtrays and 5,000 pairs of slippers, all stolen by their Ritzy guests. When did *you* last steal from a hotel?

The clergy no longer preach against theft, which they tend to treat as a form of legitimate income-redistribution. When teenage gangs used stolen cars to embark on a series of ram-raids on shops in the

Newcastle area last year, the Archbishop of Canterbury blamed it all on the government. If thieves rob churches, as they increasingly do, given the chance, the authorities simply shut the churches, one way of 'solving' the problem. Powerful, influential men, like Max Hastings and Simon Jenkins, swap stories, as readers of the Letters pages of *The Spectator* will have noted, about how many of their car radios have been pinched. Roy Jenkins, a former Home Secretary, dwells rather irritably on this point in his memoirs, but without reproaching himself for failing to deal more severely with thieves when he had the chance. The truth is our society is geared to encourage stealing. The insurance companies simply pay up. The police don't bother much, and when they do judges and JPs, with the strong encouragement of the Home Office, conspire to keep convicted thieves out of prison.

As a result, it pays to be a professional thief, and to adopt more and more daring tactics. Not long ago, about 3.30 in the afternoon, while I was working in my study, I heard a noise and went into the drawing-room. A burglar, dressed in a black cat-suit – a jewel-thief no doubt – was calmly unscrewing the bars from one of the windows. Instead of creeping back into my study and dialling 999, I stood watching this ingenious craftsman at work, until he spotted me. He then dropped like a stone on to a garden table, shattering it. By the time I got down myself, he was vanishing over the hedge. I have since asked myself what I would have done had I reached him in time. Burglars, when apprehended, once 'went quietly'. Now they resist and even attack, knowing that if the householder uses force it is he, not they, who will be charged with an offence. As a recent judicial summing-up and verdict indicated, even a habitual thief who murders a victim who hits back can successfully plead self-defence.

The widespread impression that the law is pro-crime is reinforced by our own guilt feelings, the product of decades of political and religious brainwashing on behalf of the have-nots. An affluent friend of mine recently left his home to cross the road and buy a newspaper, foolishly leaving his front door ajar. He returned a minute or so later, sank into an armchair and opened his paper. He thought he heard a noise upstairs, and went to investigate. On the landing he ran into a young man, who asked him, 'Is this the way to the post office, man?' My friend made sure his visitor had nothing in his pockets, showed him the door, and resumed his reading. After a few minutes, he became aware that there was another intruder in the house, and again investigated, this time going into each of the bedrooms in turn.

In one he saw a foot sticking out from under the bed, and pulled on it. Another young man eventually emerged. 'I suppose you are looking for the post office too?' he asked crossly. 'No, man, I want the estate agents.' This fellow too was extruded. 'Well,' said I, 'why didn't you have them arrested and charged?' My friend, who is still – just – a member of the Labour Party, explained that this was not possible. 'They were both blacks, you see. If they had been white I might have thought twice about letting them go.'

My friend is not alone in operating double standards based on obsolete guilt feelings. Last week, Jacques Delors remitted fines worth £3.7 billion for cheating over milk-powder, Gorgonzola and Provolone. The reason was that the offenders, who must have operated on a colossal scale, were Italians, Greeks and Spaniards, and thus could not be expected to behave any better. The implication was that British, Danes, Germans and Dutch would not be so favoured. We live in a world, in short, in which honesty goes unrewarded, crime is unpunished and the wicked get away with it. Who would be a just man – or a virtuous woman?

7 August 1993

Australia's fraudulent historian

If the Queen wants to needle Paul Keating, the uppity Australian Prime Minister who is her unwelcome guest this weekend, she might do worse than ask, 'Mr Keating, what is your opinion of Manning Clark *now?*' Let me explain. Keating is a streetwise bruiser of Irish descent, who left school at 14 and has educated himself while eye-gouging his way to the top of Canberra politics. One thing he has learned is that, at any rate in Labor circles, pom-bashing pays. It takes many different forms, and such boring things as historical facts are rarely allowed to get in the way of the rhetoric. For instance, Bill Hayden, the Governor-General, the sort of begrimed politico who would become president of Keating's proposed republic, has just launched a furious attack on Field-Marshal Haig, British commander-in-chief in the Great War. This monster, said Hayden, sent poor Aussie lads to their death because he hadn't troubled to learn the lessons of trench warfare, invented in 'the American Revolutionary

War'. He meant, of course, the Civil War, but what is 80 years or so between pom-bashers? Recently, too, a left-wing academic from Sydney had a go at another pom, poor Neville Cardus, the great *Guardian* writer on cricket and music, whom he accused, with no justification whatever, of being a 'fascist admirer'.

The founder of the pom-bashing industry, at least in its modern, pseudo-academic form, was Professor Manning Clark, author of the six-volume *A History of Australia*, standard fodder in many state schools. Clark's hatred of the English dated from his time at Balliol in the 1930s where, said a contemporary, he was severely snubbed, 'badly scalding his pride'. From 1946 Clark began to teach the then new-fangled subject of Australian history, and his huge tomes were a by-product of this course. His theme was the noble struggle of a revolutionary 'people' striving to break free from British oppression, and threatening repeatedly to rebel against their wicked masters and their time-serving Aussie collaborators, such as Sir Robert Menzies.

In sober fact, the history of Australia has been remarkably peaceful, the nearest approach to revolt being the 'Eureka Stockade' affair in 1854 during the Victorian gold rush. Last month I visited the site of the stockade, which has been reconstructed. It is a reflection of Australia's happy and largely uneventful history that this picturesque but trivial episode, which would have gone unrecorded in the history of less fortunate lands, has to be raised to the status of a major event. The truth is, the Australian settlements, whether originally convict or free, prospered mightily from the start and continued to get richer until, by the beginning of the last quarter of the 19th century, Australia had the world's highest living standard. Melbourne was then the wealthiest city on earth, *per capita*, and is still to this day a monument to Victorian prosperity and good government. All this has been accurately chronicled by Australia's greatest living historian, Professor Geoffrey Blainey. The country's relative decline set in at the end of the 19th century, with the rise to power of the Australian Labor Party and the even more disastrous trades union movement.

However, Manning Clark told a different tale, and one more congenial to the ears of the Australian left, with its Irish folk-memories and its chippy outlook on life. As each succeeding volume of Clark's *History* appeared, his standing with the Labor establishment rose, his fame spread and the Melbourne University Press zealously pushed his books. Clark, in turn, developed a left-wing celebrity persona, growing a sage's beard, wearing a huge black hat, cloak and broad leather belt, pronouncing on public events, genuflecting to the Soviet Union, and surrounding himself with adoring followers. His work became wilder and noisier, and less and less anchored in any historical facts. He himself was inclined, during his drinking bouts, to roam the university campus, shouting, 'Bloody poms! Bloody poms!' But none of this did him any harm, either with the Labor Party or the academic Left. On the contrary. People like Hayden and Keating were brought up on his message, and saluted him publicly when, covered in honours, he died two years ago. His pupils found their way to top jobs in the university history departments, where they waged ferocious warfare against scholars who disputed the Clark line. One victim was Geoffrey Blainey himself, driven into early retirement from his Melbourne chair by a vicious campaign of campus vilification.

Clark's inflated reputation did not go wholly unchallenged in his lifetime. In 1982 Claudio Veliz of La Trobe University published a review of Clark's fifth volume, under the simple heading 'Bad History', a masterpiece of demolition which ought to go into the anthologies. But most Australian academic historians were too cowardly to risk the fury of the Left by pointing to Clark's countless factual errors, appalling prose and sheer inventions. His followers ruled the historical roost and today form the spearhead of the republican movement.

Now, however, Clark's work has received a death-blow from an unexpected quarter: the man who published it. In the September issue of *Quadrant*, Australia's leading intellectual magazine, Peter Ryan, who ran the Melbourne University Press throughout the gestation period of the *History*, admits that he knew all along that Clark was a fraud and his books largely works of fiction. Now an old man, Ryan seems unwilling to go to his grave without admitting his share in a large-scale imposture on the public, perhaps the most successful – and tragic – of all Australian hoaxes. He writes: 'Of the many things in my life upon which I must look back with shame, my chief shame is that of having been the publisher of Manning Clark's *A History of Australia*.' His confession is an extraordinary document, unique in the story of publishing. Where it leaves the Australian republican movement is the big question, since it shows that the school of history on which its case rests is fundamentally bogus. In reaction to Ryan's apology, there has been some angry spluttering from Messrs Keating, Hayden and Co., followed by an embarrassed silence. That is why it makes an intriguing topic for the Queen to raise at Balmoral.

18 September 1993

Magic island

If I were asked to name the most delectable house in Britain, I would pick Eilean Aigas, a pink granite mansion on a rocky, wooded island in the middle of the River Beauly in Inverness-shire. The only approach is over a grand stone bridge which spans the tumultuous river, where salmon cavort in season. Then, as if to provide further protection from unwelcome visitors, the island itself greets you with a notice stating firmly: 'Danger: Children at Large'.

Centuries ago, the island was the site of a castle of the Clan Fraser. In 1838, the year Dickens published *Nicholas Nickleby*, the head of the clan, Lord Lovat, built the present house for the Sobieski Stuart brothers, who claimed to be the legitimate descendants of Bonnie Prince Charlie. Their pretensions have since been demolished in a celebrated essay by Hugh Trevor-Roper, but while they lived their claim was believed by many Highland landowners, including Queen Victoria herself. On the island they held miniature court, compiled a huge tome of clan tartans, and designed gothic furniture, which is still there. A splendid painting over the fireplace in the library shows the pair, bedizened in Highland rig down to the last cairngorm, surrounded by their clan regalia. By a self-denying ordinance, they remained unmarried, so their contentious claim would die with them. The property became the dower-house.

The last dowager to live there, Laura Lovat, was the daughter of Lord Ribblesdale, subject of Sargent's most flamboyant portrait. In the house she kept a court of Catholic writers, which included Compton Mackenzie, G.K. Chesterton, Hilaire Belloc and Maurice Baring, who spent his last years there and is buried in the windswept little cemetery up the glen. Tucked into books in the library are innumerable letters from Edith Somerville and Rose Macaulay, Dame Ethel Smythe and other famous guests. Then, from the late 1950s, a new circle of writers and artists congregated around her daughter-in-law, Lady Antonia Fraser. She herself wrote her celebrated *Mary Queen of Scots* in a wooden cabin overlooking the river, constructed on the lines of the writing huts George Meredith and George Bernard Shaw had built for themselves. The glitterati lounged round the swimming-pool, bought from the profits of the unfortunate queen, played charades in the evening or engaged in desperate games of perpetual ping-pong. I first visited the island in 1973 when George Gale and I were writing our book, *The Highland Jaunt*, to mark the 200th anniversary of Boswell and Johnson's trip. George recorded:

> There was tennis, fishing, a picnic miles and miles up the glen, and a great Common Market debate in which most of us, being opposed, felt unable to deal properly with the arguments of the most vehement pro-Marketeer, for he talked with the thickish accents of a European banker.

Yes: there were figures from politics and high finance too. On one of countless subsequent visits I recall a morning trying to console a shattered Reggie Maudling, who had just seen in the Sunday papers 'astounding revelations' of his relationship with Poulson, the corrupt architect, and realised this meant the end of his political career. 'Anyway, Reggie,' I remember saying, 'you're just too *nice* for politics.' There was another day when we took what seemed to be the entire Persian royal family up the glen for a sumptuous collation, served by butlers and maids in caps and aprons. The Crown Prince, then a smallish boy, persuaded or perhaps ordered the secret agents surrounding him to engage in a shooting competition with their revolvers, in which he took a prominent part. Alison Lurie, the American novelist, and I cowered behind rocks while the bullets flew.

Then there was 'The Great Sun is Red Fiasco'. Although the river around the island looks dark and forbidding, it is in fact perfectly safe for a decent swimmer, and is not even deep except in the pools, though the current can be mighty strong at times. We had been impressed by Mao Tse-tung's propaganda swim in the Yangtse River and the photo of his round, sun-like head bobbing above the waves. It seemed a good idea to Antonia, Jonathan Aitken MP and myself to have a similar photo of our three heads sticking up out of the black waters, and my wife Marigold was deputed to take the photo from the bridge. But by the time we three swam to the appointed spot, she was nowhere to be seen. The river was flowing strongly and, after treading water for some minutes, we allowed ourselves to be swept along. It emerged that Marigold had got talking to Mrs Hepburn, the cook, about how to make her famous venison stew, and had 'forgotten all about it'. So the historic snap was never taken.

The island is full of furtive creatures: roe-deer, wildcats and those rare and beautiful furry things, pine-martens. In the summer you see little of them, unless you are lucky and surprise a deer asleep in the bracken on a hot afternoon. In the winter they are hungrier and tamer; more visible too. The winters can be astonishingly mild: we have had a New Year's Day picnic up the glen in Riviera sunshine. But they can be very hard, too. The snow piles up in immense drifts for many days, and the whole land is gripped in frost like steel. Perilous ice forms on the outdoor steps of the house, and there is a particular flight, leading to the garden, of which I have a lurid memory. It was New Year's Eve, and my host, Sir Hugh Fraser MP, and I were just going out on a series of seasonal 'visits'. He went first, was swallowed in the darkness, and I heard the most almighty crash, followed by expletives. Hastening to his rescue, I slipped on the ice, too, and tumbled down in turn. Each of us, I recall, had various bruises, including a black eye or two, but we carried out our visits nonetheless. The next morning, Mrs Hepburn, with vivid memories of Hogmanay Eve, announced to the intrigued kitchen, 'The Lord save us! Major Hugh and Mr Johnson have been fighting!'

Now this blissful isle has been put up for sale by the Major's son, Benji, and those who buy it will find they have a treasure beyond price. My hope is that it will fall into gentle and considerate hands, who will cherish its traditions, and even add to them.

21 August 1993

Sexual harassment in a cold Oxford climate

In one university in Ohio, where Political Correctness reigns, male students, in their sexual transactions with females, must observe a question-and-answer code to avoid the fatal charge of 'harassment'. Positive verbal assent must be given to each forward move. 'May I undo the top button of your blouse?' 'Yes'. 'May I undo the second button?' 'Well ... yes', etc. The code, reported in the British press, has aroused sneers at Yankee naïvety, lack of proportion and humourlessness. But those who laugh are obviously unaware of what is going on here.

At Oxford, for instance, there are now 267 'harassment advisers'. There are 93 university departments – ye gods! – and each has two. There is a central panel of seven. Sexual harassment advisers are compulsory, for instance, even for the University Parks, the University

Archives, the Transport Studies Unit and – perhaps with some justice here – the dreaded Theology Faculty. To be a SHA is not a sinecure. You *must* fill out a form, every year, listing the cases you have dealt with. If there are too few delations, or worse none at all, it is assumed that the girls – sorry, wo-men – are too scared of you to report, so you are a bad, i.e. unenthusiastic, SHA. If, on the other hand, there are a lot, then the case is made out for more SHAs and the system expands.

To be a SHA is a constant temptation to become an inquisitor, spy and informer, indeed a blackmailer. The system ignores all the Rules of Evidence and the tenets of natural justice. In a typical case, a female student returns to college after the vacation – perhaps nine months after the event – reports it for the first time and demands, with noisy student backing, that the accused person be excluded from the college at once. For male tutors the matter is no joke since, even if they are entirely innocent, they may find themselves involved in heavy legal expenses and with no chance of wholly clearing their name.

'Harassment' is so widely and vaguely defined by the code as to make any would-be Torquemada rub his – or more likely, her – hands in lip-smacking anticipation. It is 'unwarranted behaviour towards another person, so as to disrupt the work or reduce the quality of life of that person'. Such behaviour includes not merely 'bullying' or 'verbal abuse' but 'otherwise creating or maintaining a hostile or offensive studying, working or social environment' for the victim by 'physical contact or verbal behaviour of a sexual nature, or other hostile or offensive acts or expressions relating to people's sex, sexual orientation, religion or race'. 'Abuse of authority', e.g. by a tutor, is 'an aggravating feature of harassment'. It seems to me almost any variety of traditional undergraduate or donnish behaviour can be included under one or other of these heads.

It's odd to think that, exactly 100 years ago, women at Oxford were struggling to escape from over-protection. *Oxford and Oxford Life* (London 1892) includes a chapter on 'Women's Education at Oxford' by Miss K.M. Gent of Lady Margaret Hall.

She was anxious to show that the girls had a good time. They were not forced to go to chapel, though 'a sceptical tone about religion' would be 'considered the height of bad breeding'. Anyone coming to a women's college expecting to 'find long rows of pale, heavy-eyed girls bending over books on a lovely summer afternoon' would be 'breathless with surprise' to discover 'the greater number playing "Prisoner's Base" on the lawn, with energy and enthusiasm'. Though hockey was regarded as 'too rough', the gymnasium was 'the scene of great festivity', and there were plenty of girls 'not altogether superior to a game of hide-and-seek all over the house, with the blinds pulled down'.

Sounds like Arcadia, doesn't it? No wonder, Miss Gent continues, 'the "masculine" or fast girl has been so rare that it would be almost personal to allude to her at all'. Of course, 'intercourse with male members of the university is not extensive'. But 'as long as she is with a chaperone approved by the Principal', a woman student 'is allowed the ordinary liberty in this respect'. If 'she knows men at Oxford' she can even go to their rooms, 'subject to the above conditions'. On the other hand, she can only have 'lady friends' to tea in her room, 'for even brothers are not admitted' but must be 'entertained in state in the drawing-room'.

Chaperoned girls may 'occasionally go to evening parties, dances always excepted as they are prohibited'. Most girls, concludes Miss Gent, feel that 'such a delightful period of comparative liberty will never come to them again', and she quotes one departing student: 'I shall never be so happy – the pleasantest part of my life is over.'

I'm a bit sceptical about the last, even from girls with a passion for hide-and-seek. But it's not difficult to see that young and inexperienced women would be happier observing a set of conventions reflecting age-old tradition rather than a fierce new code imposed by gender-conscious fanatics. From my own experience, I suspect that most girls who go to Oxford, having swotted like mad to get there, are rather looking forward to a bit of sexual harassment. For, after all, what is harassment but a modern term of disapproval, coined by the sex-war puritans, for the ordinary give-and-take of love-making? How can a man get anywhere with a woman without harassing her?

And how can a woman know she likes it until she's harassed? I'm not surprised that the sex-codifiers recently censured a visiting professor at Harvard for quoting with approval Byron's line, 'Who, saying she would ne'er consent, consented'. But then, what woman in her senses, then or now, would have missed being harassed by Byron?

16 October 1993

Thoughts on turning sixty-five

Paradoxically, the wet, sunless summer has produced autumn colours of exceptional glory. And, wandering round the Quantock beechwoods last weekend, I found myself in elegiac mood: how many more would I see? For I have just turned 65. A polite Scotswoman from the Ministry phoned to say that I would now receive weekly from the Government the handsome sum of £62.34. So I have passed the watershed into old age and hereafter it is downhill all the way. What have I missed, or contrived to avoid?

Well: I have never attended a pop concert or a soccer match, watched *Coronation Street* (or *EastEnders* or *Neighbours*), seen *The Mousetrap* or *Gone with the Wind*, picked up a Jeffrey Archer or a Martin Amis, sat through *The Ring* or finished *A la Récherche*, read the *Economist* or *Time Out*, owned a car, run an overdraft, bounced a cheque or appeared in court. I have never cooked a joint, used a launderette, changed a nappy, been to Annabel's, stayed at the Cipriani, supped at Maxim's, killed a fish, hunted a fox, stalked a stag or even squashed a spider – though I once threatened a tarantula in Recife. No one has ever offered me drugs, invited me to an orgy or even sold me a contraceptive. Golf, bridge, night-clubs and gambling are anathema to me. I have never had the slightest wish to possess a Picasso or a Ferrari, to be dressed by Armani or housed in Aspen. I have always given Oxfam, the RSPCA, Save the Whales and all forms of organised do-goodery a wide berth.

On the other hand, I have delivered a baby, climbed the Matterhorn, asked Kerensky why he didn't have Lenin shot ('Because I didn't t'ink him important'), smoked cigars with Sibelius – and Castro – swum in the Caspian and Lake Titicaca, made de Gaulle cross, Churchill weepy and the Pope laugh, chatted up Ava Gardner, slaughtered a bear, published 28 books and written thousands of articles. I have stood on the spot from which the Archduke Franz Ferdinand was shot, lectured from the stage where Herzl founded Zionism and held the Domesday Book in my hands. I think of myself as a typical, down-to-earth, unromantic Englishman of my day, class and age, whose views, likes and dislikes are shared by multitudes.

But I may be wrong about that. When asked what she thinks of me, my wife Marigold says, 'Difficult.'

At 65 I no longer believe that anything I say or write will have a perceptible influence on what happens, though doubtless I will continue to fulminate. The world is not going to pot, whatever I may say in a rage at the headlines. On the contrary, it will continue to get better and better for most of us, as it has for more than a millennium. I no longer have ambitions of any kind, other than the modest one of seeing a painting of mine hang in the Royal Academy. The things I now most enjoy are going to church to say my morning prayers, listening to my grandchildren and reading in bed at night. My thoughts tend to centre increasingly on the next world rather than this one. Marigold says that such an attitude is not good enough, and that I must form a positive habit of planning and executing a good deed every single day. I agree entirely. But she has spent a lifetime at the service of individuals and to help them comes as naturally to her as to breathe. I have wasted my days battling for or against trends, historical forces, classes, nations, spirits of the age, a foot-soldier in the war of ideas. I hate worthy committees, meetings, discussions. I am not even sure I like people, unless I know them. My instinct, with forward strangers, is like Harold Pinter's: to bristle and ask, 'Were we at school together?'

Marigold, asked for further guidance, says resignedly, 'Just try being nice, then.' But when, how and to whom? The last time I offered my seat to a lady in the Tube, I got an earful of feminist theory. Tubes are rather edgy places these days and all the rules have changed. One *grande dame* I know says that, when she sees a black man sitting by himself in a bus, she sometimes takes the seat next to him to show goodwill. 'But,' she adds sweetly, 'one's gesture is liable to be misunderstood.' I know what she means. When I was an undergraduate I recall a visiting potentate – I think it was Sir Stafford Cripps – observing, 'It is the sign of a gentleman always to pay a courtesy to the plainest woman in the room.' I have followed this counsel intermittently. Recently, at a gathering of Lord Weidenfeld's, I spotted a likely candidate whom I vaguely knew: a woman with a heavily lived-in face poised unceremoniously on top of a torso like a dressmaker's dummy. So I sat next to her and was polite. Alas, she turned out to be a gossip columnist and, short of something to fill her space, wrote that I had designs upon her virtue. Ye gods! What have we here – the latest politically correct phantasmagoria: dinner-party rape? A new case of Bardell *v.* Pickwick?

Good deeds, then, are more easily said than done. Malcolm Muggeridge once remarked to Graham Greene, 'I am a sinner trying to be a saint and you are a saint trying to be a sinner.' But what of the uninteresting majority like myself who desire neither notoriety nor a halo, just to slip into Elysium unnoticed with a pass degree or even an *aegrotat*?

It occurs to me that the kind of benefaction which works best is one which gives as much satisfaction to the doer as the recipient. It is a quarter of a century since I ceased to be an editor and the only thing I miss is the thrill of discovering new talent and, still more, the chance to help young authors to write better. It is a melancholy fact that, in the harsh world of journalism and letters, few possess the knowledge or the time or the desire to instruct their juniors. I come from a family of teachers and it is in my blood. So, nowadays, I take a pupil or two, to coach them through their first book. I find this among the most delightful work I have ever undertaken and a form of philanthropy entirely lacking in condescension, patronage or moral uplift. Moreover, in an age of sloppy syntax, gruesome grammar and polluted prose, there must be some merit in helping the young to honour words. Enough to give a lift to the spirit of a superannuated man, anyway.

6 November 1993

The best editor is a happy one

A survey of national newspaper editors in one of the Sundays claims that they 'command more power than ever before'. Not strictly true. None of the present lot has anything like the influence of Delane of the *Times* between the mid-1840s and the end of the 1860s. But that was mainly because the *Times* in those days had such a commanding lead over its competitors as to amount almost to a monopoly – the same reason why whoever runs the *Washington Post* today has his/her boots licked on both sides of the Potomac. What is true is that, with a weak government and opposition, and with politicians held in low regard by the public, editors appear to carry a lot of clout, at any rate of a negative kind.

Yet there is no code of conduct for editors, formal or informal.

They usually do not know what they have done amiss until they are sacked. Getting the push is far more likely to be the result of commercial failure than professional, let alone moral, delinquence. The last editor to be unfrocked was Aylmer Vallance of the *News Chronicle*, caught *in flagrante delicto* with his secretary by his outraged Quaker proprietor, 'actually on the premises', as the latter whined. But that was in 1936. Today competition has rarely been more severe, especially at the top end of the market, and I suspect most editors are too hagridden by watching the figures, and producing papers which bounce them in the right direction, to philosophise deeply about their role. So here are a few thoughts which occur to me at this time of editorial paramountcy.

An editor does not need to be a superman (or a wonder-woman). But he must be able, energetic, resourceful, quick, patient and have lots of stamina. Courage is absolutely essential – an editor who lacks it will fail though it may be some time before he is found out. He must be able to say to his proprietor, 'Sack me if you must but until then leave me alone.' Especially in an age of high-technology, an editor must know exactly how his paper is put together and be able to do it himself. He must be good enough at a pinch to do the jobs of everyone on his staff, bar one or two specialists. And the journalists must be aware of this. An editor can get by inspiring fear among them, but admiration, or at least respect twinged with awe, will· produce better work. Behind their cynical carapace, most journalists are romantics: they want to feel proud to serve a great editor, whose merest frown humbles and whose rare praise is nectar. For an editor to be good-humoured is a huge bonus, for newspaper offices are horribly crisis-ridden and laughter dissolves tension (raises circulations too). But a modicum of human wisdom is essential. Editors should keep their door ajar to harassed employees, for journalists lead messy, fraught lives and often they have no one to turn to for advice, encouragement and a bit of rough affection. A good editor is a father figure – better still, a mother figure.

Editors do not need to know all the answers. A sense of wonder, an itch to discover, are far more useful than omniscience. An editor is not required to have ideas – except about people – or be in any sense an intellectual; better not in fact, since if he is an egg-head he is fatally bound to find many of his readers ridiculous. But he needs to know how to recognise ideas and exploit them, how to suck genius dry. His own views ought to be what I call superior commonplace. He cannot spend much time in pubs, clubs, bars, canteens and buses:

but he must somehow know what is the common talk there.

An ideal editor has lots of children – and in time grandchildren – and a good stock of elderly aunts, cousins, nephews, god-daughters. A rambling family is the best conduit of unsolicited, useful information. But a good editor also listens to postmen, cleaners, constables, check-out girls, maintenance men and others who know what is really going on (not his office driver, who moves in too exalted circles). An editor may become good by giving orders but he stays good by asking questions. In short he is gregarious by day; in the evening he is frantically busy, but the real test comes between climbing into bed and switching off his light – what books are on his bedside table? An editor must be a reading man, whatever the cost.

Northcliffe held, rightly, that editors and proprietors should not get too close to politicians, especially ministers. What they thereby learn can usually be discovered by other means and is more than offset by the emotional obligations of friendship. I shudder when I hear of editors spending weekends at Chequers or Dorneywood. Today's politicians, usually socially insecure and lacking independent means, are far more demanding than they used to be in soliciting support from those they know in the media and can become quite hysterical when they get criticism instead. Not long ago a senior minister angrily assured me he 'had something' on me and that if I 'wasn't careful' I'd be 'appearing in *Private Eye*'. I wrote him a letter telling him not to demean his great office. It's a sad day when journalists have to instruct their rulers in the etiquette of public life. The only safe guide is for editors to be on no more than nodding terms with the great.

Above all, working editors should never accept honours. (Nor should any journalist so long as he is capable of holding a pen.) This rule has been broken in recent years with undesirable results for both politics and journalism. Editors may now be paid twice as much as prime ministers, hold more power than secretaries of state and be better catches for hostesses. But they don't know how to handle baubles. A proprietor told me that when one of his editors was knighted, 'he thought it made him into a different kind of person. I had to prove otherwise by showing him the toe of my boot.' The honours system is by far the most corrupt, and corrupting, aspect of our public life – rotten from top to bottom – and editors should set their faces like flint against it.

My last advice to editors is not to take the job – still less themselves – too seriously. It is the paper, which has a life, a character and a spirit of its own, which matters. Editors may feel like little tin gods but once they are 'ex' they are of no more significance than the discarded model-wife of a billionaire. I think I worked too hard when I was an editor, stuck too close to the job and worried too much about it. So I tell a new editor nowadays, 'You should behave like Alexander VI who, on becoming pope, remarked, "Now at last we have the papacy – let us enjoy it."' The paper will be none the worse in consequence. For the best kind of editor is a happy one.

13 November 1993

Time to give high fashion a bloody nose

Whenever I am tempted to despair about the state of the world, I remind myself that women, at any rate, have made great strides in recent years in taking power for themselves and transforming society for the better. I am no feminist and despise all the theoretical stuff. I believe in getting real women into actual top jobs, where they can show how good they are. Here the progress is constant. It is true I have not yet succeeded, despite repeated efforts, in persuading a newspaper proprietor to appoint a woman editor of a quality broadsheet – among the names I have suggested are Eve Pollard, Polly Toynbee, Barbara Amiel and Liz Forgan. Nor, for that matter, is my campaign making much headway to restore Margaret Thatcher to her rightful place as ruler of this country, from which she was ejected by a male conspiracy of treacherous Welsh larrikins. But most of the ground, once gained, is kept and the ladies are inching forward everywhere, even in Japan, where I have hopes that the advent of women to positions of power will make that xenophobic country far more outward-looking, culturally receptive and civilised.

All this being so, I am irritated by the failure of women – rich, educated, powerful women, too, in many cases – to throw off the chains of male oppression in the one field where women have absolute power to raise or destroy. Why do they put up with their twice-annual degradation at the hands of overwhelmingly male fashion-designers? High fashion is a tyranny in which men are contemptuous masters and women are willing, grovelling slaves. In recent years, it has become even more of a display of sado-masochism than in its classical period in the late 1940s and 1950s. Indeed the latest fashions coming out of Paris and elsewhere suggest a sniggering conspiracy of *les pédés* to see how far they can go in forcing women to make monkeys of themselves.

Much of the material for these multi-million dollar shows appears to have been dredged up out of a down-market Oxfam sale. One exquisite model is dressed in a black, ankle-length cretonne bin-bag completed by a pair of Irish bog-shoes. Others are forced to wear what look like grungy McDonald's aprons or the kind of pinnies forced on underprivileged Victorian children. A girl with a wire-wool haircut is strapped into a sawn-off tweed jacket long since discarded by an unsuccessful Haute-Marne poacher, or nailed into a string vest hand-knitted by Peruvian convicts, her bruised toes painfully crunched by down-at-heel Rochdale clogs.

One of the leading designers displays an outfit consisting of a shrunken old Woolworth sweater, a dirty brown hanky-skirt and an uneven pair of black wool golliwog socks. Some of the dresses seem to have been designed by a committee composed of Old Breughel, Hogarth and Jerry Bosch, with Shirley Temple as Consultant Toddler. There is a mendicant's medley of grubby bits of yellow lace, greasy armchair covers and stained satin gents' waistcoats rescued from a Bowery old-clothes shop, and four or five different versions of the pyjama-suits and nighties currently worn by experienced Calcutta street-dossers. Paint-splodged patches, hacked-out bits of Turkish fire-rugs, barbed-wire wool scarves, frayed thermal vests as worn in the Chinese Gulag, ripped bodices, holed cami-knickers, even tartan chippings from the Balmoral ash-heap – these now seem to be the favoured textiles of the Avenue Montaigne.

Now I know that some of the way-out ideas displayed on the cat-walks never find their way into the *salons*, let alone the shops. Only some of the clothes shown at the collections are actually bought by the super-rich or made into *toiles* for sale to the mass-manufacturers of New York and London. So much of this rag-bag stuff will never appear on the streets. Or at least I hope not. The fact is that the latest collections are so uniformly ugly, so unremittingly contemptuous of women, so obviously designed – or so it seems to me – to take the mickey out of the fair and foolish, as to constitute a revolution as big as the New Look of 1947.

No doubt in the old days men like Balmain and Captain Molyneux had reservations about female intelligence – and taste – and liked to play a joke or two. But they also loved to display their skills at making beautiful women look still more splendid. In the days when I followed such things, I often noted the enormous trouble Christian Dior took to ensure that the very best fabrics, the most delicate colours, and the finest cutting, stitching and pressing, went into his outfits, many of which were indeed masterpieces of craftsmanship. His workshops contained perhaps the most accomplished team of people ever brought together to make women happy. And Cristóbal Balenciaga, the greatest artist of them all, used to say that, while anyone with a bit of flair could make a skinny 18-year-old look ravishing, his peculiar delight was to transform a 60-year-old Chicago millionairess, or a cross old duchess from Touraine, into a cynosure of all eyes, entirely by the magic of his clothes. The aim then was not to belittle the female sex but to make silk purses out of sows' ears.

So how much longer will women tolerate the arbiters of *haute mode* spitting in their faces? It is not as though the leaders of female opinion still turn their backs on beauty and elegance. The new feminists like Naomi Wolf are proud to be good-lookers and admit that a big part of a woman's fun in life is to lure men. If a few hundred women in positions of influence stamped their feet together, the entire Paris fashion industry, and its surrogates in London, Rome, New York and elsewhere, would come to heel.

The foot-stamping does not need to come from the Madame de Rochefoucaulds or the Lady Rothschilds or the Mrs Vanderbilts, or any of the female *gratin* who patronise the collections. It can be done by the fashion correspondents and editors whose professional job it is to judge high fashion. It seems to me that these generally hard-bitten women are the most gullible and brainwashed of all – Lowri Turner of the *Evening Standard* is an exception – though probably the majority of them are embittered feminists at heart, with long histories of worthless husbands, divorces, beatings and abortions behind them. So what are they waiting for? Here is a chance for women to stand up to the cultural-sexual tyranny of the city where, after all, chauvinism had its origins, and give the frogs a bloody nose.

20 November 1993

Curious Christmas cards

Some things about Christmas have not changed, I thought, as I climbed the stairs into the Great Hall of the Knights of St John to attend the *TLS* annual party. Halfway up, one was hit by the full roar of sound, as several hundred literary types gave tongue – the authentic, uninhibited tones of the chattering classes braying for broken reputations. I attended my first London literary party exactly 40 years ago. There have, to be sure, been one or two sartorial changes. That elegant young woman in a suit of jeans – a poetess perhaps? – has sawn off the sleeves of her jacket to reveal, on her right upper arm, a floral tattoo. Is it one of those you can wash off? Dare I ask her? Otherwise, I decide, surveying the throng, the dance to the familiar music of time goes on. Isn't that Hugh Moreland over there, tanking up? And X. Trapnell, showing his teeth? And Lady Molly, talking to Widmerpool?

Nor have Christmas cards themselves altered in any essential in the whole of my lifetime, at any rate for those of us middle-class types who celebrate the season by sending each other specimens of Great Art. I recall, in the 1930s, puzzling over the appearance of Balthasar, Melchior and Caspar wearing the full-length, buttoned-up leggings then *de rigueur* for all the little girls I knew, but which also seemed to be the height of fashion among Magi in 6th-century Ravenna. And lo! those kings in the leggings pop up as usual again this Christmas, still holding out their gifts, still stretching their elegant limbs, though nowadays I can't help noticing that Melchior and Caspar are also dressed in what I can only call embroidered and bejewelled Y-fronts, worn, as John Major is supposed to do, outside their trousers.

These three, oddly enough, do not include the statutory black beloved of politically correct Old Masters. It was a chance for them to put in a delicious splash of ebony right in the middle of their composition. The young black prince in Hans Memling's *Adoration of the Magi*, one of my favourite Christmas card perennials, is gloriously garbed in ultramarine silk with long sleeves of scarlet and gold, and he has a beautiful powder-blue velvet cap, which he doffs elegantly in salute to the Christ child. I have always liked this painting for its crowded complexity. The actual visit of the Magi is only one of a whole series of disconnected incidents taking place in what appears to be the suburbs of a prosperous town. In a municipal playing-field ringed by beech trees, knights in full armour are preparing for a tournament, and they will shortly be joined by their competitors, who are riding in full panoply through the town's open portcullis. Meanwhile, a delegation of PLO leaders, some atop pantomime camels, are moving off for a sporting expedition into the desert.

The manger itself is as delightfully mysterious to me today as when I first scrutinised it in 1935. Situated as it is by itself in the midst of Euro Disney rocks, it appears to have been purpose-built as a ruin, rather like an entry for the Turner Prize which did not quite meet with Nicholas Serota's approval. Alternatively, it may be the house Laurel and Hardy were supposed to complete in *The Finishing Touch*. Certainly, it exhibits the stigmata of their handiwork. The roof has four holes and an uncompleted eave. A perfectly sound central European stove sports a smoke-stack but Laurel has forgotten to put in a chimney. Doors lead nowhere, columns support nothing and the architecture hovers uneasily between late Romanesque and early Denys Lasdun. Still, it is the ideal setting for the exercise of Memling's riotous imagination since its open-plan design enables him to include not merely the Holy Family, ox and ass, kings, attendants, sword-bearers etc. in full view, but buyers and sellers in what appears to be an international horse-fair taking place in the foreground. The sales-men are tall, handsome youths, fit for a Mayfair Aids day demo, with magnificent knee-length soft suede boots, amber dreadlocks and M & S cashmere sweaters in periwinkle, moss-green and pimento red.

More subdued is the manger in Hieronymous Bosch's *Adoration*. It is, as you would expect, made of stage-set lath and plaster flats, full of large rat-holes, through which enigmatic and sinister faces peer. I don't recall this particular card, now issued by the Royal Marsden Cancer Fund, cropping up in my childhood, perhaps because it raises too many awkward questions. The statutory black is the grandest figure, dressed from head to toe in ivory white of such sumptuous elaboration that the tassels of his ballooning sleeves riot all over the stable floor. He carries a matching white orb surmounted by a golden pterodactyl straight from *Jurassic Park*. Is this his gift?

The senior king is a less pleasing sight: totally bald, a *capo di mafia* figure whose bodily imperfections are mercifully enveloped in a huge heliotrope cloak from which misshapen black feet protrude. His headgear, a diver's helmet in white metal, is placed at the Virgin's feet, and the third king, a lugubrious New Age traveller with designer stubble, has an even more mysterious hat of perspex, imprisoning tiny figures. The real enigma of the painting, however, is that this decorous scene of adoration is about to be invaded by three drunken revellers, rather as Irish males surge into Midnight Mass when the pubs shut. Their ringleader is also dressed as a monarch, or rather is stark naked, and has flung a regal cloak of shocking pink over his limbs. He carries one crown, suspiciously like a papal tiara, in his left hand, while another is perched precariously on his head. Who is this unruly fellow and whence his irruption? The oddest thing about him is a decoration on his right thigh. I thought at first he was tattooed, like the girl at the *TLS* party, but it turned out to be a large pearl attached to a gold ring actually sewn into his flesh. Yes: they had creepy fashions in the late-15th century too. Incidentally, the *TLS* girl noticed my inquiring glance and said, as she swept by, 'No, it doesn't wash off, nosey.'

11 December 1993

London isn't burning but getting better

Since the Left cannot persuade enough voters to let them rule the country, they try to get their revenge by making us all depressed. Their stock-in-trade is no longer socialism – no one believes in that these days – but pessimism. In their sectarian press, and papers like the *Guardian, Observer* and *Independent*, and of course in the many television programmes they control, their message is unrelieved gloom. Everything is bad and it is going to get worse. You think life in 1993 is a horror story? You've seen nothing yet, comrade. One of their horror stories is the collapse of the Big City, for which of course there's plenty of anecdotal evidence.

London is burning, disintegrating, sinking into a morass of poverty, class hatred and violence. 'A third-world city', 'the New Calcutta', 'Doomchester', 'the Death of Megalopolis'. The transport system is breaking down. The poor are sleeping in the streets. The muggers and druggies are taking over. Crime is triumphant, the civic spirit gone, government impotent, the police baffled, the ordinary citizens angry, despairing and terrified. The villains, of course, are greed, capitalism, materialism, Thatcherism, the market, all the usual suspects. On BBC TV last week, Melvyn Bragg was putting this line across, and trying to get it endorsed by some American pop-sociology professor, supposedly an expert on metropolitan sclerosis.

In fact London is doing very nicely, if only people would stop taking its temperature and pronouncing it dead. I have lived or worked in the place since the early 1950s and I can think of dozens of ways in which it has got better. To begin with, you can breathe in the place. Forty years ago, especially at this time of year, London had one of the most dangerous climates in the world. Ever since the 16th century, when the city began to consume 'sea coal' from Newcastle in large and growing quantities, carboniferous smoke accumulated in the atmosphere during periods of high pressure and, any time from October to February but especially in late November and early December, formed the basis of the 'London Particular'.

This was a killer fog, which made life in London horrible for all and was often fatal for the bronchitic and asthmatic. London traffic came to a standstill, London Airport shut down for days, sometimes weeks, at a time, but it was the poor, living in unheated and substandard accommodation, who suffered most. The big fog of the early 1950s killed many thousands of people in London. It was a disgusting yellow-brown in colour and even smelt evil. But that was the last of these scourges. The Clean Air Act, making the use of smokeless fuel compulsory, was having a direct and perceptible effect by the mid-1950s, and by the end of the decade the London fog was a thing of the past. Most Londoners under 40 have never experienced a serious fog. As a result the London Particular has been virtually expunged from the collective memory of the city. But its disappearance is the single biggest improvement in British urban life for half a millennium and we should not forget it.

Then again, there have been big changes, all of them for the better, in London's river. Half a century ago, it was a black, oily, noisome, impenetrable and opaque stretch of water, carrying under the noses of Londoners a vast quantity of rubbish including untreated sewage. At certain conjunctions of tide and weather it was liable to burst its embankments and flood thousands of houses and there was always the chance of a major catastrophe. That was why we built the Thames Barrier, a most ingenious and, to my mind, beautiful piece of modern engineering. It provides Londoners with a security against flood they had never before enjoyed and in this respect makes the city one of the safest metropolises on earth.

Equally important is the improvement in the quality of Thames water. The river is not exactly sparkling clean and I do not suppose ever will be. But the effect of numerous anti-pollution measures has been to banish the oily blackness and reduce the disgusting smell, especially in summer. Fish are returning and breeding, and for the first time in centuries salmon are now occasionally caught up-river in some of the Thames feeder streams. The river now looks handsome, as it did in Shakespeare's day, and the foul flood described by Dickens in *Our Mutual Friend* is, like the fogs, a thing of the past. If you want to see what it was like, take a look at Dublin's Liffey, an unreformed river like the old Thames.

The huge reduction in London's atmospheric pollution has made it worthwhile to clean the city up, and modern high-pressure hoses have made it possible. This was the brain-child of André Malraux when he became minister for the arts in France in 1958, and London was quick to follow Paris's example. The cleaning of London's public buildings has transformed the capital over the past 30 years. Not only does it enable us to appreciate the quality of the original materials, brick as well as stone, in all their pristine glitter, it also brings out the quality of the architecture and, still more, the richness of the decoration. Uncovering London's treasures in this way has revealed the splendour of our architectural heritage from the 17th, 18th, 19th and early 20th centuries (and, by contrast, the poverty of what we have built in the last half century). Barry's Houses of Parliament, for instance, is now recognised for what it is – one of Europe's finest buildings; likewise, we can enjoy at last the subtle pastel colours of Waterhouse's magnificent Natural History Museum. London has been transformed from a city of charcoal-grey to one of gold and pink, so successfully indeed that it is now hard to remember the dark and dingy past.

I have listed only three ways in which London has been radically improved in my time. There are plenty of others, to set against the growth in crime and violence. The Left complains about the ubiquitous evidence of homelessness, which certainly did not thrust itself on your attention 40 years ago. But poverty has always existed in London in prodigious quantities. In the old days we tried to tidy it out of sight: in grim asylums for the mentally disturbed, in workhouses and doss-houses, cellars and slums – particularly in the greatest slum of all, the East End. That no longer exists, thank God: poverty is no longer fenced off in ghettoes but out in the open, where we can see it – and, perhaps, do something about it.

18 December 1993

A touch of the Gay Gordons

The urge to dance is one of the most powerful of human instincts – so fierce that society found it advisable to give it formal expression, and so discipline it, from the earliest times. Ritual dances figure on the first pictorial artifacts. The pharaohs of Egypt's Old Kingdom, celebrating their jubilees, danced to the awed delectation of the Nilotic multitudes, and King David himself capered and cavorted in front of the Israelites of Jerusalem.

Dancing, thus civilised, underpinned society, drawing all its members together in harmonious, formal arrangements. Nearly all dances, from antiquity to the 19th century, had one important, common characteristic. They alternated between collective movements and solo turns, in which every dancer or couple in succession would become the centre of attention and then merge back into the throng. Thus dancing expressed both the cohesive and the individualistic impulses of humanity, holding them in delicate balance to the benefit of a healthy society. A volume of political theory could be written around the history of the dance.

Dancing indeed was democratic even in the hierarchical age: Queen Elizabeth I, the most regal of monarchs, made a point of participating in the court dances even when she was an old lady. She was particularly fond of masques, in which theatrical entertainments, performed by professional actors and musicians, were punctuated by formal dances, in which all joined. The Queen figured prominently in these majestic sarabands, which required assiduous practice and even athletic skill, with the climaxes involving graceful jumps and bounds. She was proud and competitive about her dancing, and once inquired eagerly of the Scottish ambassador about the dancing prowess of her rival, Mary Queen of Scots, whom she had never met. The envoy replied that his mistress the Queen was indeed a bonnie dancer, adding diplomatically, 'But she does not dance so high or disposedly as Your Grace.'

The Court in those days was an extended family, with the Queen arranging suitable matches, not hesitating to send maids of honour who married without her permission for a spell in the Tower. She led the dance as a symbol of her matriarchy, her status as head of the governing family. And dancing remained a family affair. In Jane Austen's *Emma*, when Miss Woodhouse set about organising a dance for the entertainment of Frank Churchill, she constructed it around the male and female offspring of the 'four or five county families' Jane Austen regarded as the natural components of her novels. Dancing was a family affair, in which all took part, if only as critical observers. Emma's joy was complete when even Mr Knightley, who had ranged himself with the older generation as a spectator, graciously joined the dance and showed he knew exactly how to do it.

Dancing today, it seems, is not so much the open expression of an orderly society as a subterranean pandemonium, its hellish nature underlined by the darkness, noise and smoke in which it is conducted. It could be said to express with devilish accuracy the fragmentation, indeed disintegration, of society. There are no real formal steps, let alone collective figures, and one dance merges into another without apparent distinction. The dancers fill the available space in a disorderly mob. They are disconnected. So far from forming social patterns, they reject even regular partnerings, so that each dancer performs alone, gyrating autonomously in a zombie-like trance. These dances stress the fearful isolation and solitary despair of the individual in the modern age, reminding us that Hell, however crowded, is a lonely place.

Yet it is possible, even today, to take part in dancing which nourishes, brings together, heals and reinforces society. I spent the New Year in the Highlands, as I often do, and delighted again in the splendid and historic rompings with which the Highlanders celebrate the season. I say rompings because everyone enjoys them so much. There was a time when I foolishly saw the Highland dance as a barbarous survival, along with dirks and claymores. Now I recognise it as a bastion of civilisation, a precious institution which still reflects the values and habits of a settled, integrated society.

These dances are often mounted with great solemnity, as at the so-called Northern Meeting of the Clans. But they are also held at short notice in the neighbourhood, bringing together local families in a way which Jane Austen would have applauded. Boys and girls learn the steps and figures at an early age, and jealously guard their skills until they are old enough to see their grandchildren take the floor. A Highland dance is a meeting of families, friends – sometimes enemies – in which every generation joins, the sexes enjoy perfect equality, and young and old can match their dexterity. The Highland dress is uniquely becoming for men and women alike, and the Highland dances display this sartorial magnificence at its best, kilts and skirts swirling, scarves flying, cairngorms, silver and diamonds flashing. The Highlanders are tall, sinewy and swift in their movements, their womenfolk sinuous and graceful, and they dance together with stately and purposeful elegance which, as the evening wears on, acquires dynamism and climactic gusto.

Historically, such dances had a political purpose too, bringing together in friendly concord clansmen who were sometimes – quite literally – at daggers drawn. On this visit, I was privileged to see the horrific full-length portrait of the 2nd Earl of Moray, which is normally kept behind wooden curtains. This young man, tall and handsome, and so known as the Bonnie Earl, was brutally shot and knifed to death, outside his burning castle, by the followers of his hereditary enemy, the Earl of Huntley, in 1592. His mother caused the portrait to be painted while the corpse was still fresh and the wounds livid, and it is still shocking 400 years later. It reminds us of the savagery of those times which the dances were designed to mitigate. Well, our own times are pretty savage, and getting more so. Perhaps Mr Major, in his attempts to get back to basics, to heal society, to make it classless – or whatever it is he is up to – should study that binding and healing phenomenon, the Highland dance. He might try to introduce it into our ravaged inner cities. It would be an illuminating experiment.

8 January 1994

Making bricks with the last cheese-straw

We have got the Brickies on the run. By Brickies I mean the arrogant and until recently all-powerful supporters of Modern or Brick art. I prefer the term Brick because Modern is vague and inaccurate: the works it describes are no longer, strictly speaking, modern at all, but out-of-date, *passé*, defunct, yesterday's junk. 'Brick art' is more evocative because it conjures up the Tate's load of bricks, which epitomise the con man's aesthetic of modernism. Years ago, when they were first displayed, I used to wait until no one was looking and give the bricks a hefty kick, pushing some perceptibly out of alignment. No one noticed, proof that they were not a work of art at all but an imposture.

The reason I think the Brickies are on the run is that they have begun to squeak in fear. A few years ago, when their power was unchallenged, they would not have bothered; now they howl. There was a caterwauling, for instance, a few weeks ago when the Government hinted it was disinclined to renew the lease the Serpentine Gallery holds on its splendid and well-placed group of buildings in Hyde Park. Instead of using this privilege to bring the joys of painting and sculpture to the many thousands who frequent the park, those who run the gallery have filled it with the usual dreary Brick items, including, in one case, exhibits so obscene that the police insisted the windows be blocked so that children could not see them. The minister responsible wants to turn the place into a riding school, and that may be a good idea because it is so near Rotten Row. But personally I would like to see it become a splendid restaurant of the kind that adorns the Champs Elysées in Paris, and I wish some gifted gastronomic entrepreneur, like Hugh O'Neill, Mark Birley or Christopher Gilmour, would take it on.

So much for the Serpentine Brickies. The real scream of terror, however, came last week in that collective letter to the editor of the *Evening Standard*, protesting about the writings of its art critic, Brian Sewell, and calling for him to be silenced: 'Enough of Sewell's Off-the-Wall Remarks' was the headline over their complaint. Sewell is one of the few critics (others include *The Spectator*'s beloved Giles Auty and the *Sunday Telegraph*'s John McEwan) who are not part of the Brick racket. He knows a great deal about painting – proper painting, I mean – and has for some time been conducting a campaign against the more preposterous aspects of the art scene, such as the Turner Prize, and the way in which the Arts Council uses taxpayers' money to sponsor expensive and fraudulent trash. He writes with great energy and wit and his words have struck home, to judge by the anguish of the Brickies' letter.

It was, I am happy to say, an unusually silly epistle. Many years ago, Jack Priestley warned me never to sign a collective letter to the *Times* ('You are more likely to make a fool of yourself than do any good') and I have taken his advice. These letters are usually got up by nobodies who want to see their insignificant signatures displayed in company with those of the more famous. Not that the 30-odd signatories in this case are particularly distinguished. As the editor of *Arts Review* commented, they 'hardly represent a collection of art world heavyweights'. They do not, for instance, include the panjandrum of the Brickies, the director of the Tate, Nicholas Serota. He is too streetwise. They are, in fact, a mixed bunch of gallery owners, artists, academics and cultural busybodies. Obviously those who sell Brick art do not want a critic who dishes out anything but unrelieved praise for the wares they are trying to flog, a view shared by the people who produce it, such as winners of the Turner Prize.

But some of the signatures seem incongruous. George Melly is there. He is a delightful fellow, who wears the most outrageous suits in London, but his trade is singing jazz. Then there is Marina Warner, a delectable young lady who writes entertainingly on the Virgin Mary, but not an authority I would turn to in this field. One of the academics, I see, has published books on Dracula, spaghetti westerns and rape – amazing what the taxpayers will pay dons to study these days! Natalie Wheen is an announcer on Radio Three, and an excellent one with a genuine tony voice, but no Ruskin. In all, then, a bit of a rag-bag, who describe themselves, rather pompously, as 'members of the art world', as if it were a kind of club from which people who do not fit can be blackballed.

The text of the letter is abusive rather than reasoned, and so of little interest, but one phrase merits comment. Sewell is condemned not merely for criticising Brick art but for what is termed his 'virulent homophobia and misogyny'. I have never before heard of someone being accused of both, and would have thought they were incompatible, indeed mutually exclusive. But there it is. This complaint is a giveaway. For it implies that Sewell is not merely unacceptable as a critic but is an exponent of Political Incorrectness, with the further implication that support for Brick art is itself a necessary characteristic of the Politically Correct. Now it seems to me that if the Brickies really have to stoop so low, if they are now forced to equate criticism of, say, the Turner Prize, with racism, agism, dwarfism, sexual harassment and date-rape, making disparaging remarks about Nelson Mandela and/or Fidel Castro, or quoting Lord Byron on women (who 'whispering "I will ne'er consent" – consented'), then their cause is already lost.

As for Sewell himself, he needs no support from me. His editor, that crafty operator Stewart Steven, is delighted by the publicity. He hailed Sewell's contribution to art criticism as 'immense', adding grandly, 'Painters who can paint have never had anything to fear from his pen.' The episode persuades me that the time has come for all those who genuinely love and understand art to redouble their efforts to restore respect for quality. One more push and we shall have won. We must vow not to sheathe our swords until the Brickies have been tumbled from their seats of power, and the last Picassos *et al.* have been put where they belong, in the cellars.

15 January 1994

Well, strike me Pinker!

John Major, so I am told, has sworn a mighty oath, like Lars Porsena of Clusium, that he will not be 'hounded from office by the tabloids'. His great stand-bys these days are the *Guardian*, the *Independent* and the *Observer*, all that remains of the left-wing press. The Conservative faithful might ponder whether this tells them anything about their leader. Major's current chief media confidant, indeed, is Andreas Whittam Smith. Of course, the two men have a lot in common. Both are bunkered and beleaguered, hanging on to their jobs by their fingernails. Whittam Smith is no more likely to remain in control of the *Independent* than Major is in Downing Street, though which of them slithers into the abyss first is anyone's guess.

Personally, I am delighted that the country possesses a fine pack of tabloids to hound undesirables from office. After all, had it not been for London's excellent evening tabloid, the *Standard*, the outrageous behaviour of Jane Brown, the Hackney headmistress, in banning her pupils from seeing *Romeo and Juliet* because it was 'heterosexual', would never have been exposed. The local education committee then promptly branded it 'ideological idiocy', but a complaint had been left unattended on its files for three months before a leak to the *Standard* brought action. Moreover, were it not for the tabloids, the circumstances in which Brown was appointed in the first place would never have come to light either. One wonders how many more PC fanatics are lurking among our schoolchildren, undiscovered. So carry on the tabloids!

I'd go so far as to say that British public life will be the poorer now that Kelvin MacKenzie has been kicked upstairs to run Rupert Murdoch's British satellite television operations. I first came across him years ago when Rupert Murdoch asked me to write a column for the *Sun* to 'raise its tone a bit'. I thought this a bad idea but agreed to give it a limited trial, and one consequence was that I found myself lunching with Mr MacKenzie. He did not then figure regularly in print and I was under the impression his Christian name was Calvin, which intrigued me. 'Don't you find it a bit odd,' I asked, 'that someone with your name should be obliged to spend so much time sprucing up Page Three?' 'I'm not with you, Paul.' 'Well, let me put it this way: you won't find much guidance in your namesake's Institutes, will you?' 'Forgive me, squire, but is this a subtle attempt to extract the Michael?' And so on. MacKenzie has his faults and is a gifted writer of creative dialogue, but he brought to the business of popular journalism exactly the same blend of cheeky audacity and serious purpose which distinguished Hugh Cudlipp's long reign at the *Mirror*. In addition he has wit, a quality in short supply among newspaper editors. To raise a smile on the face of the British working man every grey Monday morning is a real public service. Then again, it is the brash courage of a few men like MacKenzie – a majority of editors, I fear, are time-servers or at least easily squared by invitations to No. 10 – which prevents second-rate political hacks like John Major developing into micro-Mussolinis.

Which brings me back to Major's oath. For one who has sworn so many times, in private at least, to sort out the press, there has been surprisingly little action. I do recall, in a Queen's Speech, hearing a much-deferred promise of a privacy law. Where is it? The last time I put this question to Michael Howard, who presumably would have to get it through Parliament, he became very evasive. Major may hate the press – none more so – but he cannot decide whether to beat it on the head or try to bribe it and, being a whip by instinct, his itch is towards the latter. So the little flattering attentions to selected proprietors, editors etc. – with the hint of something more substantial to come – will continue. In the meantime, the privacy issue is to be left to Professor Pinker.

Who is Pinker? He is a sociologist, Professor of Social Work Studies – whatever they may be – at the LSE and one of those worthy souls who figure on establishment committees. He has been on the British Library Project and the Advertising Standards Authority and the Direct Mail Services Standards Body and the Centre for Policy on Ageing – not to speak of the Press Complaints Commission. He has even sat on a Cemetery Committee. He is now to run a one-man quango on press intrusions into privacy.

Now this in itself is a sign of the times. In the 1970s, you may recall, the country was awash with quangos. I wrote countless articles deploring them. When Margaret Thatcher came in, she abolished many and declined to appoint any more, along with Royal Commissions and other bodies dear to the heart of poor Harold Wilson. However, loving patronage as much as anyone, she could not quite bring herself to destroy the principle of quango-mongering, and many of these sources of jobs for well-behaved boys and girls survived. Under Major, of course, they have enjoyed a tremendous revival and some observers calculate there are now more than ever.

Appointing Pinker is an example of a new prime ministerial trick – quango double-banking. For we already have one sociology professor to curb the wickedness of the tabloids, in the shape of Professor the Lord McGregor of Durris, chairman of the Press Complaints Commission, who has likewise chaired the Advertising Standards Authority and, for that matter, the Royal Commission on the Press. If Pinker has written *British Hospital Statistics*, McGregor is the author of *Divorce in England*. If Pinker runs the *Journal of Social Policy*, McGregor is a pillar of the *Journal of Sociology*. In recent years, outrages by the press have provoked McGregor epiphanies: he pops out of his little house in Salisbury Square to address a few, not always well-chosen, words to the television cameras. Are we now to have rival Pinker epiphanies as well? The truth is, Major's attempts to muzzle the press, like the rest of his policies, are a mixture of theoretical illiberality and practical cowardice. The result threatens to become farce and will merely intensify the ridicule in which he is held.

29 January 1994

We papists don't want to fight, but by jingo if we do...

This week I had intended to write about the male homosexual lobby and its plans to alter the law so that its more promiscuous, members can get their hands on our children and grandchildren. But the buggers will have to wait. There are one or two important religious matters which need clearing up first. As I anticipated, the realisation that the Catholics now form by far the largest Christian communion in England, and that many pious members of the disintegrating Anglican Church are returning to their ancient allegiance, was bound to provoke a wave of anti-Catholic bigotry. There was a similar outbreak in the 1850s, when the restoration of the Catholic hierarchy gave little Lord John Russell the excuse to bring back the No Popery mob. Who would be the rabble-rouser this time? I wondered. The Revd Ian Paisley? The Bishop of Durham? I confess I was a little shocked to find Ferdinand Mount applying for the job.

Now of course Mr Mount is far too genteel to threaten us with Maria Monk or any of the usual bogeys. He is very grand indeed and thinks nothing of turning down a mere baronetcy; he knows that in order to throw mud he would have to get his own fingers dirty. All the same, I think he might have spared us his condescending reassurance that he has never doubted our patriotism, and that we're as entitled to call ourselves English as he is – well, almost. And on one point he is mistaken. It may be, as he says, that English Catholics like myself are prickly, inward-looking, narrow, snobbish, anti-Semitic, paranoid, media-dominating and so on. But if he hopes we are going to continue to be 'self-effacing', he is wrong. The days when English Catholics allowed themselves to be trampled on, discriminated against and insulted are over.

All my life I have been aware of the quiet, sly but determined efforts of the Anglican establishment to keep Catholics firmly in their inferior place. Casting doubts on our allegiance was always one of the ploys. In the 16th and 17th centuries it was an excuse for racking and disembowelling us. More recently the object has been social, political or cultural downgrading. I wish I could convey to Mr Mount and others who are resurrecting the charge of disloyalty how much it is resented by Catholics. For nearly half a millennium we have not been slow to give our lives for Protestant monarchs whose very titles are an insult to our beliefs. At Stonyhurst we boys ate all our meals surrounded by the full-length portraits of warriors from the school who had won the Victoria Cross. We were always given a whole holiday when another name was added to the list. Of course the highest commands were barred to us, but we provided more than our fair share of the Other Ranks and junior officers who constituted the cannon-fodder. And it is only fair to add that Irish Catholics, too, in both world wars, volunteered in enormous numbers to serve kings whose official rubrics dismissed their church as the Scarlet Woman and the Whore of Babylon.

It is still lawful to discriminate against Catholics. Until recently, no Catholic, for instance, might hold the office of Lord Chancellor, and if you think this rule was academic you are misinformed: that is one reason why my fellow-Catholic, Lord Rawlinson, missed his chance. More frequently, Catholics fail to get jobs because of a nudge or a wink, a whispered aside, a confidential letter. Thirty years ago, the election of Jack Kennedy to the presidency of the United States dealt a blow to anti-Catholic prejudice. As a result, I was able to beat off a determined attempt to prevent me becoming editor of the *New Statesman* in 1964. It was led by Leonard Woolf, Virginia's relict, who assured me there was 'nothing personal' in his opposition. He objected solely on the grounds of my religion and the 'alien allegiances' it implied. The hidden bias continues to this day. There are plenty of jobs at the top of British public life to which no Catholic can realistically aspire.

Moreover, Catholics, more than members of any other faith, are daily exposed to casual and sometimes deliberate assaults in the media and showbiz, against which a Protestant state offers us no protection. I have lost count of the times when the body of Christ and the crucifix have been blasphemously and obscenely presented by depraved film directors and the like. Nuns are constantly held up to scatological ridicule, and a shameless harlot regularly paces across our stages in her role as 'Madonna'.

Only this month an obscene anti-Catholic musical has been put on in an Islington Congregationalist chapel. This features full-frontal nudity, nymphets in lingerie, a woman being raped on a Catholic altar and the Pope telling his cardinals to 'f— off'. The woman minister of the chapel, the Revd Janet Wootten, read the script in advance, so she knew what was afoot. Of course Congregationalists, or Independents as they are sometimes called, were always notorious baiters of Catholics. Oliver Cromwell himself was a member of this sect and swore in so many words that, wherever he had power, Catholicism would not be practised. He put Catholics to the sword, hanged them or burned them alive. Today the tactic is to pour filth on our beliefs.

We are not going to put up with this kind of thing any longer. The Catholic hierarchy, led by the monk-cardinal Basil Hume, is anxious to avoid a scrap and never utters a squeak of protest if left to itself. But it is high time Fr Hume went back to his monastery and concentrated on saving his soul, thus clearing the stage for a more doughty champion. For the truth is the entire Christian character of our country is now threatened by its innumerable enemies, external and internal. The Anglican Church, with all its privileges and resources, has surrendered to secularism without a fight and is leaving the battlefield in fear and disarray. It is the Catholics who are taking over the struggle against the horrific paganism of the 1990s, and I can assure Mr Mount and anyone else who is listening that we know how to fight.

5 February 1994

A walk in Canaltopia

Walking along a canal is to see the city undressed, in its underclothes as it were. When the canals were built in the second half of the 18th century, nobody would conceivably have done it for pleasure. The workers did not walk at all, except of necessity to get from A to B. The upper and middle classes were beginning to ramble, but they did it in the Lake District, which had the right picturesque views and 'stations' from which to admire them. Towpaths were strictly for the bargees and their horses. Pubs would sometimes open a dingy back room for their use, but their smart façade was on the roadside. The only one I know actually put up to quench the thirst of the canal-diggers or navigators – the 'navvies' – is The Shovel near Uxbridge, but that was a low joint in its heyday. Nobody cared what their factory or workshop looked like 'from t'canalside'.

So now, walking along the towpath, you can see industry at its most dishevelled: back-ends of machine-rooms which have never been repointed since they were built, dingy stores without a lick of paint, hut-ments redolent of dry rot, their windows last glazed before the Boer War, above all back yards in all sizes and conditions of decay, crowded with rusty engines, crumbling heaps of tiles 'which may come in handy one day', broken old statues and fallen chimney-pots, rotting packing-cases and, everywhere, sturdy weeds, blackberry bushes, nettles and even sunflowers thrusting up and adding a touch of nature.

Canals are not dead things – far from it. A short walk from my house in Bayswater and you are in the heart of what I call Canaltopia, teeming with its own peculiar life. Here are fishermen, not just boys with a pin on the end of a string but serious, well-provided men, with bags or hampers of elaborate hooks and baits. They evidently catch substantial fish to judge by the wide nets on poles they bring with them. One man last Saturday had a high-tech rod nearly 15 feet long, so he could trawl the far bank. Substantial investment has gone into this activity.

Then again, there must be sustenance in the Grand Union Canal because there is plenty of bird-life: mallards upending themselves to get it, then wagging their brilliant green heads in delight, a couple of majestic swans giving the waters a bit of class, and big, greedy Canada geese, who appear to be taking over every watering-hole in London. Along the towpath you meet that inveterate canalside denizen, the unaccompanied dog. These creatures, mostly mongrels of the rougher sort, are canine jigsaws, products of bizarre mis-cegenations: a terrier with a suspiciously grim Doberman mug, an Alsatian head attached to two pairs of basset-hound legs, a sort of failed Dalmatian. These dogs are the animal unemployed of the canal, not so much looking for work as getting through the day. The cats are more purposeful, going about stealthy business but occasionally meeting trouble. A plaintive notice states: 'Lost, a brown-and-grey tortoiseshell cat called Jessie, with a phosphorescent collar and a black magnet attachment'. The notice had evidently been there some time and had a despairing look about it. I ran my eye over the turbid waters and wondered how exactly they could have swallowed such a well-equipped cat.

This stretch of the canal runs under or near a gangling network of London's main arteries. Not far away Brunel the Younger began his great iron thrust to Plymouth, and overhead are the immense concrete canopies of the western motorways. It is quiet by the canal itself, but the murmur of traffic is continuous. Little bridges, too, remind you that the canal is a backwater to the boundless London ocean of money-making activity. The bridges are mostly plain, utilitarian affairs of girders and iron plates, designed by practical engineers on the backs of old envelopes. But I love them. So, evidently, does Westminster Council, because it keeps them freshly painted in satisfying colours: here, pink and grey; there, blue and white; or one entirely in terracotta. Sometimes the big, bold bosses are picked out in gold.

Underneath the bridges there are shadowy patches on this bright February day, where the graffiti-obsessives can work in secrecy and safety. They fancy canals as much as I do, and seem to come from a wide spectrum of the population, both sexes, all classes and ages. Obscenities are rare: the graffitiosi of Canaltopia are old-fashioned types, not aiming to shock but to inform, even to edify. They often strike a quasi-religious note. Last Saturday I was told: 'Coming Soon: the Total Destruction Krew'. Others are intended perhaps to provoke thought: 'Lapis Lazuli is best'. But this had a touch of the pseudo-intellectual about it. If Prince Charles were to take to scrawling graffiti, he might come up with something similar. A few are reassuring. Under one of the darker bridges, in a more juvenile scrawl, one read: 'I love my auntie'. Well, so I should think.

A walk along the canal is not specially productive of major aesthetic experiences. I came across only one church likely to impress John Betjeman or the great Gavin Stamp. But that indeed was a fine one, with a grand, high Victorian nave and a tall tower and steeple banded in red and white, the whole dedicated to that glamorous and yet enigmatic and obscure lady, St Mary Magdalen. For the most part, however, Canaltopia is for aimless musing, the mind scarcely ticking over, the spirit at rest, unless occasionally jerked into warm nostalgia by a reminder of the past: a forgotten advertisement for Bisto, the carcase of a T-model Ford. As I walk, all is peaceful bliss. Then, suddenly, a sinister sign: a smart lady, her shiny brown leather coat tightly belted round the middle, like an earwig, with a PC artificial-fur hat and bright blue Persian boots, walking her borzoi – no unaccompanied jigsaw dog he. What has happened? Almost imperceptibly, I have walked through the *terrain vague* of Canaltopia proper and have struck the outskirts of Little Venice. No more backyards but barges with all mod-cons and satellite dishes, voluptuous garden centres, new post-modernist flats, sumptuously painted mid-Victorian terraces and gentrification everywhere. The walk is over; time to head for home.

19 February 1994

Elegy to a tall Highlander

The worst thing about growing older is not the decline of physical powers – I can steel myself to that – but the loss of friends, which leaves gaping holes in your life you know can never be filled. It is particularly hard when the friend you lose is younger, someone you'd counted on to see you through to the end.

Last Saturday, Simon Fraser, my Highland walking companion for more than 20 years, died without warning. His going was, in a way, glorious. He was mounted on his favourite horse, in full hunting pink, in which, as always, he looked magnificent, a figure from pure romance, and he was leading the local drag-hunt in the park of his castle, its rose-brown granite glittering in warm spring sunshine. There was no pain, just the swift closing of a full, strenuous and happy life. He was more than a decade younger than I am, superlatively fit, always riding, climbing, skiing, voyaging all over the world, never ill, ready for any challenge or adventure. It was a constant struggle for me, puffing and panting, to keep up with his long, effortless Highlander's stride. I felt, 'So long as I can still walk with Simon, and not fall too far behind, I'm not really an old man.'

We climbed chiefly the big hills at the head of the glen he owned, especially Sgorr na Lapaich, the tallest (3,773 feet) and most varied, with as many queenly profiles as there are angles of approach up her tawny flanks. I have painted them all, hurrying ahead of Simon to get ten minutes' grace for a quick sketch before his relentless stride overtook me again. I have scores, perhaps hundreds, of little watercolours of the glen, sometimes with Simon in them, sitting on a rock, at his feet one of his majestic succession of black labradors, especially the lithe and graceful Roly, whom he loved so much.

One thing I envied even more than his stamina was his eyesight. Like an African tracker's, his eye was constantly and systematically roaming over the hills, so that he could spot the red deer from a mile or more away, long before they saw us. This was the fruit of many years stalking. He could no longer bear to cull the fine creatures, but he retained all the instincts of the sport, especially a keen feeling for the wind and its abrupt changes of direction, and a sense of what a watchful herd was thinking. So often we would get close to a great mass of them, resting and blending totally with the ground, before they finally became aware of us. Then they would rise, a hundred – sometimes a thousand – strong, and it was as if the entire hillside suddenly came to life and raced for the shelter of the horizon.

It was our good fortune, almost always on a long day's walk, to spot a pair of golden eagles, creatures he knew intimately. It was his theory that their devastating power and mastery of the air currents made them preternaturally lazy, so that they preferred to glide and gyrate for a mile rather than flap one giant, languorous wing. 'But,' he added, 'they are most curious birds.' We saw this for ourselves once, when we were out climbing with Simon's enchanting wife, Virginia. We were planning to go up our second favourite mountain, Sgorr a Choir Ghlais, but first Simon, who had a portable rod, descended to the lochan to the north of it, in hope of finding a trout. I went with him, while Virginia lay down and dozed in the bright sunshine on the col above. After a few fruitless casts, we were climbing up again when we became aware that an enormous eagle – the largest we had ever seen – was circling low over Virginia. He had spotted the sleeping beauty and was slowly descending to investigate further. Would he have seized her – he looked strong enough – and carried her off to his eyrie? I shall never know, for our shouts startled the noble monster, and with a few beats of his enormous wings he was off into the stratosphere.

Across the glen, high among the primordial pine-forest, there is indeed an eyrie, sometimes occupied, which we often studied from above through field-glasses. Simon believed it was of great antiquity, going back to the 17th century – musty, archaeological layers of twigs supporting in turn generations of fierce eaglets. It was already old when Prince Charles Edward, with a few hunted followers, straggled up the glen after the catastrophe of Culloden, heading for the west coast and safety.

Indeed, everything is old in these parts. Simon's castle dates from the 12th century, though it was rebuilt in the 1930s, after a disastrous fire. On a recent visit I talked to the old master-mason, who as a lad helped to match and set in place the granite ashlars of the main façade. Simon liked to jest about the fire: how the clansmen had hurried from the neighbourhood to rescue the castle's contents before the flames consumed them; but, being simple Highlanders, had brought out what they themselves most valued, so that priceless portraits and heirlooms were left behind, while the men staggered out carrying vast stuffed heads of 12-pointer stags.

Simon had a strong sense of his responsibilities towards his great inheritance and sought earnestly to give it long-term protection by anchoring it in the future. Among other enterprises, he built a salmon fishery and the most modern water-bottling plant in Europe. He was always devising schemes to provide well-paid, secure employment for the clansmen and women.

When I was last there, in January, he took me up to a wild stretch of moorland where he planned to erect a wind-farm. He had carefully chosen it to be out of sight and earshot of any human habitation, and so that the tall sails would not spoil any of the horizons we cherished. It was a day of fierce cold and intense sunshine, and the entire gigantic wilderness was under deep snow and ice. I had never seen Simon's kingdom looking so spectacular, as though it stretched to Arctic infinity, and I am glad I had the hardihood to sit down and record it in watercolour. This will be my last visual record of our times in the big hills of the north, but the figure of the tall Highlander I loved will stride through my memory until my own time is come.

2 April 1994

Another little book goes down the slipway

Next week I publish a new book, my 29th I think. Books are landmarks in the life of a writer, but they leave variable impressions on the memory. Some I cannot recall writing at all. But images of my first are vivid enough, one in particular. It is evening, early in January 1957, and I am putting the finishing touches to *The Suez War*, a political quickie written in ten days. The setting is the flat in Cadogan Place I share with Hugh Thomas, then in the Foreign Office. We rent this elegant apartment for the princely sum of £8 a week, which includes the services of a hard-working Italian chambermaid, Maria. Scattered around are the evidences of self-indulgent bachelorhood: a half-opened crate of champagne, letters in scrawled feminine hands on scented writing-paper, a mantelpiece crowded with invitations and unpaid bills.

I am not only finishing my first book, I am courting, and in two months will be married. Marigold, a fragile slip of blonde beauty, curls up, quiet as a mouse, in a corner of the drawing-room, enjoined to strict silence. Hugh slumps in an armchair, saying, over and over again, 'Eden has gone mad. We all think so.' Dominating the tableau is the gaunt, angry figure of Colonel George Wigg MP, immense, elephant ears flapping with excitement, eyes staring, vituperative phrases tumbling from his lips: 'No, sir, they will not get away with it this time ... I will have their guts for garters!' He has formed the habit of dropping in at our flat, knowing I am writing this book, to supply me with the latest titbits of arcane gossip, garnered from his plentiful sources in 'the War House', about the mismanagement of the doomed expedition. Suddenly, his eye focuses on Marigold, whom he has not noticed before, and a bony, accusing finger points in her direction: 'Has that woman got security clearance?' 'Oh yes, Colonel,' I answer promptly, and give the secret sign meaning, 'Hush! Member of the SIS.' The colonel relaxes. 'That's all right then.'

The book, calling for Eden's resignation, appeared a few days before he actually did resign. It made me quite a bit of money and was variously translated: *La Guerra di Suez, Suezkriget, La Guerre de Suez* and so on; there is even a Japanese version. Aneurin Bevan, from the kindness of his heart, wrote a preface to it, and the book was marvellously launched with a savage feature article by Peregrine Worsthorne in the *Daily Telegraph*, describing it as the most disgracefully subversive document ever published. This had my publishers hopping about with joy: 'Good for a thousand copies at least!' Arnold Goodman, as he then was, had vetted the text for libel, declared it 'a breach of the Official Secrets Act from start to finish', and had warned, all his chins wobbling ominously, that it was 'thoroughly unsafe to publish one jot or tittle of it as it stands'. The Worsthorne attack resurrected all his fears and he declared mournfully to me, 'You will get us all arrested.' But nothing happened. The excitement gradually died down. Life returned to normal.

Even today, there is no disguising the tiny bat-squeak of excitement I get when the first advance copy of a new book arrives and I scan it anxiously for egregious errors. But I have long since learned to take publication calmly. For 20 years or so I have avoided reviews, having learned by experience that all notices, good, bad or indifferent, somehow contrive to irritate. Not reading reviews of your books takes considerable self-discipline. Indeed, in one sense it is impossible since, if a particularly vicious, damaging or hurtful one appears, you can be perfectly certain that kind friends will draw it to your attention, if necessary by force. None the less, it is a sensible practice and I strongly recommend it to all writers of books, tyros especially.

The publishers eventually send you huge batches of reviews, and after a considerable time, when the work is thoroughly afloat and is coming out in paperback or in a new edition, it is safe to glance through the pile on the off-chance of discovering corrections which ought to be incorporated. By then the power of the reviewer to hurt is gone.

The new book is curiously like my first one: short, topical, a tract for the times. I have subtitled it 'A Latter-Day Pamphlet', in honour of Thomas Carlyle, a long-unfashionable writer whose day, I believe, is soon coming again, and whose angular integrity shines through all his works, even when he is being (to our eyes) ridiculous. Like Carlyle in his time, I have never before felt so concerned about the state of Britain. I believe this feeling is shared by a large number of people, high and low, of all parties and none, who love our country and are genuinely scared about what will happen to it unless we do something quickly. It would be absurd to pretend there are complete, let alone easy, answers to our multitudes of problems, and I am not arrogant enough to believe that I have any miracle solution. But I have set out, as plainly as I can, what I think lies at the root of our trouble – a lack of real democracy in the way we do things – and I have made some practical proposals for putting it right. In this sense the book is a small work of piety, offered to the country I love in the earnest hope it will serve some purpose. Now it is out, I feel that I have 'done my bit', as they used to say during the war.

Therein, of course, lies the wonderful pleasure and privilege of being a writer. There are countless people around today, much more worthy than I am, who feel just as strongly about the plight of Britain and are bursting with frustration because there is no way they can unleash their emotions. It is the writer's good fortune that in the very act of describing a horrible experience, or ventilating a fear or expressing indignation or offering a remedy – however slender the chance of its being adopted – he undergoes a catharsis, a metaphysical purgation which leaves him feeling exorcised or cured. Now that *Wake Up Britain!* is actually in being, a slim little hardback with a modest, jolly cover and exactly 200 pages, I feel better already. Anyone for tennis?

23 April 1994

The grandest living Englishman

Who is the grandest living Englishman today? I am using 'grand' in
its primary sense, meaning 'chief, highest in rank or office; pre-
eminent, most properly so called' – as in 'grand duke'. I am also
using it in the sense of 'most successful', in that this man, by his
own efforts and piety and capabilities, has attained the highest
position, in terms of sovereign power, open to an Englishman, not
merely nationally but internationally. Interestingly enough, you will
not find him in *Who's Who*, no doubt through his own choice, though
its *Companion Guide* to titles, ranks, forms of address and so forth tells
you how to pronounce his surname.

By now you ought to have guessed. No? Well, he is called His
Eminent Highness the Grand Master of the Sovereign Military Order
of Malta, Fra Andrew Bertie (pronounced Barty). Strictly speaking,
he ranks as a reigning prince, and is treated as such by the 50-odd
governments with which the Grand Magistry in Rome has diplomatic
relations. The order goes back to the very early 12th century and is
thus older than most of the royal houses, indeed nations, of Europe,
and Fra Bertie, born in 1929, is the 78th Grand Master in unbroken
succession. But he is the first to be an Englishman, though Englishmen
have served with the knights since the beginning. By all accounts,
however, he is an exemplary Grand Master, who has overseen
important improvements in the fortunes of the order in the last few
years.

Since Bonaparte, that scourge of all things good and venerable,
displaced the knights from their sovereign territory of Malta, they
have had no home but Rome, where they exist in uncomfortable
proximity to the papacy. But Fra Bertie, a simple friar but also, it
seems, a considerable diplomat, persuaded the Maltese government
in 1991 to hand back to the knights the famous fortress of San
Angelo. This figured in the ferocious siege of the island in the 1560s,
when 540 knights, 400 Spanish troops and 4,000 Maltese held at
bay the entire forces of the Ottoman Empire, then at the height of its
power. So, thanks to Fra Bertie, the knights are back in Malta again
after nearly two centuries.

Now I know that the Knights of Malta are no great shakes in the modern world and that they have some pretty odd ideas of what is important. They are, to begin with, tremendous snobs. One reason Fra Bertie was elected is that he is one of the few Englishmen who can 'prove' 16 quarters of nobility. A new book just published about the order (*The Knights of Malta* by H.J.A. Sire, Yale UP,) devotes an entire coloured plate to these, and very quaint they look. There are 10,000 knights today and becoming one is like joining a club. You have to be supported by four existing knights but there are three categories of admission – Honour and Devotion, Grace and Devotion, and Magistral Grace. For the third, and lowest, category you don't need any quarterings at all, and that now comprises most of the knights. But for Honour and Devotion you have to have 16, and obviously these knightly animals are more equal than the others.

I first became interested in the knights back in the early 1950s, when I heard rumours that Cardinal Canali, the last Roman cardinal to be cast in the heroic mould of a Renaissance scoundrel, was trying to take over their possessions. This monster was a master of intrigue, a commodity much in use during the last years of old Pius XII, and he very nearly succeeded in his object. However, one of the order's highest officials, Count Cattaneo, leaked the story, complete with authenticating papers, to the French novelist Roger Peyrefitte. He presented the tale, suitably dressed up, in a sensational *roman à clef*, *Les Chevaliers de Malte* (1957). It caused quite a stir and I read it with avidity but couldn't quite believe that all the skulduggery it revealed was true. However, Sire claims that, in all essentials, Peyrefitte described exactly what happened. The novel effectively did the trick for the knights, frustrating Canali's plot, and the next year Pius XII died, thus making way for a modern Vatican where the Canalis have no place.

Obviously the order is very rich, otherwise it would not have been worth Canali's while to try to grab its property. And today it is much richer and bigger than in Canali's time, with nearly 40 national associations and thousands of valuable properties all over the world. Indeed I suspect it is much richer than Opus Dei, and in many ways as influential, though it is careful to attract much less attention. It is no longer a fighting order, of course, though a surprising number of the knights have seen active service (Fra Bertie was in the Scots Guards). The nearest it now has to a navy are the ambulance boats it runs on some of the big lakes of Africa and the Americas. But the ambulance service it operates all over the world, its hospitals, clinics, dispensaries and health centres form what is almost certainly the largest voluntary network of medical care the world has ever seen. In short, it is a modern monument of do-goodery, served up, as it were, on a silver salver.

One of the features of its charitable work are the caravans of the sick and dying it takes annually, from all over the world, to the miraculous shrine at Lourdes. This is where the women come in. The top knights of the order have to be celibate but the lower knights marry, and their wives and friends, whether quartered or not, supply the nurses. Working on one of these convoys is therefore frightfully smart, but the duties are no more agreeable than any other form of nursing.

My talkative little friend who goes to Lourdes with them reports: 'Some of the sick people we take are awfully old and decrepit. They're all tremendously sweet but – you know. Well, I don't at all mind wiping their bums and washing down the latrines and all that sort of thing. But I draw the line at sharing a room with one of the other nurses. Why, the last time my room-mate had smelly feet and I *nearly died*. Can you *imagine?*'

Well, I can, actually. So the knights and their ladies go soldiering on, and good luck to them and their work.

7 May 1994

Prince Charles and the Wyf of Bath

Prince Charles has launched a new architectural magazine – *Perspectives* – with a call for the people to be consulted. He wants the design of houses to reflect the wishes of those who will live in them. Who could quarrel with that? But then how do you discover what people want when they do not know themselves?

Most people see houses from the inside out: they can give a pretty specific account of what they need in the way of rooms, services, space, light etc. but have no notion of how they expect all this to be reflected in the exterior. Once they get outside the house they think in terms of the garden and garage. But there are a minority, of whom I am one, who visualise their ideal house as a building, rather than a collection of rooms, and see it from outside, in its setting. I can draw an exact picture of the house I want, down to details of brickwork, mouldings and chimneys, but I am hazy about what goes on inside it. I like that kind of thing to come as a surprise when I open the front door and go in. If an architect undertook to build me my perfect house, I suspect the first thing I would do would be to quarrel with him. And, come to think of it, the historical record shows that is what usually happens. Building your own house, even if you find an architect who is not a bundle of imperiousness and impracticality – and that is rare – is an exercise in frustration, financial ruin, disillusionment, and sheer bad temper.

So most of us buy second-hand houses and make the best of what we find and can afford. This brings variety at any rate. In the last 40 years or so I have inhabited the following: as a young man in Paris I lived (leaving out hotels) in a brick-and-stucco Art Nouveau studio in Montparnasse, a huge 18th-century studio in Montmartre which had once been a chapel and was built over a night-club, and a 19th-century flat carved out of a medieval palace in the Marais. In England I moved first to a late-Georgian flat in Knightsbridge, then an 1880s brick-and-terracotta one behind Harrods, followed by many years in an early Georgian (1719 actually) house in Bucks. More recently I have bought a very early Victorian (1840) villa in Bays-water and a 1950s conversion of a coach-house in Somerset which is a perfect example, down to the light fittings, of what I would call Attlee-Truman Modernism.

I have taken great delight in the varying styles and moods of all these domiciles, and have been happy in every single one, but none remotely corresponds to my ideal. Like Cathleen Moreland in *Northanger Abbey*, I have wanted all my life to live in a Gothic castle, Revival rather than Medieval – or, better still, both – with plenty of towers, turrets, machicolations, dim passages, newel staircases, a chapel, a piscina, an aumbry and a flushing garderobe, not forgetting squints, meurtrières and a solar. Such a vision is not so unrealisable as might be supposed, since, in my experience, anyone who actually owns a Gothic castle is only too ready to unload it on to anyone else. But whenever I have been seriously tempted, my wife Marigold has put her foot down firmly, and the cloud-capped towers have instantly dissolved.

Few people now, I fear, like the Gothic, and my dream of a Second Gothic Revival sweeping away the last modernist boxes and packing cases and restoring a world of spires and battlements is not likely to be realised. There seems to be a class division over architectural styles. Above a certain line, running halfway through the middle class, there is a distinct preference for Georgian. A duke or earl who tires of his ancestral pile and decides to build himself a more convenient abode is sure to commission a neat Georgian rectory-style house, with long, light, many-paned windows, perhaps with a few Palladian flourishes in stone *à la* Quinlan Terry but essentially a red-brick 18th-century mansion. Most well-to-do members of the professional classes think along the same lines. Their idea of the good life is to wrap themselves in Georgian brick and white paint, and live as they imagine Parson Woodforde did or Mr Bennett or Archdeacon Grantley.

Down the social scale, one travels backwards in time. The lower-middle or working classes may insist on all mod cons, even more emphatically, these days, than anyone else, plus a disco too. But they like the flash of an exposed beam as well. For over a century now, the popular preference, to which generations of mass-produced houses built for sale testify, is for some kind of Tudor. Not, indeed, the sophisticated Renaissance Tudor of John Smythson or Longleat, but something earlier, earthier and quainter, with an atmosphere of black-and-white lath-and-plaster rather than carved stone ashlar.

It is odd, but the bulk of the British seem to see their ideal house emerging from early Tudor times or even from the later Middle Ages. It springs from a child's storybook, illustrated long before the age of political correctness, the kind of house where Goldilocks met the Three Bears or where the Wolf ate Little Red Riding Hood's grandmother – a cottage with casements and eaves and diamond-paned windows, sunflowers and hollyhocks in the garden. This is how ordinary British people visualise Arcadia, and they attempt to recreate it by patronising 'Henry VIII Nights' at the local pub, where they are served food on 'platters' by 'wenches' and there are robust jokes about multiple wives, axes, heads and hauntings. That the Golden Age is dated in the popular mind somewhere towards the end of the 15th century is further demonstrated by the extraordinary passion for garden gnomes, whose dress and headgear suggest they could easily have been spectators at the Battle of Bosworth Field.

Why do people want to transport themselves back to those dubious times? There is no answer to the question. One should ask, rather, why they reject so emphatically all the aesthetics of the Modern Age and the answer is all too obvious. They may be forced, by cruel councils and brutal architects and planners, to live in tower blocks or concrete bunkers designed by heartless intellectuals who see a house as a machine for living in. But no one can make them like it. They regard modern architecture as merely the latest form which the age-old tyranny of the ruling class takes. If Prince Charles can free them from that, and help them to inhabit a Utopia where the Wyf of Bath or the Merry Wives of Windsor feel at home, then he would be well on his way to becoming a popular monarch.

19 March 1994

Capitalist Michelangelos and Beethovens

What is power? I have been reflecting on this as a result of an episode involving my third son. He is a young entrepreneur who, among other things, has achieved a reputation for rescuing companies in financial difficulties. Recently he heard of a case in Blackburn, where a chain of shops specialising in wedding clothes was about to go into liquidation. Convinced that the firm was fundamentally sound and that its plight arose merely from poor management, he dashed up north and talked the key bank into a financial restructure. Then he dashed back to London and cleared the deal with the bank's head office. As a result he and his partner were able to save 150 jobs.

Now that is what I call real power. Few possess it, certainly not writers. I suppose I have had a certain influence through my articles and books but it is hard to be sure about it and quite impossible to quantify. Most politicians fear the same. Cabinet ministers often tell me how powerless they feel. When Dick Crossman was a secretary of state and I was an editor, he used to say to me, 'You have a damn sight more power than I do.' 'Nonsense,' said I, and we would argue hotly. But the truth is neither of us had much. Even in the matter of jobs, when a politician embarks on a job-creation scheme he is seeking short-term popularity and piling up long-term mischief. But for a young man to make secure 150 jobs and bring relief to all those families, just by making efficient something which was badly run, is a marvellous exercise in real power.

It is also, in a curious sense, creative, and this is a point that is often missed about the capitalist system. We have been taught to see it, particularly by Marxists and their contemporary successors, entirely in financial terms, 'shuffling bits of paper about' as they often say in the left-wing press. But capitalism also involves starting from nothing, building vast factories, digging mines and launching exciting new products on the market. I am deeply grateful, for instance, to whoever designed and marketed this typewriter I am using. It is the best I have ever had, I have written huge books on it and countless articles and it suits me perfectly. To me, the man or woman responsible for getting it on to the market is a creative person of a high order. Again, in America, South Africa and Australia, I have had a fascinating time talking to a specialist category of mining engineers, who actually design deep-level goldfields, or those complicated mines where various base metals are extracted on conjunction (sometimes with silver added). The design of the mine is the key to its success, but the engineers have to work in the dark because, despite the most modern instrumentation, no one really knows what lies in the bowels of the earth until they dig deep enough to find out. So the mine designer has to use his imagination and often work by intuition. He is rather like a playwright who doesn't know what reception his lines and effects will have until they are presented to a live audience.

When I was writing my last big book, *The Birth of the Modern*, which among other things dealt with early industrialisation, I had to study the lives of a large number of entrepreneurs, and I became convinced that the desire to make a lot of money was only one of their motives, not necessarily the most important one. The elder Brunel, who built the world's first production line in Portsmouth, was a creative spirit if ever there was one, and his son, Isambard Kingdom Brunel, was a major artist as well as a great engineer.

The titans of early industry did not see themselves – as they are often now presented – as the destroyers of beauty but as its creators. Bringing good wages to a family hitherto living at subsistence level was to them creative. To mark the fact they hired fine artists and designers to embellish their mills and mines and forges. The passionate love of good, clean design which Thomas Telford put into his bridges and toll-houses, docks, locks and road-furniture – much of which happily still survives – amounts to a major artistic achievement. And the first Stephenson, though illiterate until his son, who had been to school, taught him to read and write, took constant trouble to make his engines beautiful. But he also made his business pay, through hard-headed entrepreneurial skills, knowing full well that any businessman who can't meet the wage-bill at the end of the week is no good to anyone.

The sheer creativity of capitalism has in recent years become the theme of a number of fine American writers, such as Thomas Sowell and George Gilder. Michael Novak, who has presented democratic capitalism as an important expression of the creative Christian spirit, has now had his work recognised by the award of this year's Templeton Prize. These writers, and others pursuing similar themes, are today well known in the United States, and their message is getting over at some of the more vigorous universities, such as Adelphi in Long Island, Temple in Pennsylvania and Southern Baptist in Dallas. Their ideas are also spreading outside the United States; for instance, the huge new University of Latin America now being planned in Miami, which will move to its permanent headquarters in Cuba as soon as the failing Castro régime disintegrates, will have a special department called after Novak, in which the creative aspects of capitalism will be explored, taught and developed.

We do not seem to get any of this here in Britain, where most dons – who, of course, know little or nothing about the subject – present capitalism to their pupils as a horribly materialistic activity characterised by greed and dishonesty. Some of them positively discourage their brighter charges from going into industry. First-year students who tell their tutors that they hope to make a career producing motorcars or household appliances are soon likely to be sneered out of it. Yet these dons are exactly the same people who criticise Margaret Thatcher and the Tories for 'destroying Britain's manufacturing base'. We will keep a manufacturing base into the next century and beyond only if we can persuade our cleverest, most imaginative and innovatory spirits to work in it. That means we must develop the habit, at various levels of our society, and especially in our education process, of presenting capitalism as a creative activity, akin in its own way to writing symphonies or novels, or painting great landscapes.

28 May 1994

Vultures gather for their D-Day feast

As the D-Day celebrations move to their climax, and the Draft Dodger, the Grey Man and the Old Repellent gather together to squeeze whatever political kudos they can out of the honourable dead, I have been trying to imagine what the Iron Duke would have said about it all. He was not a man for celebrating occasions like this. Wellington hated war and it was some satisfaction to him, at the end of his long life, that his active career as a warrior had ended in 1815 when he was still only 45. Up to that point, it is true, he had witnessed more scenes of slaughter than any other man of his time, Bonaparte alone excepted. Unlike Boney, however, who did not care tuppence for his conscripts, the Duke regretted every man who died and took immense pains to minimise casualties – one reason men preferred to serve under him, as later they did for General Montgomery.

Wellington often said that the only thing worse than a battle won was a battle lost. Even he, with all his experience, was profoundly shocked by the carnage of Waterloo, where two huge armies, both under determined commanders, were jammed into a tiny space and under fire all of a long June day. The Duke was amazed that he and his wonderful horse Copenhagen survived their 18-hour exposure – 'I really think the finger of providence was on me' – especially as so many of his colleagues, including his cavalry commander, Lord Uxbridge, who was talking to him at the time, were cut down or maimed. The annual Waterloo reunions he held thereafter, at Apsley House or Windsor, were not celebrations at all but meetings of brave men who had gone through hell together and wanted to thank God for their survival and drink to the memory of dead comrades.

The Duke particularly disliked politicians or anyone else horning in on Waterloo for their own purposes. He did not even fancy the idea of David Wilkie's *Chelsea Pensioners Reading the Waterloo Dispatch*, until the painter satisfied him about his good faith and accuracy. Wellington detested George IV talking about the battle, especially as the king, under the influence of cherry brandy, would persuade himself that he had taken part in the famous charge of the Royal Scots Greys. He often recounted his personal experiences of the battle to a crowd of embarrassed courtiers, who knew he had been safe in bed in London, ending his narration: 'And that's how we licked 'em, eh Arthur?' The Duke, who also hated the monarch calling him Arthur, would grit his teeth and wearily reply, 'As Your Majesty has so often observed.'

So we can be pretty sure the Duke would not have approved of Bill Clinton trying to hijack D-Day. Indeed, there is something peculiarly mean-spirited about the way in which those who were not present at the battle, or in any way related to those who were, have been jostling each other to get in on the act. There have been disturbing reports that men who were actually on the beaches and distinguished themselves there were left out of the invitation-list, or added to it grudgingly only after protests. Tory ministers used to be especially sensitive about the rights of veterans and their dependants. But that was because they had seen military service themselves and knew what it was all about. Hardly any of the present lot were in the second world war. Some were not even born. Few are old enough to have done two years' peacetime conscription. For them, the services are just things to be cut so that more money is available to bribe their constituents. When an event like the D-Day anniversary comes along, their instinct is to send for a PR firm and ask, 'What's in it for me?'

One veteran who was nearly overlooked was Brigadier Lord Lovat, who led the first wave of Commandos ashore, accompanied by his piper. I have talked to him about that morning and found him modestly anxious to play down his role, which he thought had been exaggerated. But he undoubtedly was one of the heroes of the occasion, and if ever an age needed a few heroes it is this one. Lovat is old and frail and unable to leave his house, though still keeping an eagle eye on the world. But his family were surprised that his invitation was so long in coming, and hurt when a plan to have him represented at the banquet by his 17-year-old grandson and heir was obstructed by the minister concerned. That is typical of the way the whole thing has been handled.

There are other shadows over the affair. The prominent role being taken by François Mitterrand will certainly offend some people, since parts of his wartime career remain an impenetrable mystery. Despite much recent controversy, we still do not know whether his heart lay with the Resistance – as he has claimed for the past half-century – or with those who then ruled France. Perhaps both. Or perhaps he does not have a heart at all, merely a political calculating-machine. I hope he has the decency to say as little as possible on the day.

No such chance with Clinton of course. The politician who fled abroad to avoid Vietnam, and who once said publicly how much he hated 'the military', will be beating his own big drum, like the tipsy George IV. The more one examines this dreadful man, the more unsuitable he seems in the White House. The American presidency has often been associated with the highest military honour, quite apart from the fact that the incumbent is also Commander-in-Chief. In addition to Washington himself, five other presidents have been general officers of distinction, and many others have had fine war-records. The idea of a politician who wriggled out of his military obligations to his country being elected to the White House would have been unthinkable only a decade ago. It stains the entire D-Day ceremony and I hope some of the veterans who attend it will give the President a piece of their minds, as did Herbert Shugart last week. At a ceremony to present posthumous Congressional Medals of Honour to the widows of two soldiers who died in the Somalia intervention – a typical Clinton mess – Shugart, the father of one of the boys, refused to shake Clinton's hand and told him, 'You are unfit to be the President of the United States.' That is a sentiment with which all of us can agree.

4 June 1994

The siege of Saltwood Castle

'With every flick of Max Clifford's wrist,' wailed David Mellor in the *Guardian*, mankind was 'doomed' to be 'sent spinning further into an abyss of semi-fictionalised voyeurism masquerading as news.' Mr Mellor, himself a victim of Max Clifford's black art, was of course commenting on the publicist's latest creation: the sexual gavotte said to have taken place between the former defence minister, Alan Clark, and three female members of the Harkess family. But most other columnists – who have not themselves suffered at Clifford's hands – just lay back and enjoyed it. 'We should be grateful to these clowns,' wrote Woodrow Wyatt in the *News of the World*, 'for the vast entertainment they've given us.' All things considered, Alan Clark got a marvellous press. Peregrine Worsthorne was so entranced that he gave Clark two rave notices. In the *Daily Telegraph* he described him as 'a writer of genius'. 'Whereas David Mellor,' he added in the *Sunday Telegraph*, 'came across as sleazy and rather ridiculous, Alan Clark has succeeded in presenting himself . . . as an authentic Cavalier.'

It is true some of the down-market gossip columnists felt they had to be censorious. Allison Pearson in the *Evening Standard* denounced Clark as an '18th-century Loutish Leftover', a 'Bionic Bounder', 'a Forty-Million-Pound Phallus' and a 'Caveman'. Sounds as if the lady would like to meet him, doesn't it? There were more sour grapes from Henry Porter in the *Daily Mail*: 'In the life of every Romeo,' he wrote, 'there is a moment when he can move – perhaps lurch is a better word – from ageing roué to dirty old man.' He added: 'Clark is curiously without style'. I'm not sure Porter would be my first choice as an arbiter of morals, or style for that matter.

Another self-appointed moral heavyweight holding forth was Edward Pearce in the *Standard*. But he decided to go for Clifford as an easier target: 'He is a subterranean creature reminiscent of H.G. Wells's Morlocks, who were four feet tall, bloodshot-eyed, browless and crept about in a hunched, arm-drooping simian posture. They lived in caves underground and were cannibals. That is a little kind to Mr Clifford, but gives a good idea of his moral standing.' The trouble with such journalists as Pearce is that they lack the imagination to see themselves as others see them. Many years ago, feeling sorry for Pearce, whom I scarcely knew, I invited him to a lunch party at my house. Afterwards, my wife, said, 'Please don't ask that man again.' 'Why?' 'I don't really know, but I could see the other guests edging away.' Yet another of the gossips, Peter Hillmore in the *Observer*, actually had the nerve to dismiss Clark's writings as of 'tabloid quality' and to define him as 'a fellow of low vulgar manners and behaviour'. Most people, I imagine, would consider this an apt summation of columnists like Porter, Pearce and Hillmore.

There were some surprises. The *Times*, in a leader, dismissed the whole business under the headline: 'Sex romp comedy: Clark and his coven are earning public cheers not pity'. The story was 'adding to the harmless gaiety of nations'. This seemed odd from a paper which once insisted, apropos the Profumo affair, 'It *is* a moral issue', and its editor, Peter Stoddart, confessed to me he was not so sure of the line he had taken. He may be right to have second thoughts. On the other hand, censoriousness towards Clark did not ring true. His luxurious lifestyle, complained Suzanne Moore in the *Guardian*, was particularly hard on 'those among us who have to huddle in doorways with tattered sleeping-bags and beg for a living'. My God – I knew the *Guardian* was mean, but is it *that* mean? Here was I imagining Ms Moore, the paper's star woman moaner, comfortably settled in Swiss Cottage with a glass of Bulgarian chablis in hand, and all the time she was underneath the Arches!

Jane Clark was awarded the crown of 'Heroine of the Week' by most columnists, led by the *Mail*'s Linda Lee-Potter, that faithful litmus-test of middle-class suburban opinion. By contrast, no one had a good word to say for the Harkesses. The *Sun*'s Richard Littlejohn summed up the general opinion: 'They will be remembered – if at all – as a couple of silly bitches and a pathetic cuckold. They've had their fifteen minutes. They can go home now.' Dr Raj Persaud, a Maudsley Hospital psychiatrist hired by the *Mail* to give an expert's view, dismissed the Harkess women as suffering from 'low self-esteem'. However, I was not impressed by this shrink's homework. He wrote that it was 'Clark's imperviousness to what others think which made him a difficult Cabinet colleague'. But the whole point about Clark, as I thought everyone knew, is that he never got into the Cabinet – not even Mrs Thatcher, who had a soft spot for him, would put him there – and it was this failure which led him to resign his seat and publish his *Diaries*.

Indeed, in general I was disappointed by Fleet Street's inability to investigate the background to this story properly. Why did no one point out that the Mr Hyde side of Clark's character comes from his dreadful mum, another Jane? She quite literally used to crash into a room and is the only woman I think, at any rate in the present reign, who toppled over while curtsying to the Queen, did a spectacular cartwheel, and landed on her bottom, drawing from the monarch the laconic comment: 'That was quite a bump.' Again, I think the reporters ought to have done a better job on the legalities of Clifford's business. He is, by any definition, a public nuisance who should be brought to book if possible. And, since he makes a habit of taking a percentage from women who cash in on their adulterous activities, is he not in danger of a hand on his collar? Why has no one suggested to Ms Barbara Mills, that unimaginative and far from hyperactive director of Public Prosecutions, that there may be a case for doing Clifford for living on immoral earnings? The prosecution and conviction of this egregious manufacturer of half-truths and lubricious fictions would be a fitting end to the Siege of Saltwood Castle.

11 June 1994

It's always tea-time in Chile

The performance of the Chilean Ballet at the Festival Hall earlier this month revived all my love for their country and its people. These stunningly beautiful girls and ultra-athletic young men cavorted with matchless energy and grace for over two hours, performing dances from all over Latin America – tangos, sambas, rumbas, cuecas, galoperas, lambadas, chapecatos, romps from Colombia and Paraguay and rituals from the age of the Mayas, Aztecs and Incas. The costumes were delicious, and there was some haunting piping and drumming. My hands were quite sore with clapping at the end. As I normally attend the theatre in thunderous silence, my wife, Marigold, was amazed.

But then I have been a Chile fan for more than 30 years. I love its absurd shape, the sombre lakes of Valdivia and the Antarctic glaciers in the south, Santiago with its spectacular views of the High Andes in the middle, the burning tropical desert in the north. Valparaiso has been to me the most romantic port on earth, ever since as a child I heard it glowingly described by my father, who ran away to sea when he was 12 and found himself there. Chilean women, peasants and grand ladies alike, have an elegance you find nowhere else in the Spanish-speaking world, and the men of all classes a noble dignity. They all laugh a lot, however sad life may be. The food is delicious, the wines sublime and the courtesy impeccable.

Not least, the Chileans take tea-time seriously. This may be because of the English connection. To be of English descent is the grandest thing in Chile, though Welsh, Scotch and Irish is not bad either. The 'liberator of Chile' was Bernardo O'Higgins, whose father came from County Meath, and who licked the Dons at the Battle of Chacabuco in 1817. And it was Admiral Lord Cochrane, flying his flag in the battleship *O'Higgins*, who completed the destruction of Spanish naval power in the eastern Pacific. The Royal Navy helped to bring the Chilean navy to the high standards of efficiency it still maintains, and only last week its head told me that Chilean naval officers, to this day, wear black mourning ties on the anniversary of Nelson's death at Trafalgar.

So, it's not surprising the Chileans enjoy tea-parties. The first I attended, in 1960, was a memorable one. I had spent the afternoon at the Santiago race-track with Salvador Allende, then a senator. He was a clever, jovial, likable man, who smoked a pipe, wore a tweed jacket and might have been a prewar economics lecturer at the LSE. But he was rather keen on the Sport of Kings.

Together we had one or two successful flutters, but just before the last race he studied the card with unusual care, disappeared for a few moments to consult some shifty-looking men, and, on his return, said, 'We'll give this a miss.' He proved to be well-advised. The favourite, easily in front, was pulled back in the most outrageous fashion just before the post, and a dark horse came from nowhere to win. The crowd went mad with fury and surged on to the track. The argument was still raging when we left.

We repaired to the Senate to take tea. What a repast! There was not only tea, India, China or Ceylon, coffee, wine and home-made lemonade, but sandwiches and muffins and crumpets and trifles and cakes and jellies and blancmange. It was also what the late Henry Fairlie called 'a knife-and-fork-hot-cooked tea', and in the middle of the buffet was a mountainous pile of exotic fruits of all descriptions. While we tucked into this feast, Allende gave me the facts of life about Chilean politics. He was already favoured as the presidential candidate of the Left, but told me he just didn't have the votes to win unless the predominantly conservative electorate was divided by a split in the Right. Then, he thought, he might just make it, but heaven knows what would happen.

As with the last race, Allende was proved right ten years later. He was elected president with only 36 per cent of the popular vote, the split anti-socialist vote totalling 62 per cent. On the principle of Thomas Jefferson, a man he much admired, that great innovations should not rest on slender majorities, he should have admitted that he did not have a mandate for social revolution and concentrated on good housekeeping.

Instead, he was pushed by his more extreme followers into a vast programme of absurd changes, and, not content with this, they began to take the law into their own hands and seize estates and property. The result was economic crisis, hyperinflation, mass unemployment and a revolt of the middle class. A reluctant head of the army, General Pinochet (Chile has no tradition of *caudillismo*), was persuaded by the conservative civilians to take over and avert civil war. In the process, poor Allende was killed.

Two decades later, the General invited Marigold and me to tea in his Santiago HQ. His mandate was now complete and he had retired from the presidency. But he remained in charge of the armed forces, and he asked some of his most brilliant officers to meet us. This time we sat round an enormous table, with Marigold on his right: as she was an expert on the IRA, he was anxious to pick her brains about fighting terrorism.

Under his rule, the Chilean economy was restored and prospered mightily; the country is the richest in Latin America – so rich, alas, that the fumes of countless cars now make it impossible to see the snowy summits of the Andes from the Santiago streets – and a model for all its neighbours. But, thank God, the tea-time fare has not changed. We began with apricot ice-cream, progressed to Welsh rarebit and honey-cooked ham salad – interspersed with rich pistachio cake – and, if the orderlies had suddenly brought in a smoking-hot steak-and-kidney pudding, I would not have been at all surprised. As the general said, tea-time is an important meal in Chile. Long may it remain so.

18 June 1994

Saving parents from their children

Cyril Connolly was an ugly child from a far from distinguished and not particularly wealthy family. But he was a dazzling success at Eton, not primarily because he was clever and good at Greek – that helped of course – but because he learned how to make the bloods and aristos laugh, and so got into the Eton society Pop. It ruined his life. As he wrote later, the last school year of a successful Eton boy is so blissful that life thereafter, however well the fellow does, is a descent from Elysium, an expulsion from the Garden of Eden. Connolly once said to me, right at the end of his days, 'My adult life has been a purgatory, lit by a few flashes of remembered heaven.' A lot of other Old Etonians meet the same fate. One sees them littering obscure corners of London clubs or slinking in and out of City merchant banks, looks of profound melancholy on their stupid faces.

The hidden curse of Eton has now become the curse of all children. We over-indulge our offspring to the point where they inhabit an illusory paradise, and we then dump them into the real world of competition, unemployment, housing shortage, crime and tricky personal relationships. The spoiling process begins at the earliest possible age at which pandering is possible. That excellent maxim, 'Children should be seen and not heard', has been reversed. They are not merely allowed to be present on all occasions, but to dominate the scene. Recently I heard a Cabinet minister, a newspaper editor and the chairman of a big public company, who were enjoying a civilised conversation on how to get rid of John Major, suddenly shushed into silence by parents because 'Felicity [aged nearly three] is trying to say something'. Well: we waited and it eventually came: 'My doll is called Nobbie.'

Some good things I do not grudge the young. They now have comfortable and pretty clothes, whereas I still remember the agony, aged 12, of trying to put on starched collars with studs. Our part of London is crowded with adventure playgrounds of dazzling ingenuity, where kids riot in joyful high spirits and learn to be courageous and enterprising the easy way. They eat wonderful food and as much of it as they want (does any British child now know what it feels like, as I certainly did, to be really ravenous?). Reading and many other kinds of learning are made fun. None now experiences the toils of filling in a copybook with pen and ink. Their treats are Babylonian and never-ending. Recently I took a grandchild to see (and, my word, hear) the mechanical dinosaurs at the Natural History Museum, and marvelled at the amount of expertise and cash which now goes on amusing the brutes – the kids, not the monsters.

In addition, we increasingly bend the law in their favour. It is now very difficult to prosecute tiny-tot thugs at all, even when they commit murder, as they increasingly do. Not only is the infamous Children's Act 1989 on the Statute Book, but its provisions are becoming well known to teenage horrors. The recent riot at St Mary's, Wantage, could not have occurred on such a scale without it. For the staff got wind of what the fifth form was planning after exams were over – that they had, for instance, been stockpiling powder paint and giant water-pistols with which to spray it – and accordingly raided the ringleaders' lockers and confiscated the munitions.

In the day of Angela Brazil, Dorita Fairlie-Bruce and Eleanor Brent-Dyer, that would have been chalked up as a famous victory for the beaks and the end of the matter. Instead, the new brand of dormitory lawyers pronounced this pre-emptive strike an unlawful 'invasion' of their 'private sphere' under the Act. Some complained to Childline, others threatened to go to the police, but the hardliners said, 'No – revenge.' So these fiends went back into Wantage, bought oil-based paint this time, plus 100 glass stink-bombs and other North Korean-type ultimate weapons, and in due course launched their D-Day, signalled by setting off the fire-alarm at 2 a.m. They wore IRA stocking masks knowing that the staff would hesitate to tear them off, as this would expose them to charges of assault under the 1989 Act. As a result, the head, the Revd Pat Johns, one of the fat ladies recently made into priests, expelled all 51 of them – well, sent them home until the end of term – a response which was variously described as draconian, courageous, vindictive and over-reactive. This school is not, as the papers have said, a nest for children of decadent jet-setters, but a perfectly ordinary middle-class school for the daughters of pious Anglican parents.

Of course, as with Connolly's world of Pop, once children are booted out of this favoured existence into the real world, they hate it. But the booting out is now often delayed for decades, grown-up children squatting in their parents' comfortable homes well into their 20s, even 30s, citing the accommodation shortage as an excuse. Some parents, in despair, buy their off-spring flats, or sell their houses simply to get shot of the incubi. One divorced lady I know, with three children ranging from 25 to 35, all of whom live at home free when they feel like it, finds herself acting as a kind of unpaid valet, lady's maid, cook and laundress to her indulged brood. Me: 'You should not be such a doormat.' She: 'I know. But if they go they might never come back. I don't mind, really, but I do wish Laura would not borrow all my best clothes without permission.'

There speaks a typical member of the newly downtrodden parental classes. But nemesis comes to the oppressors in the end, as it must. In the real world at last, they find themselves condemned to, among other things, sexual permissiveness. Increasingly, they discover it is not acceptable to have boy/girlfriends, affairs and flings, or even harmless friendships. They are forced by the opinions of their peers into gruesomely permanent 'relationships' with members of the opposite sex, variously described as 'partners', 'live-in lovers' and other unappetising terms. The girls find themselves drudges and the young men are often role-reversed – and henpecked to boot. Last week, at a party, I asked a girl in her mid-20s how she was liking London. 'Not bad,' said she, 'but I have to begin cohabitation next week and, between ourselves, I'm not looking forward to it.' So there's some justice even in a youth-dominated world.

25 June 1994

Sex is becoming a laughing matter

The first recorded laughter in history occurred at the end of the Early Bronze Age, about 2000 BC. Significantly, it was a woman who laughed. The Book of Genesis tells us (xviii, 10ff) that, when Sarah overheard the Lord inform her husband Abraham she was to have a son despite her age, 'Sarah laughed within herself, saying, after I am waxed old shall I have pleasure, my lord being old also?' So the first joke was female and concerned sex, and it is significant also that Sarah made it to herself. When the men – that is, the Lord and Abraham – crossly accused her of laughing, she denied that she had, 'for she was afraid'.

It is a remarkable fact that from the Bronze Age to this day women have been inclined to find sex funny, and men have resented their lack of seriousness. I know a woman whose husband strictly forbids her to laugh or make a joke while they are making love. He considers it most improper. One can imagine D.H. Lawrence taking exactly the same line with Frieda – indeed, I think it is actually recorded that he did, as well as making her wear old-fashioned, humourless bloomers to do it in. Lawrence too went banging on and on about love-making being a sacrament, something dreadfully solemn and portentous, quite unsuited to humorous commentary. It is notorious that when men attend a sex-show they always sit in oppressive silence, punctuated by heavy breathing. When women hold a hen-party and engage a male stripper, they hoot with laughter the whole time. What does this tell us?

Well, the first thing it tells us is that, while life is hard for everyone – we live *in hac lacrimarum valle* as St Anselm put it – it is much harder for women than for men, so they need jokes even more than we do. When surveys are taken of what women want in a man, 'sense of humour' always comes at or near the top of the list. Men by contrast do not particularly relish humorous women: they are afraid of being laughed at. That, I suspect, is why Nancy Mitford, the wittiest person I ever came across – making jokes was her life – found it so hard to get or keep a man. Come to think of it, Jane Austen experienced exactly the same difficulty. Laughing women have been liable to come croppers throughout history. There is much contemporary evidence that Anne Boleyn was a fun-loving girl, always giggling or in shrieks. Henry VIII would not have liked that in the end. Though he was the last king of England to employ a professional jester, I do not recall any accounts of him ever making jokes himself, except of the ghoulish, hangman's kind which Stalin, too, loved. St Thomas More, who must have laughed as often as any other Lord Chancellor in history, treated Henry as humourless. Anne Boleyn's sense of humour, indeed, may well have contributed more to her undoing

than her putative adultery. Asked recently to describe the experience
of being made love to by a certain fat MP, his former mistress replied,
'It is like being under a very large wardrobe with a very small key
in the middle.' If Anne made jokes like this and they got about – as
such jokes do of course – then it is no wonder Henry cut her head
off. No wonder, either, that their daughter Elizabeth I steered well
clear of sex, though she too had a notable sense of humour, inherited
from her mother, naturally.

Prince Charles's confession of his affair with Camilla Parker Bowles
last week led to much regurgitating in the papers of adulterous
liaisons by heirs apparent. But no one pointed out that, while royal
mistresses make jokes, royal lovers are singularly humourless. An
exception was Charles II, though it is not clear whether even he
made jokes about sex. Certainly his girls did, from the charming
Louise de Kerouaille to 'pretty, witty Nell', who flabbergasted a mob
stoning her coach by popping her head out of the window and crying,
'Fools, I am the *Protestant* whore!'

The first two Georges were gruesomely grim in their pursuit of
female flesh and the fourth, though frivolous enough when he chose,
made sex so arduous that his long-time companion and possible wife,
Mrs Fitzherbert, referred to her dealings with him as 'twenty years'
hard labour'. His dreadful brother, the Duke of Clarence, gave an
equally hard time to Dorothy Jordan, the funniest as well as one of
the most beautiful women in Europe. Edward VII was no better. He
expected Mrs Keppel to amuse him but it is not recorded he ever
made *her* laugh, except inadvertently – the story of the wardrobe and
the key again. It was the same with Edward VIII and Mrs Dudley
Ward and, I suspect, with Prince Charles and Camilla. Rumour has
it that what holds him spellbound is her earthy humour; it certainly
can't be her looks.

The bifurcation of masculine and feminine senses of humour is
very ancient. It must have begun in the Stone Age. Once men and
women developed even rudimentary manners, they adopted different
modes of intimate discourse, especially in talking about sex. This
development of parallel vernaculars lasted thousands of years and
they began to converge only in the 20th century. Virginia Woolf
relates that, when she and her sister Vanessa were living in Gordon
Square, about 1906, 'the somewhat sinister figure' of Lytton Strachey,
whom they scarcely knew, called on them when they were alone.
Even before he had given them his hat and stick, he noticed a damp
stain on Vanessa's white dress and, pointing a bony finger at it,

asked, 'Semen?' The girls laughed, and so Bloomsbury was born, its vivifying characteristic being that its male members used exactly the same speech whether or not there were ladies in the room.

It has taken the best part of a century for the practice of Bloomsbury to percolate through to the nation as a whole. But it is now plainly happening and will soon be complete. 'Hush! Ladies present!' is rapidly becoming an anachronism. Women now dominate the coarser kind of comedy on television. The clergy and the stiffer element in society may well deplore this new tolerance (or use) by women of the language and lore of the barrack-room. I'm not sure I like it myself. But it has one compensation. It means that, increasingly, sex will be treated as it ought to be – as a laughing matter.

9 July 1994

The cave of a Christian Aladdin

The greatest treat a civilised person can enjoy in London today is a visit to the Pugin show at the V&A museum. It is truly sensational; arranged not only with glittering skill, but with manifest love, and crowded with extraordinary and beautiful objects. Those who think the British race has declined may well argue that we could not produce such a man as Pugin today. Even the Victorians, accustomed as they were to giants, knew he was exceptional. 'Genius and enthusiasm in every line of his face,' wrote one. And another: 'His energy was boundless, his powers of application almost unrivalled and the versatility of his powers inexhaustible.' At the age of ten he was already hard at work, drawing, painting, designing, inventing. Thereafter, in ceaseless procession, came churches, altars, vestments, holy vessels, jewellery, frames, tapestry, wallpaper, book-bindings, tiles, furniture from thrones and pulpits to the humblest stools, carpets and scarves, cushions and covers, ceilings, candelabra, stained glass, crockery and goblets, swords and forks, fireplaces, tombs – an entire Aladdin's cave of precious things. Much was wrought by his own busy hands; the rest by the incomparable craftsmen in which the Victorian age abounded, jealously watched by the Master as they worked from his meticulous drawings. All this proceeded with ever-increasing speed until this English Leonardo, soon after his 40th birthday, was abruptly swept into Elysium, like Elijah, on a whirlwind of madness and death.

The life of this amazing man was driven by a consuming passion for the Gothic, which frog-marched him into the Catholic Church and forced him to conjure up a world transformed into one gigantic pointed arch and its endless transmutations. It even determined his singular – and for a man of his time, robust and varied – sex-life. When he married his third wife Jane, he exulted: 'I have got a first-rate Gothic woman at last!' 'Driven' was indeed the word. His diary entries, mostly brief and to the point, record a frenetic life spent dashing all over Britain and the Continent, on stagecoaches and brigs, later on steamboats and trains – like Trollope, he found rapid motion conducive to creative work – in the execution of myriad commissions or in search of inspiration. He was short (5'4"), muscular, with a tall forehead and a beautiful mouth which made him a devil with women, a commanding voice, restless movements, dauntingly energetic, prone to bursts of furious temper when thwarted.

Like all Englishmen of his generation, born (in 1812) at the height of our naval supremacy, he loved the sea. From the Gothic mansion he built for himself at Ramsgate (recently on the market, I believe, at £300,000), he ran a succession of sizeable boats which he mastered himself, engaging in contraband, wrecking and treasure-hunting. He even dressed like a sailor, favouring a navy-blue overcoat with colossal pockets in which he could conceal folio volumes, monstrances, brass crucifixes and other items he picked up on his voyages, and his one spare shirt (he travelled light). He must have seemed an odd figure. Landing at Dover and entering 'as was his custom' a first-class compartment, he was greeted with: 'Halloa, my man, you have mistaken, I think, your carriage.' Pugin: 'By jove, I think you are right – I thought I was in the company of gentlemen.' The Master was not easily crossed in matters of manners, taste or anything else, and was quite capable of 'decking' an opponent with his huge fists.

Pugin believed trustingly in an almighty, all-caring merciful God, but there is no disguising the fact that he associated Gothic with inspissated gloom. His diaries show he delighted to record disasters, personal, financial, artistic. He always noted, for instance, when a West End play closed abruptly after bad reviews. Entries read: 'Sixty bankrupts this day.' 'Lady Erskine forced to apply to the Lord Mayor for relief.' 'Chartres Cathedral burned.' 'Dreadful thunderstorm.' 'The iron roof of Mr Maudsley's Manufactory fell in, burying a great number of persons in its ruins, some of whom died immediately and the rest removed to the hospital on shutters, with slight hopes of their recovery.' 'The French libertine play not well received.' 'Aladdin opera not successful. The machinery wretchedly worked.' 'During the evening a cluster of lamps fell, covering the Lord and Lady Mayoress with oil.' And so on.

Despite his taste for the lugubrious, it was part of Pugin's genius that he contrived to make his form of Gothic light and airy, at times ethereal, almost gossamer. There is grace, elegance, gaiety in his lines. In his church screens, for instance, he uses an ultra-light-grey background, which brings out the power of his rich greens and reds, while avoiding heaviness. His tables, even at their most massive, seem spare and springy. His delicate touch makes his work immensely attractive today, and it is one of the merits of this display that so many of the items are available in reproduction. Tiles, jewellery, cups and saucers, chairs and desks, wallpaper of course, even richly worked hangings are for sale. I set my heart on a three-foot-high reliquary of brass and gilt. With its columns and porticos, architraves and spires it is an encyclopaedia of Pugin Gothic, its central crystal eye waiting for a piece of the True Cross. Alas, the price is £4,000.

But what is, or was, money in Pugin's magic, or rather miraculous, world? His great patron, the Earl of Shrewsbury, gulped when he discovered that the tremendous church Pugin built and decorated for him at Cheadle was costing him not the £7,000 he expected, but £40,000. So what? There is nothing like it on earth: the combined fortunes of Packer and Soros and Goldsmith would not buy it now. We spend half a billion on the hideous, cheap-looking and still unfinished British Library, but we could not afford a Pugin, even supposing one existed. None does exist: that is the point. We have artists of consummate single talents. David Hockney draws almost as well as Ingres and Glynn Boyd Harte achieves effects with water-colour which make me weep with envy. But the mould which brought us the omnicompetent genius like Pugin, Ruskin and Morris seems broken. Or is it? Perhaps some special boy or girl will be taken to this scintillating treasure cave at the V&A and emerge, transfixed and empowered, determined to devote a life to doing even better. The history of art is full of such improbable, thaumaturgical events.

23 July 1994

There's a lot to be said for a big family

Last week, just round the corner from my house, I saw a family setting out for a day's expedition. The mother, tall, thin, blonde, who looked no more than a teenager herself, was festooned in various bundles, satchels and hold-alls. The biggest boy, ten perhaps, had a cricket bat and a set of stumps. His sister, nineish, carried an enormous plastic bag containing the family lunch. The four smaller children, the last a mere toddler though stumping along unaided, had each a packet to carry, plus a much-loved stuffed bear or lion, all the worse for wear. The smallest had the largest bear, almost as big as herself. I do not think this was a one-parent family. The father was probably working, or serving abroad, rather like Commander Walker, father of John, Susan, Titty and Roger in *Swallows and Amazons*. The mother and her brood had no car. They were catching a bus. What struck me about them all was their air of purposeful collective content. Here, indeed, was a happy family. They were so clearly going to have a jolly time that I was almost tempted to say, 'Mind if I come along too?'

Now I am not saying that being a member of a large family is easy. Money is usually short and you have to do without a lot of things, or get them second or third hand. This can go on almost into adulthood. I once admonished a 20-year-old, whom I had seen walking in Fleet Street with a rather disreputable older man, and pointed out that he had been the lover of no fewer than two of her elder sisters. 'I know,' she said fiercely, 'and *I've got him now*!' Big families are usually competitive and members have to learn to fight for their share. One girl I know says, 'You can always tell a person from a big family. When they sit down at table they instinctively stick their elbows out to make sure they get enough space.'

On the other hand, members of large families quickly learn useful lessons about collegiate living which don't come the way of others until much later, perhaps never. They waste little time crying and complaining but simply get on with it. One of my nieces, a gifted artist in stained glass, has five little ones already, living in bohemian cosiness in a small Oxford house (their father, like Commander

Walker, is often away on duty). But they never quarrel or cry, except for a few brief seconds to make a rhetorical point: the atmosphere of the household is one of busy serenity. I stress busy: big families are full of interest; there is always something doing. It cannot have been easy to be one of Mrs Bennet's many daughters in *Pride and Prejudice*. But they were never bored, like the solitary Miss Darcy.

And genius fizzes in big families, or is thought to do. I met a lady at an impromptu Highland dance last New Year. She was plainly no longer young but still beautiful, in the etiolated, epicene way of some Englishwomen – she was what Pugin would have called 'a first-rate Gothic Woman.' 'I don't suppose you have any children,' she began challengingly. 'I do, I have four.' 'Ah, do you indeed? I have ten. And every one a genius. That one' – she pointed to a young lady exactly like herself – 'is another Menuhin.' Surveying her Gothic progeny, who suddenly became instantly recognisable all over the room – ranging in age, size and style from Early English to Late Perpendicular – I was awed into humble silence, for once.

It is not sufficiently known that Hollywood was the genius-child of the large family. A wayward, sometimes an evil genius, no doubt, but indubitably creative, colouring the whole of our century in tints which are garish and even false but indelible. Take away Hollywood from our century and it becomes, you must admit, a much emptier time. In the last 40 years of the 19th century, Jewish-Ashkenazi families in eastern Europe probably had the highest birthrate in the whole of history. Many of these children arrived in New York as unaccompanied immigrants with just a label tied to their necks, to be picked up by relatives and then plunged into the maelstrom of the Lower East Side until they could surface, break out and capture a wider world. Carl Laemmle, the first of the movie tycoons, was the tenth of 13 children. William Fox was one of 12. The Warner brothers were among the nine children of a poor Polish cobbler. These and others – Loew, Mayer, Goldwyn, Cohn, Schenck, Schary, Zukor, Zanuck – products of the amazing Ashkenazi family system, created or dominated all eight of the big Hollywood studios. No wonder the place has always, in its odd, sometimes twisted, way worshipped and upheld the family, and long may it continue to do so.

The large family is touching as well as happy. Until quite recently, those little ones were fragile, might easily disappear and be buried unceremoniously in a family vault. The iconology of medieval tombs in our parish churches shows not only strings of sons and daughters praying earnestly for their parents lying above, but cocooned babies who did not survive infancy. Family tears were soon dried: in an age of faith, they knew those children would be waiting for them in Heaven when their own time came. The young Dickens saw dead babies being laid out, 'like pig's trotters', in drawers. Faded Victorian photographs show large broods draped around their mothers, fathers, uncles, aunts, on the garden steps, awaiting fate: TB would claim some, especially the daughters, wars and adventures would pick off sons. But there were always plenty left in those days. Forsyte 'Change, epitome of weekly gatherings of the extended family throughout comfortable Britain, was never less than crowded.

So if large families register inevitable losses, the ranks soon close up and seem as serried as ever. As you grow old, you realise that the pains of age are nothing to the loss of friends, who cannot be replaced and leave huge, ragged holes in your waning existence. It is at this point that the sustaining role of the family, especially if it is large, is so reassuring. For the family does not stand still and wait to be hit by death. It breeds, it reproduces itself. New, smiling faces come along, pop up as if from nowhere, claiming relationship – 'I'm Amelia, don't you *remember?*' – suddenly transforming themselves from toddlers, to teenagers, to undergraduates, becoming persons, then personalities, bringing problems, difficulties, needs, requests – above all, bringing interest, filling what Dr Johnson called 'the great vacancies of existence'. A big family ensures that life remains worth living.

30 July 1994

Victor Hugo's magnificent machine

Whenever possible nature should be allowed to take its course. This applies to the old as well as to everything else. Hospitals are not being cruel in wanting to get rid of patients for whom they can offer no treatment and who are simply occupying beds because they are decrepit.

We medicate and treat the aged too assiduously, keeping them alive, or half alive, against nature, often against their wishes. This is because society, being officially Godless, treats death as the ultimate enemy; whereas to the Godly, death, like any other natural event in its due time and place, is a friend. The old should be allowed to die in dignity and meet death meekly when he comes in season. Three scores years and ten is our lot, and we should be grateful if we enjoy them fully in reasonable health. Anything extra should be treated as a bonus.

No doubt the bonus can be worth having. I rejoice at the good fortune of the old lady of 92 whose poetry is about to be published, for the first time, by the Oxford University Press. Recently, on a cruise up the Norwegian fjords, I made friends with another old lady, who celebrated her 85th birthday on board. I discovered we had similar views on a wide range of subjects, especially crime, punishment, dealing with hooligans, hanging etc. – amazing how sensible the very old are on these issues! And this week I have been celebrating the 100th birthday of a friend's mother who must be one of the few survivors – almost certainly the only woman – to have seen active service in the Great War. She lives happily alone and is a delight to her friends.

There is indeed something satisfying about elderly prodigies who, unlike the infant variety, soothe rather than irritate one's feelings. Good luck to old Gladstone, for instance, for keeping the entire British Empire in uproar over Home Rule when aged 84 – and to Marshal Radetzky, who is said to have fathered a child and invented a new march when in his nineties. Far from being disgusted, one ought to be encouraged to hear of old men, or old women for that matter, disporting themselves. When I lived in Paris in the early 1950s, an ancient man told me that, as a child of four or five, he had a vivid encounter with Victor Hugo, then over eighty. It took place in the early morning, before six in midsummer, in an old château, on the bare boards of the top corridor, where the children and maid-servants slept. The little boy, bored, had got out of bed to explore the castle and he met Hugo, in his nightshirt and bare feet, padding around in search of the sleeping quarters of a pretty housemaid, whom he had spotted at dinner the night before. The sunlight streamed in through the curtainless, cobwebby windows, making the bearded old rogue look like an Old Testament prophet transfigured. He seized hold of the little boy's hand, placed it on his triumphantly erect member, and said:

Tiens ça, mon petit – il parait que c'est très rare à mon age! Alors! Tu aurais le droit à dire à tes petits-enfants que tu as tenu à la main le machin de Victor Hugo, poète!

The anecdote did not relate whether Hugo was rewarded for climbing up all those castle stairs. But one hopes so. Why? Because there is something splendid about the very old going down fighting – as Dylan Thomas put it, 'Old age should burn and rave at close of day.'

It is a different matter, however, for us officiously to strive to keep alive the frail, the bewildered, the imbecile and the helpless. Yet that is what, increasingly, we are doing. The financial cost will soon be crippling, when one in four will be over 65. The human cost is increasing even faster, as the lives of middle-aged children, especially women, are tied to the breathing corpses of their parents, kept in this world by a medical profession whose philosophy has failed to keep pace with its technology.

I use the word 'philosophy' advisedly. Our growing ability to preserve people, even when they are in what is termed a persistent vegetative state, is forcing us to reinvent medical ethics. Unfortunately, the subject has been left largely in the hands of the doctors themselves, who are floundering, and lawyers with a forensic taste for ethics. To be sure, they are monitored by the theologians, especially the Jews and papists, who have strong views on the subject, which may well prove right in the end, but which ought to be subjected to the strictest scrutiny. What we lack is a thorough-going philosophical investigation of medical ethics, or rather a philosophical analysis on which a practical system of ethics can be built. But hardly any professional philosophers are working in the field. One of the few who does, Dr Sophie Botros of Birkbeck College, London, has been giving me tutorials on this topic and I am beginning to grasp the immensity and complexity of the problems.

These are real, life-and-death conundrums, moreover, not the verbal parlour games played by most academics under the guise of philosophy. We have scarcely yet, for instance, subjected to philosophical analysis the ethics of using or cutting off life-support systems for incurables or those in Persistent Vegetative State, one of the tricky areas in which Dr Botros is working. An agreed solution to the dilemma is becoming more urgent as our ability, for instance, to keep alive victims of horrific road accidents increases.

Then there is the even more difficult problem of allocating funds to research into killer diseases. Should we, for instance, adopt a philosophical position of pure utilitarianism, in which the greatest needs of the greatest number are, in numerical order, the criteria of priority? At present the matter is determined very largely by lobbying. That leads to anomalies, even scandals.

For instance, a huge and growing percentage of available resources is being devoted to what many see as a fruitless search for an Aids cure. This looks like a classic case of throwing money at a problem. Many would argue that such funds should go rather on methods of treating Parkinson's or motor-neurone or other horrific diseases, or forms of cancer or heart disease, both exceptionally fruitful fields of research. Others would add that, since the chief beneficiaries of an Aids cure would be promiscuous male homosexuals and drug-addicts, its priority for the general population is low anyway.

But all these points are, at present, subjected to rancorous and often abusive argument, rather than cool philosophical inquiry. In the end we may find that the best solution is to allow the market, like nature, to take its course. But we ought to debate the issue first, properly, scientifically – and philosophically.

20 August 1994

Bimbos immortalised in marble

Despite the philistine sneers of some of our less educated leader writers, Mr Stephen Dorrell, the new Heritage Secretary, is right to make a fuss about Canova's 'Three Graces', and John Paul Getty II should be given a bar to his KBE for allowing us to keep it.

It is the masterwork of a superb sculptor, for Canova (1757–1822) deserves to rank with Praxiteles, Donatello, Michelangelo, Bernini and Rodin among the greatest practitioners of this difficult craft. Malcolm Baker of the Victoria & Albert has at last pointed out, in a letter to the *Guardian* on Monday, that our 'Three Graces' is not a mere copy of the one in St Petersburg but, rather, another version and a much better one, of finer marble and with a more meticulous finish. Canova did the one now in Russia first, and learned from it, as he learned from all his experiences, and the intertwining of the ladies – all fantastically difficult to sculpt in marble – is done with far more confidence and aplomb in the Woburn example.

Canova has been underrated in Britain for the last 150 years. Bonaparte made no such mistake: he rated him as Europe's greatest sculptor on a par with his favourite painters, David and Ingres. Wellington and Castlereagh were equally enthusiastic, and it was because they listened to his tearful pleas that Canova, as papal commissioner, succeeded in 1815 in getting the French authorities to disgorge the antique and Renaissance masterpieces Bonaparte had looted from the Vatican, plus many other Italian art treasures which were now put back in their rightful homes.

With the possible exception of the great anonymous artists of the Egyptian Middle Kingdom, no sculptor has ever possessed such technical skill as Canova in working with difficult material. He acquired it from infancy as the brilliant offspring of a family of stonemasons at Possogno in the Dolomitic foothills of the Alps. What is more surprising is his daring and originality. In the years 1783–87 he ended baroque sculpture almost at a stroke, replacing it with neo-classicism, by producing his stupendous tomb of Pope Clement XIV in Rome. Tombs of the exalted were big news in those days. He followed this up by producing another epoch-making tomb in the Augustinekirche, Vienna, which houses the Habsburg dead. This was to honour Maria Christina, daughter of the great Maria-Theresa and sister of the executed Marie-Antoinette. Canova was a devout Catholic and a conservative, never happier than when employed by popes and legitimate sovereigns, but he was also an artistic innovator of unsurpassed courage, and perhaps this is why he appealed so strongly to the family which was trying to overthrow the established order of Europe.

At all events, Bonaparte's pretty younger sister, Pauline, adored him as she believed he had a unique gift for making perishable female flesh immortal. She was narcissistic, obsessed with the beauty of her body, especially her small and delicate feet. She married as her second husband Camillo Borghese, head of one of Rome's oldest families, and even when she was far from young the Roman nobility and famous visitors, especially Englishmen, were invited to the Palazzo Borghese to see '*la toilette des pieds*'. She issued printed cards.

Many years after, Augustus Hare published a description of these occasions which he had from Lady Ruthven, who had attended one. The guests found Pauline with her little, exquisitely white tootsies displayed on a velvet cushion. At her command, her maids entered, touched the feet with sponges and dusted them with powder. The women guests were just as fascinated as the men, though less proprietorial. The Duke of Hamilton, a regular worshipper at the shrine, would take up one foot and tuck it into his waistcoat 'like a little bird' (a feat, if I may put it that way, quite difficult to accomplish, unless the Duke had a special waistcoat).

Once Canova was under her spell, Pauline determined to get him to immortalise her whole body. Like her elder sister Caroline, she was proud of her long, elegant back. Caroline had used her favourite artist, Ingres, to make it famous all over Europe, once in 'La Grande Odalisque' actually inserting three vertebrae too many to heighten the sensation. Not to be outdone, in 1808 Pauline ordered Canova to sculpt her naked, as Venus Victoria, the archetypal sex-goddess. The pious sculptor at first refused. Then he compromised by offering to present her as Diana, more or less naked but associated with chastity. Pauline insisted on Venus, and Canova, used to dealing with absolute sovereigns, obediently complied. He did cover up her private parts, but the splendid back is displayed to the cleft of her buttocks, and there can be no question that the statue is erotic. He placed her on a mattress sculpted of marble, like her body, but he used as a plinth a real bed of painted wood, to heighten the realism.

Canova carved his portrait-statues not just to be seen from afar but closely inspected from a distance of inches, and the plinth-bed has a mechanism which allows the entire work to be turned around for minute scrutiny. During Pauline's lifetime, it was the custom, after dinner, to take friends of the family and honoured guests to look at the statue by candlelight – this was how Canova wanted all his works to be seen – and the treat had an additional thrill when the princess was in charge of the party and drew attention to her finer points. The then pope was particularly down on sex and actually banned trousers in the papal states as being too tight-fitting, but he could do nothing about Pauline's self-presentations, which continued under his nose until her death in 1825.

Canova's eroticism, then, is to be enjoyed, not just admired, with the help of darkness, candles, shadows and chiaroscuro, and I hope this is borne in mind when our 'Three Graces' find a permanent setting. Then the multitude will rediscover him again. It is true that, like most sculptors, he made egregious errors. Asked to sculpt Washington for the state house in Raleigh, North Carolina, he depicted the President delivering his final address to Congress with bare knees and wearing a Roman toga. This, I think, was destroyed in a fire but you can still see, in Naples, Canova's odd presentation of the ferocious Bourbon, King Ferdinand I, as a transvestite, dolled up like Minerva and on a colossal scale.

However, there is nothing incongruous about the 'Three Graces'.

It is a joyful hymn in marble to the delights of the female body and we are very lucky to have it.

27 August 1994

A still, small voice in the stinks lab

Recently a stinks don from New College, Oxford, has taken upon himself to raise the standard of militant atheism again. In this capacity he has been popping up on the wireless and television and even in the columns of the *Spectator*. Among other things, he has accused me of being told what to think by 'an elderly Pole'. He is called Richard Dawkins, and I would not bother with him had not a Christian lady, for whom I have the highest respect, said she was impressed by his arguments and challenged me to refute them.

Dawkins is an expert on genes, which are currently the fashionable objects of scientific inquiry. His colleagues are constantly discovering 'new' genes which explain aspects of human behaviour. Thus they recently unearthed a gene which makes some people homosexual; eliminate it, and there will be no more queers. Last week we learned they have found an 'ageing gene', which determines how we grow old; if they can get to work on this fellow they will be able to cure Alzheimer's and Parkinson's. No doubt in time they will discover a 'religious gene' which makes people believe in God, and if they can get rid of that one we will all grow up to be like Richard Dawkins. But it could be that, by this time, genes will have been succeeded by another scientific fashion.

In any case, I distrust the way in which people like Dawkins set up scientists and believers as polar opposites. Like Darwin, I am sure there is no necessary quarrel between science and religion. In fact science is a working tool of religion. The medieval universities treated theology as the queen of the sciences, and rightly so, for what can be more important than to discover how we, and everything, came into existence, and for what purpose, and what will ultimately happen to us all? The overwhelming majority of great scientists have always believed in God and regarded adding to our knowledge of Him as a central part of their work. That great 12th-century doctor, Maimonides, who has strong claims to be considered the father of psychiatry, was also the greatest of Jewish theologians. It seems to me significant that Sir Isaac Newton wrote two defences of belief, *A short scheme of true religion* and his *Irenicon*, though he published neither. He drew none of the distinctions Dawkins seems to think matter so much. Indeed, come to think of it, Newton's library contained 138 books on alchemy and he wrote at least 650,000 words on alchemic topics. It proves nothing except that Newton had an inquiring mind and never ruled out possibilities, thus setting a good example to us all. I was educated by the Jesuits, who since their inception in the 16th century have engaged in every form of scientific inquiry all over the world. My school had a famous observatory and the most respected member of the community was an ancient Jesuit who had spent almost all his life examining the heavens through a giant telescope. It never occurred to him, or to any of us, that there was a conflict between his work and our beliefs.

Scientists like Dawkins, who argue that the physical sciences inevitably lead to a denial of God's existence, seem to me to fall into two errors: materialism and determinism. They are obsessed by big numbers, rather like military dictators and multimillionaires. Writing in the *Spectator*, Dawkins seems to think that the sheer size of the universe refutes the truth of Christianity, since knowledge of Christ, travelling at the highest possible speed, can have reached as yet only a tiny corner of it. But there is a reality even greater than the universe, however large it can conceivably be, and that is eternity. Indeed, compared with eternity, past, present and to come, all creation is nothing, a tiny notch on Dawkins's slide-rule, a bubble in one of his test-tubes. Yet eternity and its infinite perspectives of time are the warp and woof of Judaeo-Christianity since it is the realisation that this life – this world, this universe, everything in fact in the Dawkins compendium of actual and possible knowledge – is merely the flicker on a microsecond in God's scheme of things, which underlines every aspect of moral and dogmatic theology. The fact that we are eternal is far more important than the fact that we are, for a time, material. Materialists shut their eyes to all except a tiny fraction of existence. They forget that God plays the numbers game on an infinitely bigger scale than anyone else.

The determinism of the scientific atheists is even more dismaying than their obsession with matter, for it is precisely this baleful philosophy, whether in its Marxist, Nazi or other forms, which has ruined the 20th century, at its dawn the most promising of human epochs. Our behaviour is no more determined by minute changes in our chemical components than it is by our class or race or any other crazy theory that deprives us of free will. Nor are events fixed in advance by irresistible forces. A lifetime's work as a historian has convinced me that we human beings are masters of our fates. Nothing is won or lost in advance: the game is to be played by each one of us. But, as Einstein wisely observed, God does not play dice: the game of life is played with the counters of love, forbearance, fidelity, compassion, patience, acceptance of suffering and imagination, not least with courage, all of which are powerful, real forces in our lives but which cannot be quantified or even identified by the instruments at Dawkins's disposal in his lab.

Indeed, the most important single element in religious faith is belief in free will. We are free spirits. True, our hearts will never be at peace until we have submitted our wills to our maker's. But that act of dissent or assent is voluntary and cannot under any circumstances be taken away from us. It was still possessed by a Jew on the threshold of the Auschwitz ovens or today by a black child scrabbling around in the filth of an African refugee camp. Our material impotence, however total and degrading, is belied by the fact that, by an act of our uninhibited will, we send a signal to the architect of all existence, across the infinities of time and space, which is instantly received and registered. It is a comfort to me, and, I think, to all who believe, that this power of communicating with the Almighty cannot be taken away from us by the Stalins or the Hitlers or the materialists or the determinists or the scientific humanists or by any combination of those who have the power of the world on their side but who lack awareness of the spirit.

3 September 1994

Painting God's image in the human face

Portraiture is the most humane and fascinating of all the arts. In fact if I had my time again I would become a professional portrait painter. I love gazing at people's faces in the tube, to see if I can penetrate their mystery. The Bible says that God made us in His image so that to paint people's portraits is, in a metaphysical sense, to paint God Himself. Yet most painters despise portraiture and always have done.

They do it of necessity, to live. In Tudor and early Stuart times painters had no alternative: English royalty, the nobility, gentry and merchant classes would commission nothing else. They were a philistine lot, not prepared to pay good money except for mugshots of themselves and theirs. If you think of what was happening in Italy, and even France, in the 16th century, and then compare it with what we had to show, as displayed in the *Dynasties* exhibition at the Tate, England was a miserable artistic backwater then. In fact take away the Holbeins and there is little of value left. As François I sneeringly observed of the court of Henry VIII, 'Their idea of beauty is to cover everything in thick coats of gilt or gold paint.'

One reason why painters did not like doing portraits even in those days is that convention demanded that anyone sitting for a portrait had to wear their best clothes and put on mighty serious expressions. The Tudors in particular look a grim lot, though we know for a fact that they often laughed their heads off, sometimes quite literally by making jokes about Henry VIII's appearance. Even Lord Cobham's six delightful children look morose, though they are tucking into a delicious bowl of fruit and have their pet parrot and marmoset on the table. One of the saddest portraits of all is of Tom Durie, Queen Anne of Denmark's jester: he looks as if he carries the sorrows of the entire world on his shoulders and is about to drown them in the enormous cup of wine he is holding. Isaac Oliver did an exquisite miniature of his wife Elizabeth smiling gently, but this work was an intimate family likeness, probably worn next to the painter's heart. For public consumption, levity was frowned on. After all, when looked at closely, the 'Mona Lisa' is not really smiling and Hals' 'Cavalier' certainly does not laugh. What makes Hogarth's sketch of the shrimp girl such a landmark is that she is not just a comic grotesque, she combines beauty and grace with laughter.

The seriousness rule of portraiture gradually disappeared in the 17th century but plenty of other conventions remained and that is why painters find the genre so irksome, especially since the rules are applied not by their peers but by often ignorant sitters. Those who were paying insisted not just on flattery but on sartorial correctness. Even the patient Sir Thomas Lawrence, one of the few masters of portraiture who seemed happy in his job, was irritated when the Duke of Wellington told him he couldn't paint a sword 'for toffee' and insisted it be corrected. 'Yes, Your Grace, I shall attend to it presently.' 'No, attend to it *now*!'

Yet if painters do not like portrait-work it is often what they were made for. It is a fact, and the 20th century has demonstrated it beyond peradventure, that a majority of painters really do not know what to do with their skills and need patrons to set them subjects. The more detailed orders they receive the better they paint. It is hard to think of any major 20th-century artists – except the landscapists – who would not have benefited from a stricter, old-style dependence on exacting patrons. Henry Lamb, whose portrait drawings were almost in the Ingres class, tried all kinds of 'real' subjects and mastered none of them. It was the same with the gifted Glyn Philpot, who was lost outside a routine portrait commission. Even Sir William Orpen, best of them all, could never think of subjects worthy of his genius. And when artists do not really know what to paint they are liable to take to booze – look at John, and Orpen himself.

These reflections are prompted by another new exhibition in London, the large retrospective of David Hockney's drawings at Burlington House. Hockney is a splendid fellow, immensely funny and illuminating on all artistic matters – there is no one with whom I would rather visit a gallery – and his technical skills both as draughtsman and colourist are phenomenal. But he was born to be a portraitist and outside portraiture it seems to me he has never quite found a role. His portraits do not always come off. I looked at the one of Stephen Spender with his widow Natasha and we both agreed the nose was too big and coarse – though she observed that, oddly enough, it was a marvellous likeness of one of Spender's uncles. Next to it, however, there is a drawing of surpassing brilliance of old Auden, deadly accurate and quite devastating.

Hockney's drawings of his mother are wonderfully moving, and there are two drawings of 'Celia' I would give anything to possess: rumour has it that Hockney tried hard to fall in love with this succulent creature before surrendering in despair to the horrors of queerdom. Be that as it may, these drawings are great and poignant works of art. I wish that Hockney, so marvellously endowed by his creator – for I doubt if he learned anything much at art school – would devote himself for a few years, in the service of God, art and posterity, to a prosopography of England in the last years of the millennium – leaders, beauties, geniuses, the smart and the unfashionable, the grandees and the common folk.

He could do for our times what Van Dyke did for Cavalier England or Lawrence for the Regency or Sargent and Orpen for the Edwardian and Georgian ages. He knows very well, for he has studied this exact point deeply, that he can record these human images infinitely better than any photographer, however skilful. And he has the dazzling speed required for this great work (by comparison, Baron von Thyssen told me Lucien Freud required over a hundred sittings for his portrait). But will Hockney do it? Of course not. Artists are not biddable these days, more's the pity.

18 November 1995

The coming triumph of Madame Butterfly

As we approach the 21st century, signs are beginning to appear that we may be experiencing a fundamental change in the way humanity conducts its affairs. Until the present, however well or badly the human race has fared, there can be no question that its direction has been in the hands of men. From the beginning of recorded history, we know that all the key decisions, and an overwhelming majority of the minor ones, have been taken by males, in all societies and at all periods. For huge stretches of history women have been virtually invisible, except as breeders and unpaid menial labourers. The intellectual input of women has been insignificant, and it is still tiny compared with its potential magnitude, though it is now accelerating with dramatic speed.

In short, throughout its existence the human race has been operating with only half its creative energy. We have tended to see this loss in terms of individual tragedies, and sympathise with the frustrations of countless women of talent and even genius whose lives were thrown away. Our hearts go out to those gifted women who, by courage and persistence, did contrive to intrude a little into a man's world.

Was it not monstrous that Jane Austen, our one perfect novelist, had to remain silent for so many years of her short life, never had a room of her own and had to use a corridor to do her writing, covering it up hastily whenever she was interrupted? Why was Sir Joshua Reynolds's painter-sister, perhaps more talented than he was, never allowed to follow her career? And why did Gwen John, whose art was so much finer and purer than her brother Augustus's, die neglected and hungry, while he roistered his way through a long, misspent life? Thomas Gray, lamenting the unseen gems of purest ray serene or the countless flowers born to blush unseen and waste their sweetness, thought entirely in terms of village Hampdens or mute, inglorious Miltons or guiltless Cromwells being wasted. Would he not have written a far greater poem if he had pondered the fate of the multitudes of unknown Janes and Elizabeths – and Françoises and Gretchens and Carlas and Natashas – who from the dawn of humanity have been denied the right to use the brains their creator gave them?

But these are just sad tales of frustrated women. And it may be that, with feminine ingenuity and stoicism, they were not so frustrated after all, finding compensations in all kinds of ways. Jane Austen, for instance, does not strike us as an unhappy, unfulfilled woman; like Nancy Mitford, another victim of the system, she was never short of a laugh. But what of the much wider, unmitigated tragedy of mankind as a whole, advancing only at half-speed, perhaps less? What have we missed by keeping women off the bridge and out of the engine-room – how much further would we have travelled by now? This question is never considered.

In a hundred years' time, however, the misuse or non-use of female talent will be judged the most glaring and incomprehensible mistake of human history. Because by then it will have become blindingly apparent that women are not just the intellectual equals of men but in many respects, perhaps in all important respects, their superiors. Why this should be I cannot say: part of God's ultimate providential plan, I suppose, since He certainly made women the moral superiors of men. In plenty of other species females are the driving and directing forces, and I don't myself find it difficult to imagine a world society largely run by women.

What is harder is to see quite how we will get there, granted that at present, and for the foreseeable future, women are still brutally handicapped by their biological role as the carriers and rearers of children and – dare I add? – by the huge and irreplaceable satisfaction they get from this role. This year's school exam results confirm the fact that 16-year-old girls are cleverer than boys of the same age, or at any rate better at ordering and disciplining their skills. They also provide overwhelming evidence that girls in single-sex establishments perform far better than girls exposed to the world of sexual competition. The GCSE performance figures, reproduced in many other countries and providing, for the first time, definite evidence that the females are intellectually superior to males, have to be qualified by figures for 17- and 18-year-olds, which reflect stronger motivation for boys and a falling-off in the academic concentration of girls as the sexual urge begins to bite.

But this merely underlines the burden, or braking effect, which women's sexuality imposes on their performance. And this can gradually be eased by social and other changes. My own observation suggests to me that there are many able women in the world today who are uneasy because they are not married and having children, and who remain unhappy about their predicament. But they are not sufficiently unhappy to marry unsatisfactory men, as they would have done a generation ago, because they are no longer prepared to enter a submissive arrangement with someone who is manifestly their intellectual inferior. This is the great force for change today: the growing self-confidence of women in their capacities, their willingness to display this pride in practical ways, the first stirrings of female triumphalism. The process will be pushed forward by many factors: the decline of submissive marriage, the collapse of male self-confidence, the ability of scientific commerce to provide a shopping market for women who want marriage, children *and* careers right to the top, and the greater influence of women on the political decisions which hasten all these processes.

People who blithely assume that the West, having given birth to feminism, will continue to provide the forcing-house for such changes are in for a shock. Feminism is, and has always been, an irrelevance masking far more fundamental changes which have enabled women to perform better and be seen to do so. The Asian people are now taking the lead in learning how to organise their societies more productively and efficiently, and I expect them to play the female trump card first. The Japanese, in particular, who have shown they can move at amazing speed when they so determine, will leap-frog the West by enabling women to jump directly from a posture of supine subservience to aggressive leadership. The Vietnamese, Koreans, Chinese and others will not be far behind.

The 21st century will be the age of Madame Butterfly – still beautiful, I hope, but no longer the victim, more the perpetrator.

10 September 1994

Remembering J.B. Priestley

Who speaks for literature these days? I ask, but answer comes there none. By speaking for literature I do not mean the squeaks and cavortings of those incestuous people who preside over Booker Prizes and other stage-managed cultural non-events in the annual publicity circus, or the smarty-bootsies with manicured provincial accents who front the television book-shows. None of your Braggery, sir! No: I mean those genuine heavyweight men of letters who, resting comfortably on a shelf-full of achievement, used in former days to raise an occasional and dignified voice when the interests of the craft came under threat or when an issue on which writers had a legitimate view was put before the public.

Such were Dr Samuel Johnson in his day or, in the mid-19th century, Dickens and Thackeray and Tennyson or, a generation or two later, Hardy and Kipling. When I first came to London, T.S. Eliot was still around to be looked up to and certainly listened to attentively on the rare occasions when the oracle spoke. Then there was C.P. Snow, not necessarily to everyone's taste but someone whose background in science-politics, Whitehall and government, as well as in writing and publishing, gave his voice resonance. And, of course, there was J.B. Priestley.

The centenary of Priestley's birth has served to remind us that no one has quite taken his place. It was a definite and distinctive place too. Two or three times a year I used to see him sitting comfortably in it when we were guests at Kissing Tree House, just outside Stratford. There he lived in some style. The fine wines were carefully chosen by his wife, Jacquetta Hawkes, the devoted staff served delicious food, summer shadows lingered long on the croquet lawn and the perfumed shrubberies, and deep, leather armchairs invited you to sit in the big library where books were king and ran in thousands up to the high ceilings. Some of them, you were surprised to discover, concealed the entrance to a well-stocked cocktail bar into which Priestley would retire, to re-emerge with a trayful of potent and icy martinis.

There was no attempt to play the country squire: quite the contrary.

He loudly censured literary men who, in his opinion, tried to do so, selecting Evelyn Waugh as a notorious example and so setting off a lively row. No, Priestley's models, rather, were those ancient grandees of the French literary scene, who lived in *haut bourgeois* comfort in their country châteaux, occasionally communicating with a deferential public by means of an essay in the *Revue des Deux Mondes*, or trotting up to Paris to loll splendidly in their chairs at the Académie Française. It was his view that French men of letters got a much better deal than their English equivalents, carried more weight and were more carefully listened to. Why, he wondered aloud, could not people such as himself be treated more like André Gide or Paul Claudel or François Mauriac? 'Would it help if I wore a skull-cap?' he pondered.

It was not that Priestley wanted honours. He was happy with his OM, having turned down offers of peerages from both Clem Attlee and Harold Wilson. Nor did he want money. Quite apart from his spectacular success with *The Good Companions*, he once had three plays running simultaneously in the West End: he told me that, in the Thirties, he used to earn £30,000 a year from the stage alone, at a time when income-tax was two shillings in the pound. He felt, rather, that literature was the real glory of England – always had been – and that those who represented it had a duty to speak and a right to be heard. He was disgusted with the gross materialism of the modern world, what he called Admass. He thought that not just the Conservatives but even the Labour Party were too concerned with getting and spending and were ignoring the metaphysics of old England, the words, rhymes, sights and sounds which vibrated in the nation's heart and the deep, romantic emotions which occasionally shook it to its core.

Priestley could play on these emotions like no one else of his time. And, despite his grumbles, he was listened to. The *Postscripts* he gave on the BBC in 1940 and at other times during the war were probably the most successful examples ever of the spoken word being used to raise spirits, not with tub-thumping but with gentle, penetrative philosophy. They made even Churchill jealous, and it was widely believed, though probably unfairly, that he used his power to have Priestley taken off the air.

Of course Priestley was, certainly at that period, a propagandist for the Left: years later he even did a Labour Party Political Broadcast, showing how the thing ought to be done. But he was not really a party man and never, in any sense, an ideologue. He started the campaign for nuclear disarmament from a posture of common sense. The essays he contributed on public matters were entirely personal. He called them 'Thoughts from the Wilderness' and he saw himself as a lone voice, even in a way a reactionary one, celebrating a better, simpler, nobler England, prizing ancient virtues, landscapes and customs, rejecting the new varieties of Vanity Fair which, from the Sixties on, took over Admass.

He died on the eve of his 90th birthday and the peculiar chair he occupied has remained vacant since. No one speaks for literature. All we get from Kingsley Amis is the occasional bark. V.S. Pritchett is too modest, Stephen Spender and Iris Murdoch too diffident. The phenomenon of the disappearing laureates and mandarins is not confined to England. In the United States, no one has taken the places once occupied by Edmund Wilson and Lionel Trilling. In France Jean-Paul Sartre, André Malraux and Raymond Aron were the last of their line. Most of these grand voices came from the Left, and it may be that the collapse of all the old causes, such as socialism, and the current refusal to believe in any kind of utopianism, helps to account for the demise of the public intellectual. It would certainly explain why there is no Bertrand Russell today.

But surely the world of letters, which is neither Right, Left nor Centre, just important, ought always to have an illustrious figure to speak on its behalf. Who, then, is to claim the throne, nowadays a bed of nails too?

17 September 1994

Americans used to say what they thought

The editor of the *Spectator* was right to draw attention to the censorship of race discussion being imposed on Americans. It is not only wrong and unnatural in itself, being contrary to America's tradition of outspoken debate, and the letter and spirit of the First Amendment, it is also dangerous because behind the wall of silence an explosion of race hatred is in train. Unless Americans start discussing their race problems frankly and truthfully, drastic solutions will emerge, and the victims will be precisely those the silence is intended to protect: the blacks.

There was a time when Americans led the world in saying what they thought. That is how they are portrayed by Dickens, Trollope and Thackeray. That is one reason why the squeamish Henry James fled from them to seek refuge in European reticence. Their archetypal journalist, H.L. Mencken, set new world standards in vituperation and persiflage. Now educated Americans, especially the ruling class of businessmen, politicians, academics and media people, are terrified of opening their mouths on any topic even vaguely connected with race.

The effect is often ludicrous. Recently I was a member of a panel holding a public debate in New York on the teaching of American history. The question, 'How do you define an American?' came up and immediately everyone became nervous. A black man got up and said, 'I am telling you this not as a matter for debate but just as an assertion. A few years ago, I called myself an American. Then I called myself a black American. Then I called myself an African-American. Now I call myself an African.' This absurd remark was received in reverent silence. I almost felt like retorting, 'Well, why don't you go and live in Africa and see how you like it, old man?' but I did not wish to get my hosts into trouble.

And trouble, big trouble, would have been the result. The penalties for stepping outside the agreed codes for racial references are severe. Some time ago, drunken black women caused a small-hours rumpus in the residential quarter of the University of Pennsylvania. An Israeli student poked his head out and told them to pipe down and 'stop behaving like water buffalo' – a mild term of Hebrew abuse, it seems. In a sane society the women would have been disciplined for being drunk and disorderly. In today's America it was the Israeli who had to go through hell.

A few radio phone-in hosts, like Rush Limbaugh and Bob Grant, break the taboos and let ordinary Americans speak. Terrific efforts are made by the ruling intellectual establishment to silence them. Limbaugh has 20 million listeners and so far has survived. Grant is more vulnerable: it remains to be seen whether a campaign led by *New York* magazine to force advertisers to withdraw their sponsorship will take him off the air. (*New York* does not exactly smell of roses: a major source of its revenue is explicit advertising by the City's prostitutes. But then there are no taboos on sex, especially of the perverted variety.)

Censorship of speech does not, needless to say, apply to blacks themselves, who seem to be allowed to say anything they please. Jesse Jackson has never been penalised for calling New York 'Hymie-town'. Louis Farrakhan, an anti-Semite in the Goebbels class, continues to rant unscathed. One of his disciples, head of 'Afro-American Studies' at a New York university was suspended following public protest against his anti-Semitic outbursts. He has now been vindicated in the courts, reinstated and awarded huge damages. In universities and media establishments, in the public sector and in any workplace where state or federal contracts are sought, blacks are a privileged caste. To meet a quota of employment of minorities, they must be hired, whatever their qualifications; and it is increasingly difficult to discipline or fire them.

Black privilege is now undermining America's judicial system too. If a black kills a white, even in front of witnesses, it is becoming difficult to secure a conviction. Some black jurymen and women will not vote against a fellow-black for murdering a white, whatever the weight of proof. And, since the affair of the three Los Angeles cops, the unspoken threat of a black mass-riot hangs over all controversial big city trials. It is increasingly improbable that justice will be done in the O.J. Simpson case because California does not want another multi-billion-dollar uprising by black looters. Now Simpson is likely to walk free. It is an odious commentary on the damage race taboos are inflicting on America that its colossally expensive courts are now less likely to produce a fair verdict than the lynch law of the old South.

I believe, however, that a change may be coming. The publication of Charles Murray's *The Bell Curve* marks a turning-point in the race debate. The book's prime focus is not on race, but it does discuss such forbidden topics as relative scoring by different races in IQ tests and, in particular, the consistently poor performance of blacks. For this reason, various efforts were made to suppress the book. Murray was dropped by the Manhattan Institute, and it was only through the courage of the American Enterprise Institute in Washington DC that the book came out at all. It has been savagely and repeatedly attacked in establishment newspapers like the *New York Times* (its Book Review was a brave exception, publishing a fair notice). Attacks on Murray have been highly personal, mendacious and directed to making him unemployable.

Nonetheless, the debate has begun and will continue. For the first time in over a generation America has an opportunity to learn again how to talk about race openly and sensibly. The change comes none too soon. Under the regime of no debate, ordinary whites were, indeed still are, building up resentments against blacks which could eventually acquire overwhelming force. If they get angry enough, Americans are capable of thinking the unthinkable and voting the impossible. There are obvious lessons here for Britain too.

26 November 1994

Bygone literary Donnybrooks

'Barbarians. Yahoos. *Untermenschen. Canaille.*' The speaker was Cyril Connolly coolly surveying a literary party in the 1950s, from just inside the door, and addressing his remarks not so much to me personally – I scarcely knew him – as *urbi et orbi*. A second later he was gone.

I gather from a new life of Connolly by Clive Fisher, due in 1995 – I have been reading the proofs with delight – that he didn't really enjoy parties unless he was giving them himself, and so in control. In any case, I could not agree with him. London literary parties, in those days, seemed to me immensely exciting and privileged occasions. Looking around a room, I could hardly believe the evidence of my senses. Was that really T.S. Eliot, or 'Tom' as I longed to call him, holding forth on the power of pentameters? Could it actually be W.H. Auden listening to him, none too patiently? And did my eyes deceive me, or was that not Ivy Compton-Burnett wagging a bony finger in the face of Rose Macaulay?

Unfortunately, such parties were not as decorous as these illustrious names might imply. They were always potentially, sometimes actually, explosive. Before the evening ended there was liable to be blood as well as broken glass and cigarette stubs on the carpet. I recall one evening when a leading academic critic, having made an interesting point too vehemently, was knocked bleeding and unconscious to the floor, while his wife, also the worse for wear, walked straight into a glass door in the ladies' loo and shattered it. Both ended up in hospital. Dylan Thomas and, still more, Brendan Behan set high standards of literary misbehaviour. I have an ineffaceable image of

Behan pouring neat whisky into his ear under the impression it was his mouth.

Then, too, there were some notorious bruisers loose in those days. Maurice Richardson was a peaceable man, not easily roused. But once enraged by what he called 'pipsqueak bad manners' he was always ready to 'sort out' the offender, and then one realised he was a former heavyweight boxer. John Davenport too had fought in the ring to some purpose. His high-pitched voice belied his massive strength, and when he began to address a minor poet or detective-story writer (classes he abhorred) as 'short-arsed' or 'jumped-up', you knew trouble was on the way. Davenport was famous for putting the Lord Chancellor on the mantelpiece of the Savile Club bar ('Sit there, you short-arsed little swine'), an outrage for which he was expelled from the club. Evelyn Waugh was likewise expelled from the Savile, for smashing in the glass cigar case with his walking-stick when the porter was slow to arrive with the key to it. He too was around in those days, though more likely to provoke a fight with well-directed insults than lay about him first. Gilbert Harding was another sharp-tongued conversational warrior, around whom chaos swirled. And then there was Constantine Fitzgibbon, who gave premonitory signs of aggression by swinging his right arm slowly and menacingly from side to side, a bellicose Irishman worthy of King Brian Boru.

One reason fights were frequent was that literary parties were then still primarily masculine affairs. Bimbos and floozies were scarce, but there were just enough pretty girls around to provoke intense competitive jealousy and so, from time to time, fisticuffs. Literary men were happy to scrap for such delicious morsels as Sonia Brownell or Barbara ('Tears before bedtime') Skelton, not to speak of the ravishing Edna O'Brien, then fresh from the wilds of Ireland. There was always, at a typical literary party in the Fifties, an air of sexual tension, as hungry young men hovered, elbowed and jostled around the few honey-pots.

Literary occasions today are much tamer because women pre-dominate. I have been to three so far this Christmas season and the girls were in a majority at all of them: at one, indeed, they out-numbered men by more than two to one. Then again, today's masculine contingent leaves much to be desired. It is not yet as bad as New York, where recently I heard a tipsy woman address the throng: 'Aren't *any* of you guys straight for Christ's sake?' but we are moving in that direction. Gays they may call themselves, but they certainly do not add to the tensile gaiety of a booksy shindig. As one frustrated female put it last week, 'I call the buggers *glums.*'

Another and perhaps more important reason why London literary parties now tend to sink without trace is that no hosts serve the hard stuff. In the Fifties, the late Jock Murray, entertaining the elite in that matchless Albemarle Street drawing-room where Thomas Moore burned the only manuscript of Byron's *Memoirs* in the grate, used to dish out an endless succession of the strongest and iciest martinis this side of the Atlantic. Until the end of the Sixties at least, a writers' soirée without whisky and gin would have been unthinkable. Today it is always champagne – or plonk at the downmarket gatherings. The spirit or spirits of literary London have fled. Indeed orange juice is spreading almost as fast as sodomy, though I don't say the two are connected.

However, we must not generalise too much. The most notable party I have attended recently was given by my colleague Auberon Waugh at Simpson's. He is quite a showman is young Bron. His 'Bad Sex' awards had the London *literati* rolling, especially when a delectable young lady read extracts from a novel by Edwina Currie, in which the heroine (Mrs Currie herself, I assume) ate strawberries and cream spread over the private parts of a fellow-MP. Marianne Faithfull, an amazing creature, gave the prizes – and kisses. There may or may not have been whisky but the champagne certainly flowed. While the 'Bad Sex' stuff was going on, I repaired to the bar and asked for a Coke. 'You'll 'ave to pay for it.' 'What do you mean?' 'Mr Waugh's orders – champagne free, soft drinks to be paid for.' 'Good God. How much?' 'One pound fifty – in advance.' 'Did Mr Waugh tell you to be rude to teetotallers as well as charging them?' 'Count yerself lucky, I 'ave to fetch it.' The waiter took the money and was away for some time. When he finally handed me the Coke, he said, 'That's yer lot, I'm not going back again.' From all of which I concluded that Bron's campaign in favour of smoking and drinking has got going early this year; his father, up above, would have approved.

But it will take more than one eccentric host to bring back the literary vernacular of yesteryear. 'Excuse me, but are you by any chance the unspeakable anonymous coward who reviewed my novel so despicably in the *TLS?*' 'Well, I wouldn't go so far as to ...' 'Take that, you brute!'

10 December 1994

The eleventh commandment of Karl Popper

Philosophers have not been of much use to us in this century. Ideally, a philosopher ought to be a thinker of pure and penetrative intelligence, who uses it both to seek truth and acquire wisdom and to convey them to the rest of us in ways we can use in our life and work. By this definition we have been ill-served, or rather scarcely served at all.

Bertrand Russell wrote innumerable books and magazine articles aimed at the general public, but it is impossible to point to any salient message of his which has stood the test of time. Most of his assertions in fact are contradicted by other statements, following one of his abrupt changes of opinion. And he snootily held that his 'serious' work, by which he meant his *Principia Mathematica*, had nothing to do with ordinary people. For 70 years he entertained us as one of the leading actors in the intellectual soap opera 'What's Cooking Among the Eggheads?' but as for conveying wisdom he might never have lived.

Jean-Paul Sartre was less snooty and genuinely tried to make a philosophy of life available to the young. But half a century after he launched Existentialism there is nothing to show for it except the stale aroma of hot air. And, later, he went out of his way to teach bad morality, notably in the use of violence: one of his many apt pupils in the Third World, Pol Pot, is still around killing people.

The best that can be said for Russell and Sartre is that they scorned the academic parlour tricks which occupied most 20th-century philosophers. Both Wittgenstein and Freddie Ayer, the most famous of them, went a long way towards persuading me and countless other people that modern philosophy was a frivolous affair, a sort of rarefied quiz game which had no relevance to the great tragedies of our time. The message I got from Wittgenstein was that nothing could be proved at all. Ayer, in so far as he had any influence on most people, actually did harm: as Lord Hailsham points out in his new book – a remarkable effort for a man of 86, beautifully printed in his own handwriting – Ayer persuaded many of his readers that most of the great moral and aesthetic truths on which civilisation depends are mere 'value judgments', incapable of philosophic validation, and therefore meaningless.

There was, however, one marvellous exception to this dismal showing by the professional philosophers of our time. Karl Popper, who died in London at the weekend, was not only a truly wise man but he contrived to spread enlightenment where it really matters: among men and women of affairs, the movers and shakers, people who actually exercise power or influence those who do. One would have to go back to Locke, or at any rate to Adam Smith, to find a philosopher who was more widely read and absorbed by politicians, senior civil servants, businessmen and scientists, writers and journalists. Popper was unable to prevent the monumental catastrophes of the 20th century but his teaching played a considerable part in bringing them to an end and will help to ensure they do not recur.

The messages he conveyed cover a wide area and mesh together with impressive strength. He was not a one-book man. His most famous work, *The Open Society and Its Enemies* (1945), was the most devastating exposure of the crimes of totalitarianism ever written, which should have laid to rest for ever the absolutist strain which runs through philosophy from Plato on. But he followed this with his remarkable *The Poverty of Historicism* (1957), which exposes the folly of all gigantic attempts to explain the world, history, human behaviour etc., and to give it a determinist twist. All clever young men and women should be encouraged to read these two books in their last year at school, or first at university, before they risk falling victim to the fashionable ism. Popper is an all-purpose vaccination course, a super-potent jab which, once administered, should protect the brilliant young from most intellectual diseases.

However, underlying these books, and in some ways even more important than them, is his *Logic of Scientific Discovery* (1934), which embodies his whole approach to evidence and proof. Popper learned from Einstein, the hero of his youth, to be wary of the enthusiasm of discovery. When we are working on a problem, in science or anything else, we form a hypothesis and then endeavour to verify it empirically. Human nature being what it is, if the hypothesis is exciting in embodying a new and important truth, or if it accords with our preconceived ideas, we tend to look eagerly for evidence which supports it, and to ignore or brush aside evidence which doesn't fit. Worse still, if negative evidence thrusts itself on us, we brazenly modify the theory to accommodate it, instead of bravely admitting the hypothesis is false and starting all over again.

Popper cited Marx and Freud as outstanding examples of pseudo-scientists who fought to the death for their false hypotheses rather than admit the weight of evidence against them. By contrast, Einstein deliberately constructed his General Theory of Relativity in such a way that it was easily falsified by empirical evidence and could not be considered valid until it passed the three vital tests he set it. Even so, it was no more than a provisional theory, subject to constant verification. Popper taught us that all empirical knowledge is provisional, that the pride of certitude is the deadly sin, and that the endless quest for truth requires heroic intellectual courage.

These are lessons everyone can make use of and which apply to almost all higher forms of human activity, from the art of government and legislation to the writing of history. As a historian, I have taken Popper's methodology to heart though it requires terrific self-discipline. Once you have satisfied yourself that a certain interpretation of history is correct, nothing is harder than to force yourself systematically to grub around for evidence to refute it. But it must be done, to qualify for Popper's definition of a scientist.

The piece of paper I prize above all others is a letter he wrote me last year, approving in the most generous terms of my book *Modern Times*. I have had it framed and it hangs in my study just above where I write to remind me daily that the principles of falsification and verification for which Popper stood are the Eleventh Commandment which all writers ignore at their peril.

24 September 1994

How to eat nobly and still enjoy Christmas

Christmas ought to be about God and our salvation. And we have made it about eating. I have been thinking about eating this week. For me, that is a most unusual activity. I was brought up to regard discussion of food, especially at table, as vulgar. My childhood was rather like Benjamin Franklin's in that respect. He relates that at meal-times his father always took care 'to start some ingenious or useful Topic for Discourse, which might tend to improve the Minds of his Children'. He adds:

> By this means, he turn'd our Attention to what was good, just and prudent in the Conduct of Life; and little or no Notice was ever taken of what related to the Victuals on the Table ... so that I was bro't up in such perfect Inattention to those matters as to be quite indifferent to what kind of Food was set before me; and so unobservant of it that to this Day, if I am ask'd I can scarce tell, a few Hours after Dinner, what I din'd upon.

I would not go so far as to say that. One should pay some attention to what one consumes. I agree with Dr Johnson, who insisted: 'I mind my belly very studiously, and very carefully; for I look upon it, that he who does not mind his belly will hardly mind anything else.' I like that word 'studiously'. Johnson certainly studied his food, as well as eating it: he seems to have given it his entire mind as well as his stomach:

> When at table, he was totally absorbed in the business of the moment; his looks seemed riveted to his plate; nor would he, unless when in very high company, say one word, or even pay the least attention to what was said by others, till he had satisfied his appetite, which was so fierce, and indulged with such intenseness, that while in the act of eating, the veins of his forehead swelled, and generally a strong perspiration was visible.

It is a great pity that Johnson did not, as he often threatened, write a cookery-book 'on philosophical principles'. Today more people write about eating than ever before. They advise us where to go and what to eat there and how much it will cost. They tell us *ad nauseam* how to eat well and remain slim and how to choose our food so as to prolong life. But they do not put forward a philosophy of eating.

I have, however, been reading a book which does precisely that: *The Hungry Soul: Eating and the Perfecting of Our Nature*, by Leon Kass (The Free Press, New York). The author is a doctor of medicine, and a student of Aristotle and the great Emmanuel Kant. He has thought deeply not merely about the physics of eating but about its metaphysics and its ethics. He regards the whole approach to civilised eating as one of the clearest ways in which we distinguish ourselves from brute creation and underline the fact that we are animals who 'walk uprightly'.

Considering how large a part of our life we spend eating, and how vital it is to our existence, we devote surprisingly little attention to thinking seriously and systematically about it. The Jews, as often, are exceptions. Unlike the Christians, who rather despise eating, go to some lengths to contrast it with spirituality, and whose key sacrament, the Eucharist, makes the point that bread, the archetypal food, has to be transformed by miraculous means to provide lasting sustenance, the Jews have spent 4,000 years elaborating a moral theology of food: what to eat, how to cook it, when and in what manner to consume it. For them, eating and the word of God are closely connected. As Pirke Aboth puts it, 'If there is no meal there is no Torah, if there is no Torah there is no meal.' Meal-times are quasi-sacred. Hence the Jews have always, and rightly, condemned the disgusting practice, now commoner than ever, of desultory gobbling in the open. The Talmud says, 'Whoever eats in the street or at any public place acts like a dog.'

Kass has a masterly chapter, 'Sanctified Eating', on the spirituality of food and meals, which includes a close and original analysis of the dietary laws of the ancient Hebrews. It is fashionable, I see, to laugh at the Book of Leviticus as absurd, and empty-headed actors have recently taken to tearing it out of hotel Bibles because it condemns their sexual proclivities. But, like most sections of the Bible, the more it is studied, the more rational it becomes and the more useful knowledge it yields. Kass accepts the principle elaborated by Kant in his illuminating essay, 'The Conjectural Beginnings of Human History', that the object of Hebrew moral teaching was to show men and women how to get as far away as possible from the instinctual and brutish behaviour of the animal kingdom while at the same time preserving and refining the natural appetites which keep us alive and make us creative. This approach applies to eating, to sex and to all other human activities which we perform in a state of nature but which have to be civilised.

Kass makes brilliant use of the concept of 'nobility', the practice, which once acquired becomes a habit, of rising above and transcending our animality. We can and should eat not just well, but nobly: and at Christmas in particular nobility in eating ought to be our aim. A noble meal is an elaboration of the notions of moderation, self-control, decorum and mannerly conduct. All these were first set down in Aristotle's *Nicomachean Ethics*, showing how all our doings, even eating, can promote harmony and grace. To eat reasonably and in accordance with the logos is noble. And as Kass says, nobility, like sanctity, does not require a beholder (except God of course). A lady or a gentleman, Kass insists, 'who is fully self-conscious takes aesthetic pleasure in enacting or appreciating his or her own nobility'. He continues:

> even when dining alone, and – let me push the point – even were he or she the last human being on earth eating the last meal, the virtuous human being would cover and set the table, use the implements properly, and would chew noiselessly with mouth closed.

Thus such a person demonstrates that nobility, though it has to be acquired by instruction and training, is nevertheless the natural mode of 'the truly upright animal'. I am taking Kass's admonitions very much to heart and I intend, this Christmas, not merely to eat nobly myself but to ensure that members of my family – including grandchildren – eat nobly too. A Utopian enterprise? We shall see.

17 December 1994

A playwrights' convention at the Palace

Playwrights fascinate me. Though they spend their lives, as I do, dealing in words, they fling them at a living audience watching a stage. So they require a quite different inner ear to the one I need to concoct formations of words to be read by one person in solitude.

Then there are the profound differences of structure. My books and articles have beginnings, middles and ends and are conceived, and written, as wholes. Playwrights work quite differently. They do not necessarily start with a plot at all. Tom Stoppard told me that he gets the idea for a single dramatic incident, then expands it backwards and forwards into a story. J.B. Priestley said he liked to 'shuffle people around in time to see what would happen to them'. He said to me, 'I have always felt that Ibsen worked in roughly the same way.' I asked John Osborne if he thought of a plot first. 'Good heavens, no. I start with a character and get him into messes.' (With Osborne it was always 'he': women were life-threatening appendages, a key element in the 'messes'.)

Osborne interested me particularly, as a writer, because he had a touch of what can only be called genius, which I would define as talent heightened to the point at which it becomes inexplicable. He could create a theatrical moment so intense but ephemeral that, afterwards, you could not really explain why it had seemed so magical. Oddly enough, he displayed the same quasi-genius as a prose writer. His brilliant autobiographies are dotted with such moments, amid the atrocious rancour and embarrassing special pleading. He also found, late in life, in writing for the *Spectator*, that he could produce the perfect diary paragraph, a little playlet in itself, with a magnificent curtain.

Osborne is popularly associated with anger and vituperation but the incident which remains most vividly in my memory shows him in an entirely eirenic light. It was at a large evening party which the Queen gave at Buckingham Palace last July. There were over 800 guests, I was told, a cross-section of British life, from the Prime Minister downwards – or upwards. The idea for this party, the first of its kind given by the Queen for many years, came from the fertile brain of Belinda Harley, a bouncy girl who had been advising the Prince of Wales. At all events it seemed to me a spectacular occasion. All the public rooms at the palace were open and the guests could wander at will. The band of the Irish Guards played softly. There were excellent champagne and eats. The royal librarian had gone to enormous trouble to find interesting manuscripts and drawings and put them into showcases. The Queen did her considerable best to talk to everyone present and many other members of her family were bidden to attend and make themselves agreeable. Most of those who were there, I imagine, will remember the party for the rest of their lives as a grand occasion which was also fun.

There were little tables where you could sit and talk and eat, and around one I found myself part of a group of playwrights. There were Arnold Wesker and Harold Pinter and one of the younger ones – David Hare, I think. And there was John Osborne, who has already recorded the event in *The Spectator*. He was in mellow and benevolent mood, and the following exchange took place. (Others may recall it differently, but this is my version.)

Osborne: 'Is not this delightful? On my way here, I said to Helen, "We are in for a dreadful evening – it will be a bore – we shall know nobody – and we must contrive to leave as soon as we can politely do so." And now, here we are and I am enjoying myself hugely. Music, food, drink, the company – everything marvellous. Look at us here, sitting round this table. They say that writers are quarrelsome, but here we are, on the best of terms, just having a good time. So God bless the Queen, say I.'

Myself (aside): 'This will not last.'

Wesker: 'I agree with John. However, might I take this opportunity, Harold, to remind you – you can scarcely have forgotten – that on the last occasion you dined at my house, you ruined the evening for us all by being gratuitously rude to the principal guest?'

Horrid pause.

Pinter (taken aback, being more accustomed to opening the offensive rather than being at the receiving end of an unexpected salvo): 'Have a care what you say, Wesker.'

Wesker: 'Ruined the evening for all of us. Moreover, your motive in going for my friend was simply that he was rich, and an American.'

Myself (hastily and not entirely accurately): 'No, Arnold. I don't feel that what you say can be entirely right. I have known Harold for many years and I can't say I have ever known him to be rude to anyone. Indeed, I'd go so far as to claim that he is constitutionally incapable of being rude.'

Pinter (triumphantly): 'There you are! Paul is quite right. I am constitutionally incapable of being rude. So shut your ***** gob, Wesker!'

Osborne: 'There, there, children – enough of this. We can't have the Queen coming round and discovering us at odds. [*Imitating Queen's voice.*] Auow. I thought I'd find my playwrights like a little nest of singing-birds so what is all this squawking? Stop it at once *or I'll have you thrown to the corgis.*'

Osborne's serene final period was a case of all passion spent, I think. He could not even be bothered to get annoyed with gossip columnists, though they continued to pester him. The truth is, after a lifetime of battering women verbally, and being battered in return, he had found repose in the arms of a beautiful, talented and supremely patient lady, who protected him from the world and himself and gave him a rest from the rage of life.

It could not last and it did not last, but at least Osborne enjoyed a few years of tranquillity. That is when I knew him and I shall always recall him as a wise, relaxed and gently amusing creature, a great writer taking his ease after a lifetime's work and battles. Good-night, sweet-sour prince, and may flights of avenging angels sing thee to thy rest!

7 January 1995

How one woman rejected the world and still lived to enjoy it

In a world increasingly dedicated to success and an ever-expanding gross national product, social, economic and even legal pressures combine to force women to pursue careers exactly like men. A good deal of European Union legislation, such as regulations making provision of crêches compulsory, for example, is directed to 'keeping women in the work-force'. If a teenage girl were asked today what she intended to do in life and answered, 'Get married and have children,' she would instantly be treated as a 'case'. Being a mere housewife is now thought of, by most women especially, as waste, cowardly, immoral, even – I heard the term used the other day – as 'parasitical'. In Sydney, where they are notoriously direct, one woman asks another, 'What do you do – or are you just a Handbag?'

If a housewife is just a Handbag, then, what on earth is a nun? A Prayer-Book, I suppose. Yet throughout most of the history of our civilisation, becoming a nun was an honourable calling for a lady. It was considered not merely natural but highly desirable that large numbers of young women should profess themselves – that was the expression used – in the service of Christ and His church, leading lives of prayer and austerity, sometimes away from the world behind convent walls, sometimes in it, caring for the sick and the poor, or educating children.

Until quite recently, a nun was to be found in every Catholic family. There were several in mine, ranged naturally among the aunts and great-aunts and cousins. Sometimes they would visit us, wearing magnificent habits which had scarcely changed since the 14th century, swishing into the room with a great rustle of skirt, rattling of rosary beads and crackling of starched linen, carrying with them a faint whiff of holy water and incense.

I never thought of nuns as strange, let alone sterile or frustrated. Committed to their care at the age of five, I found them warm, motherly creatures, severe on rare occasions but always loving. Nuns were part of life, among the nicer parts, certainly among the better parts. Their existence added to our security, since they prayed for us, constantly, devotedly; their orisons drifting up to heaven as naturally as the sun rose and set.

There are still, happily, many scores of thousands of these holy women left in the world, and no shortage of recruits even to the most demanding orders, like the barefoot Carmelites. Recently, I lost a much-loved first cousin, Margo, who had been a nun all her adult life, and her death has set me thinking about the survival of this ancient form of dedication in our selfish world.

Margo was older than I was, a lively, laughing girl, full of poetry and jokes and funny sketches, fertile in new ideas and suggestions for having a good time. It seemed odd, at first, that she had decided to become a nun, a Bride of Christ rather than of some fortunate young man, and sink all her liveliness in the solemn vows and dark habit of a perpetual virgin dedicated to poverty, chastity and obedience. Odd, too, that her name was changed to Sister Thomas More – many nuns are called after outstanding male saints or martyrs – as though her very sex was obliterated in her transformation from a free spirit to a woman bound for life to divine service.

Yet it was not so odd as it turned out. Anyone who has read the life of St Thomas More knows that this likable man had a extra-ordinary gift for combining intense religious convictions and absolute dedication to high principle with humour and irreverence. He romped and joked and gossiped with his swarm of children even when he was Lord High Chancellor, in an age which prided itself on its solemn pomposity. He delighted to play the Mr Bennett to his foolish wife's Mrs Bennett. He risked a crack or two even with his ferocious master, and he still had a one-liner in hand when, faint and crippled by imprisonment, he dragged his way up the steps of the scaffold. So his was not an inept name to be chosen by a serious-minded young woman who still harboured laughter in her heart.

So it proved. Margo, or Sister Thomas More, lived a life of unceasing toil and constant prayer but one lit by smiles and flashes of wit. And in many ways her existence was not so very different to that of women in the outside world. She spent much of her time teaching children and looking after them. She had a gift for interesting them in the things she loved most after God – the grandeur of history, the glories of great literature, the excitement of art. She composed poems and songs, which she set to music or matched to old folk-tunes, and the children loved to chant these spontaneous efforts. She wrote and circulated newsletters throughout her order, and kept in touch with correspondents throughout the world. She was a good typist and expert translator, an authority on the Vatican Council and the changes it brought into the Church. She became an able cook, fruitful in new dishes. Her convent house was famous for its simple hospitality and she delighted in organising outings, celebrations and sacred feasts. She was fond of barbecues, and brilliant at running them. She was active in the neighbourhood and persuaded Camden Council to have some nearby derelict houses refurbished for families in need. In her own quiet way she was a practical supporter of sensible causes.

She was a member of a group which studied the bible with Anglicans, and of another which shared scriptural insights with Jews. Every year on Good Friday she joined the Joint Witness walk which carried the Cross through central London. Her love of the psalms, her understanding of the sacred writings, her dedication to Christ's teaching were profound and reverent, but her eyes twinkled, her jokes were always ready, her relish for it all – her religion, her work, her life – was manifest. When we went to see her shortly before she died, she still sparkled, despite weakness and pain, and her resignation before death and the will of God was lit by a smile of content.

It is comforting to think that there are still many such good women left in the world, ignoring its horrific temptations, defying its abysmal dogmas of greed and ambition, brushing aside its relentless invitations to the pursuit of pleasure, and concentrating instead on the quiet pursuit of God's will. They seem to find profound happiness in it too. Best of all, they spend much of their time praying for the rest of us.

11 February 1995

Poussin: an emperor with no clothes

There is no other area in which the well-meaning public is so easily conned as the visual arts. Witness the deification of Picasso and the vogue of such obvious frauds as Yves Klein. But it is not just in the 20th century that the bogus or the incompetent have been hailed as geniuses. The canon of 'Old Masters' is crowded with third-rate daubers who, for one reason or another, have got themselves into it. A visit to the Nicolas Poussin show at the Royal Academy confirmed my long-held view that he is an egregious example of this process.

What a bad painter he was! Had he any merits – other than industry and persistence?

Poussin, like other artists whose canvases look dingy, has benefited from the superb colour reproduction processes we now take for granted. They make some of his paintings seem respectable – though they cannot save others – and anyone glancing through the exhibition's catalogue might conclude that Poussin was at least, on occasion, a gifted colourist. But the reality is far worse, and many of those respectable middle-class visitors who crowd the show must have been disappointed by the smudgy, lacklustre, seedy – or alternatively garish – state of the works on display, and the general impression of run-down cheerlessness and fuliginous gloom they exude. But of course they would not dare say they were disappointed, would they? Poussin is a Master, one of the greatest, and must be spoken of with awe. One must never say the emperor has no clothes, or the painter no talent – or not much, anyway.

Now it is no use telling me that many of Poussin's canvases have worn badly and have been cretinously restored. You have to judge paintings not by reputation but by what you actually see: no point trying to imagine into them virtues they manifestly do not possess. Besides, there is plenty of objective evidence in his *oeuvre* that Poussin's artistic shortcomings were many and radical and have nothing to do with the way his works have been treated by time and posterity. To begin with, he was visually incurious. He never seems to have actually looked at anything, being content with a series of stereotyped images implanted in his mind at an early age, never corrected by reference to nature, and reproduced, with bone-aching monotony, decade after decade.

There is, for instance, only one Poussin sky: an empyrean of an implausible colour of pinkish blue with, lower down, a collection of cotton-wool or dish-rag clouds violently lit from the left. To achieve a night or tempest effect he shoots down a lot of soot through an imaginary chimney. There is also what I call his Cadbury's cocoa sky, which serves for a distant fire effect, impending doom etc (see 'The Saving of the Infant Pyrrhus'). Part of Poussin's difficulty, as a painter, is that as a studio-bound artist he never took the trouble to ask himself, 'What is my source of light in this composition?' Three-quarters of his canvases are, in fact, underlit – hence their murky drabness – and in others, where the light comes from is a mystery. In 'Tancred and Erminia' there is no explanation for the glittering shield or the highlights on the stricken man's body because if the torches held by the *putti* had actually been real flambeaus instead of just dull red-orange splodges, the light would have come from the opposite direction. Such puzzles make me fret about nearly all of Poussin's designs. In 'The Testament of Eudamidas', the light should actually be coming from the window on the left. In fact, if anything, it emanates from the notary's flashy yellow shirt – a most unsuitable garment for a lawyer, incidentally.

Poussin had a lot of trouble with clothes, which are often prominent in his designs and tend to take them over. He is hailed as a master of composition but the linear balance is frequently upset by a triumphalist fashion show from a minor figure. Thus Mercury's red cloak dominates 'The Birth of Bacchus', and an even more outrageous habit worn by a black St Joseph shouts down all else in 'The Holy Family with Ten Figures'. Much of this high-decibel colouring may be due to poor restoration, but it looks to me as if at some stage Poussin, a notoriously warm man, bought a job lot of what we would now call Spectrum Orange and could not resist using it lavishly and often inappropriately. Clumsy colouring aggravates his even more fundamental weakness, an inability to paint the human skin. He has three basic skin colours: off-white for live women, Red Indian for warriors and men generally, and Terminal Pewter (or Agony Green) for the sick, dying, dead etc. One has to ask: did Poussin ever examine the skins of his models? (Assuming he ever used them: he worked in secret, and the overwhelming majority of his characters appear to have been painted from lay-figures. Broadly speaking, he has only one female face, itself a stereotype rather than a real one.)

But then nothing in a Poussin canvas comes from the real world. The trees are all what we used to call, in army fire-control drill, 'Bushy-Top Trees'. The palaces are 17th-century Disneyland, the houses Lego-brick. If the men ride, they are perched uncomfortably on wooden, white-painted rocking-horses. Titus has one in 'The Capture of Jerusalem', and it reappears twice in 'The Rape of the Sabines' and four times in 'Ruth and Boaz', where it is ploughing up a field of weird standing corn, a scene of total agricultural confusion. A lot of these canvases – nearly all of them, indeed – are unconsciously funny, and I fear that my occasional shouts of laughter shocked the right-thinking worshippers at Burlington House. The amazing tangle of beefy legs in 'The Ecstasy of St Paul', the whizzing up and down of *putti*, especially the artist's favourite, a button-nosed encephalitic monster with a smile of solid malice, the wriggly hands of 'The Judgment of Solomon' – Poussin, given time, is sure to provoke a giggle. How does the fellow do it? The drawing for 'The Death of Cato' in the Royal Collection shows a sword-hilt going in one side of the body and a quite different blade sticking out of the other. Poussin indeed had a gift of sorts – a positive genius for ineptitude.

If Poussin had been an Englishman or an American he would have been ridiculed and buried like B.R. Haydon or Benjamin West. Being a frog he has benefited from the chauvinistic self-promotion, especially in matters of art, at which that vainglorious nation has always shone. Leaving Burlington House and anxious to have my senses soothed, I hurried to the National Gallery to look again at my favourite painting there, Rubens's 'Château de Steen', crowded with all the magnificence of nature Poussin had no eyes to see. I looked, too, at Caravaggio's 'The Arrest of Christ', on loan from Dublin, a tragedy of heartbreaking truth at the opposite polarity of Poussin's clumsy artifices. My faith in civilisation restored, I got the bus home.

25 February 1995

So switch off the life-support, nurse

Once you get past 65, certain matters begin to demand attention. A Will? I have done that. Moral improvement? I'm working on it. The other day a friend suggested a third. 'Have you thought up your Famous Last Words yet?' I admitted I had not, and began to ponder furiously.

Needless to say, the very best exit lines are unpremeditated. My friend Simon Fraser, who died exactly a year ago from a heart attack, sitting upright on his horse while leading out the local hunt, hit the perfect note for a passionate sportsman: 'Where are the hounds?' The slight ambiguity is a neat touch: heaven has its hounds, as well as earth. So is the note of interrogation, which reminds me of the perfect farewell, from Henry James of course: 'So here it is at last – the grey, distinguished Thing?'

It is fair to assume that most appropriate last words are premeditated or embroidered or even invented by pious death-bed witnesses, or completely apocryphal. I don't believe for a minute that Renan went off with his neat bit of atheist triumphalism: 'We perish. We disappear. But the March of Time goes on for ever!' – which sounds even more bombastic in French. Nor do I believe that the last words of John Adams, second President of the United States, were 'Independence for ever!' Julian the Apostate's so-called farewell: 'Thou has conquered me, O Galilean!' was surely minted by a Christian propagandist. And another such, John Foxe, the great 16th-century Protestant spin-doctor, has St Lawrence, broiled on a gridiron in 258 AD, saying to his torturers:

> This side enough is toasted, so turn me, tyrant, eat,
> And see whether raw or roasted I make the better meat!

Those who attended Disraeli's deathbed say that his last words, carefully whispered, were in Hebrew. It is just possible that the old fox, who certainly betrayed no knowledge of Hebrew in his lifetime, had carefully planned his departure. Again, I think I believe that Napoleon Bonaparte's last words were *'Tête d'armée!'* – they are too unselfconsciously neat to be considered invention. I also accept that poor Hazlitt expired with: 'Oh well, I've had a happy life!' He had so obviously had a spectacularly unhappy life, and his sense of irony was so strong, that the saying fits.

Many famous last words have the ring of truth because they were entirely accidental and have nothing directly to do with death or summing up a lifetime. I don't know what Winston Churchill's official last words were – his biographer Martin Gilbert records none, and his final 14 days were spent in a speechless coma – but James Cameron had dinner with him not long before he died. The old lion said nothing at all. Then, as James was leaving, he nervously shook hands with Sir Winston a little too vigorously. Churchill suddenly came to angry life, his eyes blazing, and said, 'Damn you!'

Tennyson died after asking for a *Collected Shakespeare*. It was handed to him and his last words were: 'I have opened it.' Dickens said mysteriously, 'Yes, on the ground.' For Goethe it was 'Light, more light!' For Grotius it was 'Be serious!' Henry VIII went down with: 'Monks, monks monks!' (though this too could be papist invention). Louis I said, 'Out, out!' Oliver Goldsmith was piously asked if his mind was at ease, and snapped, 'No, it is not!' and died. Most actual last words, I suspect, have been simple expressions of weariness, like Macaulay's 'I am very tired' or Byron's 'Now I must sleep'. Or, for those dying violently or unexpectedly, mere ejaculations or shouts. Marat: 'Help, help!' Gustavus Adolphus: 'My God!' Richard III: 'Treason!' Gibbon (speaking in French, a bit affected to the last): *'Mon dieu!'* Richard Brinsley Sheridan said, 'I am absolutely undone!' –

which I suppose is how a theatrical type ought to put it.

A third group of credible last sayings come from those famous men wearied by sympathetic ministrations. Thus John Locke had had enough of Lady Masham, who was reading him the Psalms, and snapped, 'Cease now!' Voltaire: 'Please let me die in peace!' Princess Charlotte, daughter of the Prince Regent, who was being desperately dosed with brandy by her incompetent doctor: 'You are making me drunk – please leave me quiet!' Many angry last protests concern the dying men's desire to have priests, monks, friars etc. leave the room.

Personally, I would like to go out in the company of those who left with a jest, whether premeditated or no. One old hanging judge, Lord Chief Justice Tenterden, suddenly sat bolt upright, announced, 'Gentlemen of the Jury, you may retire' – then expired. Another judge, Lord Thurlow, explained, 'I'll be shot if I don't believe I'm dying.' Another version of this joke is Palmerston's finale: 'Die, my dear doctor, that's the last thing I shall do.' Robert Burns requested, 'Don't let the awkward squad fire over my grave' – a meaty little saying, *ben trovato* if not entirely authentic. I am thinking of something of the genre for my exit, though if I hit upon a happy formula I shall keep it to myself. Lots of writers are keen to sign off with a good one-liner, and death-bed plagiarism is, by its nature, unpunished.

The reality, however, is likely to be more dismal. Increasingly, the only deathbed sound is the click of the life-support system being switched off. Washington's last words were: 'I die hard but I am not afraid to go.' Nowadays, with all the terror-miracles of modern science, the dead not only die hard but very old indeed, and most are only too anxious to go, if they are still *compos*. An edifying death or even a simple *bona mors* is hard to pull off when you are in your nineties or hundreds, and have long since lost your marbles. Nurses in geriatric wards tell you that the old die speechless or mumbling incoherently. If you can identify a word it is most likely to be an expletive or an obscenity. So if you want to die memorably, get your last words ready now, and make sure the press-release containing them is prepared, like your Will, well in advance.

25 March 1995

A blast of the papal trumpet against death

The modern world began early in the 19th century, when the great triad of technology, democracy and liberalism first got a grip on the western world. The rest of that brilliant century witnessed its apparent triumph – free societies, the end of slavery, miraculous improvements in public health, living standards, literacy, speed and safety of travel: steady advances which kept on accumulating right up to 1914.

Thereafter, the 20th century demonstrated the dark side of modernity, the way in which the demolition of ancient and no doubt inefficient and obscurantist political and social structures could open the gates to something infinitely more horrible: totalitarianism, the two competing progressive tyrannies of Communism and Nazism, what Evelyn Waugh called 'the modern world in arms, huge and hideous'. From 1917, when totalitarianism first set up its rule in a major state to the final collapse of Soviet Communism at the end of the 1980s was three-quarters of a century, torn out of human history and made evil and barbarous.

Crueller things were done during those decades, on a larger scale and with more devilish refinement, than ever before in the sad story of mankind. It was a terrifying experience of the risks modernity holds. We have, I think, learned some at least of the lessons, though we have not yet finished clearing up the moral squalor – China is still a totalitarian state, and its gulag contains 20 million people, more than Stalin's did at any one time.

Still, the totalitarian century is behind us, and we have learned to see the state as it is: useful, even friendly when small and chained, a mortal enemy when it breaks its constitutional bonds. That will not be the problem during the 21st century. But it is already evident what we shall have to fear. In our own century, we allowed vicious men to play with the state, and paid the penalty of 150 million done to death by state violence. In the 21st century, the risk is that we will allow men – and women too – to play with human life itself. And by play I mean to use and abuse and change the life-forces as though there were no laws except those we ourselves determine.

I was much struck last September by an exchange which took

place at an Oxford conference on medical ethics which my wife organised at St Anne's College. One of the speakers, Melanie Philips, used the phrase 'the sanctity of human life'. Another, a dauntingly clever philosopher, interjected, 'Now wait a moment – let's look at that expression, "the sanctity of life". You may be right. Perhaps human life *is* sacred to us. But I don't know it as a fact. Prove it to me. *Why* should human life be sacred?'

I found this a chilling moment, and many of those to whom I described the exchange found it a chilling moment too. I had always thought that the sanctity of life was one of those 'truths' which sensible men and women 'held to be self-evident'. It did not need to be proved. It just was. Proving it is not easy. I doubt if I could prove it. But then I do not need to prove it because I know it to be true as surely as I know I am a human being. I think most of us feel that way. There are a number of beliefs to do with behaviour and morality and civilisation which are so self-evident that the request to prove them creates uneasiness.

Yet that is precisely the kind of uneasiness we are going to experience in the 21st century. All kinds of axiomatic certitudes about human life will come under challenge from the innovators who plan to use new technology to 'improve' the human condition, just as the Nazis and the Communists planned to use the state to improve it. There are of course continuities between the two forms of human and social engineering. The Nazi plan was to 'cleanse' the human race by a form of eugenics which involved eliminating Jews, gypsies, Slavs and other types of *Untermenschen*. Communist eugenics involved eliminating the exploitative bourgeoisie and introducing a new, cleansed kind of human being, without acquisitive instincts. Looking back, it is hard, now, to decide which was the more dangerous kind of nonsense. Both involved mega-murder, and both rested on the assumption that those in authority have the right to make up the moral rules as they go along. The innovators who will endeavour to take power in the 21st century and change the rules about human life have, likewise, a contempt for absolute morality and a belief that morals and laws should be relative, and changed from time to time to suit the convenience of men and women.

They are having their will already. Last year in Britain alone 168,000 unborn children were lawfully destroyed, and the number of abortions which have been legally conducted in the world exceeds the numbers killed by both the Nazi and Communist tyrannies. At the other end of the lifespan, euthanasia is already lawful in the

Netherlands, or at any rate unpunished, and efforts are being made to introduce it here and everywhere else. Abortion and euthanasia are merely the plinth on which the innovators intend, during the 21st century, to erect a system on which they will be allowed to do anything with human life which technology makes possible.

Pope John Paul II has chosen this moment to publish his new encyclical *The Gospel of Life*. It firmly restates the sanctity of human life as an absolute; it defends human life in all its manifestations in a manner which is robustly grounded in natural and divine law, unassailable, unalterable and eternal, and it identifies all acts terminating innocent human life, however speciously defended by courts and parliaments, by philosophers and even churchmen, as forms of murder. The Pope's teaching on human life is internally coherent and consistent, massively brave and unfashionable, a hard doctrine to follow – as all good teaching is – and will be resisted and ridiculed and cursed by all the evil forces of the modern world.

May this marvellous old man live to see the year 2,000, so that his frail but firm and clear voice can trumpet forth absolute truth at the very dawn of the 21st century before the agents of death get to work on it.

8 April 1995

Collapse of stout parti in the Luxembourg

Paris

Anyone whose stomach churns at what the French culture ministry has done to the Louvre, now turned into a Grand Central Station of art-tourism, should take a restorative walk round the Luxembourg. It is just as I remember it, nearly half a century ago. It even keeps its old-style *pissoir*, hygienically banned everywhere else. A clever television raconteur like Lucy Lambton could present the whole history of France just by wandering among its statuesque bric-à-brac. I associate it with fierce women, ever since, in 1953, I had a final rupture with a delectable but combative Air France hostess, walking up and down one of its *allées*.

And there are fierce women here in plenty, especially among the grand ring of statues of the French queens – Louise de Savoie, for instance, Régente of France and Henry VIII's contemporary, a formidable 'off-with-his-head' type; and Margaret of Anjou, wife of our poor Henry VI, and immortalised by Shakespeare as 'she-wolf of France'. I suppose Marie de Medici, wife of Henri IV, was pretty aggressive too. She built the palace, in the style of the Pitti in her native Florence, she laid out the gardens, with its great Medici fountain, and she commissioned Rubens to paint 24 enormous pictures tracing her life allegorically. He must have roared as he hustled up these brilliant but preposterous hoardings, now tarted up and in the Louvre. They are still good for a laugh today because what they don't record is that Marie had the guts to take on Richelieu, was worsted and ended her days penniless in Cologne; and the French, always happy to tease an Italian, have hung her life history in the Pavillon Richelieu.

The palace was afterwards used for all kinds of events, including the trial of Marshal Ney who, as his nearby statue reminds us, took part in 39 major battles and was wounded a dozen times: 'bravest of the brave', as Bonaparte said. It is now the Senate, and its members, the embodiment of the French political establishment, 'in fair round belly with good capon lined', who occasionally stroll round the *grand bassin*, in training for fresh battles at Véfour and Lapérouse.

I was delighted, on this last visit, to find a new addition to the political statuary. My first mentor, Pierre Mendès France, has now been set up in bronze: it is no great work of art but the head unmistakably conveys his charismatic obstinacy. Mendès had been brought into politics by the *chef du cabinet* of Clemenceau, head of a noble radical tradition going back to Danton himself. He would not have been surprised by the collapse of the long Mitterrand regime into a morass of corruption unprecedented even in French history. '*Le pauvre François,*' he used to say, when Mitterrand was his minister of the interior, 'he is always in trouble – *il a le goût de policier.*' As if to remind one of this, just beyond the Luxembourg Gardens, in the Avenue de l'Observateur, is the very hedge behind which Mitterrand crouched during his fake assassination attempt.

There must be a hundred or more statues in the Luxembourg, many of them rubbish artistically but none without interest. There is a big bronze lion killing an ostrich, and a tasty morsel, naked except for her long tresses, putting her hand into a monster's mouth, and a beautiful boy holding aloft a mask and surrounded by the heads of eight famous actors (the 'gays' can puzzle that one out). Here is Le

Play, whom the French claim invented economics, and Branly, said to have discovered the wireless (they have never heard of Marconi). Some of the inscriptions have long since been washed away by wind and time. Is this Watteau, being handed roses by a languorous young lady? And who is the moustachioed grandee who looks as if he introduced macassar hair-oil? But George Sand is plainly labelled and impeccably dressed as a Victorian matron, with lace and frills and looking as if butter – let alone anything stronger – would not melt in her prissy little mouth.

Not far away is Charles Baudelaire, also highly respectable, and even Paul Verlaine, most scrofulous of syphilis-ridden poets, is given a wash and brush-up. Poor Paul Eluard, by contrast, done by Ossip Zadkine, has lost his tummy and is presented as a piece of machinery. Stendhal looks as boring as, alas, I now find his novels. Delacroix is, as you would expect of an illegitimate son of Talleyrand, a mixture of the showy and sinister.

These gardens are deserted most of the time. No hissing, clicking Japanese – not a tourist in sight, indeed. It is not on anyone's list of musts. Just the odd Gallic jogger and a few plump Parisian ladies doing slow Chinese work-outs. At lunchtime, however, it fills up. There are a lot of famous high-schools in the quarter – the Lycée Montaigne the other side of the rue Auguste Comte, and the Henri Quatre just beyond the nearby Panthéon. The teenage pupils bring their sandwiches to eat near the *bassin*. Each circle of girls, I note, has its statutory male, and the gangs of boys all sport a virago, an *amazone en titre*. By contrast, the singers from the Schola Cantorum, also nearby, are decorously mingled, and so are the hectoring left-wing teachers from the Ecole Normale Supérieur.

While I make a careful drawing of the palace, I listen to the chatter of these youngsters and realise that Académie French is a lost cause. They do not say *quoi* they say *what*. Nothing is now *nouveau* or even *nouvelle*, it is *new*. They say *'t'es complètement out'* – meaning you are definitely not with it. The in people are not *le gratin* but *les tops*. They don't say *vraiment* but *honestly*. It is hard to follow them because, perversely, they sometimes studiously avoid *franglais*. Thus, they do not go on *demos*, as you would expect, but on *manis*, short for *manifestations*.

I find myself baffled by the slang and new vocabulary. What is *un meuk* – a boyfriend? And does a girl convey approval when she says her *meuk* is *flash*? What is to be *jalmince comme un cul vert*? On the other hand, when a young woman says, '*J'ai totalement collapsé*,' you know exactly what she means: collapse of stout *parti*. Except the French aren't fat any more – all that *cuisine minceur*.

15 April 1995

Animal rights and human duties

The stinks don from New College has been making trouble again. Defending abortion, he argues ('Are chimps sacred?', Letters, *The Spectator*, 15 April) that there is no such thing as 'the sanctity of human life', since under Darwinian theory this would imply that 'along the chain of 200,000 African generations, a child whose life was sacred was born to parents whose life was not'. Old Stinky dismisses the notion of absolute values and morality as 'an inadequate substitute for thought'.

I wish I could be as certain as some of these scientists are about what happened 200,000 generations ago (I suppose he means about 6 million BC). Unfortunately, being a historian, I plead ignorance. In fact, our reasonably secure knowledge does not stretch back much further than about 6000 BC, in sites like ancient Jericho, where we have some materials to work on and means of dating them roughly. Hard evidence in deep antiquity is rare. It is often questionable at much later periods. Until recently, some scholars dismissed Jesus Christ as largely mythical; but we have considerably more contemporary or near-contemporary documentary evidence about him than we do in the case of prominent figures in Roman secular history whose existence no one has ever doubted.

When I was writing my books on ancient Egypt and Palestine, I became uneasily aware to what extent our confident descriptions of what actually happened in, say, the Egyptian Old Kingdom, around 2700 BC, were based on suppositions and deductions and hypotheses, often varying dramatically from one generation of historians to another, and tentative readings of ancients texts whose language is imperfectly understood. To some extent, I fear, much of our understanding of deep antiquity is based on an interlocking series of what might be called honest con-tricks.

And of course the further you go back, the greater the uncertainties. The evolution of human life is certain to remain a mystery to us, this side of paradise. It seems odd to me that physical scientists, accustomed to working with absolute proof in their own specialities, should so glibly, on no evidence at all beyond deductive supposition, insist that a specific event occurred 6 million years BC – a change from monkey into man – simply because it fits in with their notions of Darwinian evolution. This is faith, not knowledge. And since we are dealing in faith, I prefer the creation story that God made man 'in His own image' as a deliberate act, being fully aware of and intending the infinite consequences of this act at the time. In that sense there was nothing accidental or evolutionary in the creation of man. It was indeed an absolute act, which necessarily introduced new moral absolutes, including the sanctity of human life.

Human life is sacred because we are an image, albeit a flawed one, of Absolute Goodness. But, in a sense, all created life is sacred. What do I mean by this? Like many people, as I grow older, I tend to look more closely at life-forms, being so soon to lose my own. An ordinary house-fly now seems to me, on close inspection, such a marvellous living contrivance that I cannot bring myself to swat one any more, however annoying it may be, and will go to considerable lengths to get it out of the window. I still, I regret to say, kill mosquitoes because they seem to regard me as a particular target, but I hope for the day when I will spare even them. In the meantime I am moving slowly but inexorably towards vegetarianism.

None of this makes me doubt for a second that man is uniquely valuable. Indeed living creatures of all kinds are, partly at least, valuable precisely because they make us think about the extraordinary nature of creation, of which man is the crown. And because man is the crown, all other living organic creatures are subservient to his needs. That means he may kill and eat. But he must do so intelligently, and as he uses his intelligence to refine his dependence on brute power, so he must gradually eliminate from his food supplies the higher creatures whose sensibilities make them undesirable for food production. The moral case for vegetarianism is that a growing number of affluent humans no longer need to be meat-eaters or fish-eaters or even to rely on milk, eggs and other animal products. We can improve our moral stature as the ruler and protector of the entire animal kingdom by using our ingenuity to find practical alternatives to this form of cannibalism. I have no doubt at all that, in due course, eating animals of any kind will be regarded as being just as atrocious as human cannibalism.

None of this means that animals have rights. I rather doubt if anyone has rights, except God. And if humans have rights, it is only because they have, in the first instance, duties. There is no moral possibility of animals possessing rights unless they are conscious of duties. And, unfortunately, animal duties have to be imposed by man: no animal has an autonomous sense of duty. If it sometimes looks that way, as in Millais' painting 'The Old Shepherd's Chief Mourner', that is mere sentimental anthropomorphism. So the so-called 'Animal Rights' campaign is moral nonsense, and it is not surprising it is degenerating into savagery.

Those who feel animals need more protection should switch the emphasis from animal rights to human duties. Our duties to animals are very clear, and they are beautifully set out in the new papal *Catechism*, 516–7. The Seventh Commandment enjoins respect for the integrity of creation. All organic life is intended for the common good of the created universe, past, present and future, the summit of which is humanity. Use by man of these resources cannot be divorced from respect for moral imperatives. The dominion of man is relative; he has a leasehold, not a freehold, of the planet, and all his actions must be limited by concern for his neighbour, including generations to come, and a religious respect for the integrity of creation. Towards animals we have the duty of providential care and kindness. It is contrary to human dignity to cause animals to suffer or die needlessly – and that includes the duty to prevent over-breeding. It is likewise unworthy to spend money on them which should as a priority go to relieve human suffering. One can and may love animals, but it is sinful to direct to them the affection due only to persons.

All this is eminently sensible and there is no reason at all why dutiful and conscientious farmers, shippers and the like should not abide by it. But, if man is to continue to subscribe to moral absolutes – as he must to survive – I see no long-term future for livestock farming.

29 April 1995

To Hell with Picasso

Last week Andrew Lloyd Webber admitted he was the man who paid $29 million for Picasso's 'Portrait of Angel de Soto' (1903). Easy come, easy go. If you make a fortune by writing tunes which vaguely remind people of something they've heard before, why not splurge some of it on the most successful artistic con man of the century? Webber, amazingly enough, came to Picasso via the pre-Raphaelites. He only saw the portrait three days before the Sotheby auction, so it was an impulse buy. He proposes to hang it next to a Burne-Jones. Picasso said he admired Burne-Jones and was much influenced by his line and colour. But then Picasso told a lot of lies, from a variety of motives, and I think this was just his Andalusian blather. I can detect no connection. Burne-Jones was a great artist who achieved his true level of performance quite late in life after prodigies of effort. He would have despised Picasso from the very bottom of his heart. If I hung a Picasso next to one of my Burne-Jones's, I would expect them to object vociferously, in the way good pictures do.

This particular portrait always makes me laugh. It is so confusing it is often reproduced the wrong way round. Angel was one of two brothers (the other was a sculptor) whom Picasso sponged off in his Barcelona days. Angel was an idle fellow, who pretended to paint but in fact did nothing but drink and brothel-creep. But what did he do to deserve this caricature? Occasionally Picasso took trouble over portraits of Angel. Four years before the Webber thing, he painted a sad, hung-over oil sketch of Angel (now in a private collection) and there was a revealing charcoal drawing of the lad which has disappeared – both, I suspect, reasonable likenesses. In addition, the Museu Picasso in Barcelona has two drawings of Angel – boozing in a café and engaging in mutual masturbation with a whore. They have no merit but are revealing in different ways.

The work Webber has paid so much for, by contrast, has nothing at all to recommend it. It is a clumsy daub and it is hard to say what is most objectionable about it: the gruesome colouring, the lazy sloshiness of the brushwork, or the bad drawing. I know it is often said by 'experts', and repeated endlessly in fashionable drawing-rooms, that Picasso was a consummate draughtsman. It is true that some of his drawings are better than others. But Barcelona at the turn of the century abounded in superb draughtsmen, and none of his efforts comes within a mile of the work of Casad, Rusiñol or Ribera, to mention only three. There was nothing special about Picasso's drawing even when he was trying hard, which he rarely was, and the results invite easy pastiche. I know a young lady, a genuine master-draughtsman – her *sfumato* shadows would make Sir Ernst Gombrich's spine tingle – who amuses herself and foxes her pretentious art-loving friends by doing Picasso drawings with a pen attached to a sex-vibrator. She calls them 'Prickassos'. Even at its best, Picasso's drawing has nothing special to recommend it, and in Webber's 'Angel' it is horrible. Perhaps he was tipsy.

To begin with, the glass on the table is out of the vertical and one side of it bears little relation to the other. Its perspective gives one an uneasy feeling, and the shine and shadow make no visual sense. (Anyone who wants to see how this kind of glass should be painted can look at Velazquez's 'The Water Seller', currently part of the 'Spanish Still Life' exhibition at the National Gallery.) Then there is Angel himself, poor fellow. His left arm appears to lunge out of nowhere and is attached to his body by a miracle of plastic surgery, as it bears no relation to anatomy. The right arm looks more normal but is clumsy and much too big. Both hands – Picasso was never much good at hands – have uncooked chipolata-sausage fingers which make one itch for a frying-pan. The index finger of the right hand is a Monster Show claw and the thumb has mysteriously disappeared, or been strapped inside its palm in an agonising way. This may explain why Angel is having such difficulty holding his pipe – if it is a pipe and not one of those thingummyjig pipe-cleaners or giant toothpicks sold on the *fin-de-siècle* Ramblas. If Angel is fed up, and he plainly is, who can blame him? His eyes are looking in different directions and have been rammed painfully into their sockets. Half his left cheekbone has rotted away and he seems to have a giant gumboil which is twisting up the right corner of his mouth and causing havoc with his cheek. And that right ear! Why was it hacked off his head and glued back on the bottom side of his jaw? No explanation. It must have hurt a lot anyway.

John Richardson, Picasso's official hagiographer, explains all this by saying that the 'deformations' are deliberate, enabling the Master to transcend the normal forms of portraiture and 'delve far more deeply into character'. Picasso had 'learned how to exploit his inherent gift for caricature in depth as a means of dramatising psychological as well as physiognominal [sic] traits'. The work, says Richardson, tells one all about Angel and is, moreover, 'galvanised' with Picasso's own 'psychic energy'. The great man 'internalises things and comes up with an enhanced characterisation of his subject'. Yes – well. In the words of Mandy Rice-Davies, he would say that, wouldn't he? If you are presenting your chap as the finest painter of all time, you have to pile on the verbals.

The art market is governed not primarily by quality but by rarity and hype. Most 'Blue' Picassos are already locked irrevocably into museums and his 'Angel' was the first to come on the market for five years. Hence the high price it fetched, though even the knowing were shocked by its enormity. Dealers have been massaging the Picasso market skilfully for three generations and this explains why the price keeps up. It is the same in the stamp trade. Some kinds of Penny Blacks and Cape Triangles are no rarer than plenty of other stamps but fetch top prices because dealers have talked them into celebrity class. My friend Kenneth Rendell, perhaps the greatest living authority on autographs and holographs, explains in his new book, *History Comes to Life: Collecting Historical Letters and Documents* (Oklahoma UP), how and why the celebrity factor often outweighs the rarity value. The hyping of Picasso makes the punters scramble to pay up, just as the Churchill cult transforms his signature on a photo into gold – I saw one the other day go for £12,000. So paying $29 million for the 'Angel' daub tells us a lot about collecting mania. But of course it has nothing to do with art.

27 May 1995

When Londoners ask 'Who's spouting tonight?'

Last Thursday evening, my wife and I and about 200 other people traipsed to the Tate Gallery to hear Professor Roger Scruton give the Peter Fuller Memorial Lecture on 'The Artistic Venture Today'. Since Scruton was demolishing the claims of much of the painting and sculpture featured in the Tate, its director, Nicholas Serota, the *monstre sacré* of London's modern art establishment, found it convenient to be in New York.

However, that is not my point. What struck me, glancing round the audience of personalities and high-fliers, was that so many people should turn out to hear a lecture at all. And the same thing is now happening all over London, at the National Theatre, the National Gallery, the Royal Geographical Society, the French Institute, the Accademia Italiana and many other venues. Television is dead: the public lecture has returned.

I say 'returned' because in the 18th and 19th centuries the London public flocked to lectures, often paying handsomely for the privilege. To attend a lecture was regarded as public-spirited, civilised and highly respectable. It was the secular equivalent of going to church. Indeed, Tom Paine always referred to God as the Great Lecturer. On a typical June evening in Regency London, the enthusiast had a choice between, say, Samuel Taylor Coleridge, Sir Humphry Davy, William Hazlitt and Michael Faraday. Places like the Royal Institution in Mayfair and the Surrey Institution on the South Bank were crammed.

A generation later, Thackeray was packing them in with his famous series on 'The Four Georges' and 'The English Humorists'. These could be lengthy performances: two hours, even more, was not unusual. In due course, Dickens drew audiences of thousands, in great cities all over Britain, so that the largest halls available were required to house the multitudes who flocked to hear him. But these were 'readings', not lectures: already a symptom of decline, with the focus shifting from self-improvement to entertainment.

Meanwhile, the torch had been taken up in America, where the Lyceum Movement was founded in 1829, precisely to make the public lecture the beacon of enlightenment of an expanding society. Lyceums were opened not only on the developed East Coast, but in Cincinnati (1830), Cleveland (1832), Columbus (1835) and then throughout the Midwest and the Mississippi Valley. Ralph Waldo Emerson's famous Boston lecture of 1837, 'The American Scholar', was later termed, by Oliver Wendell Holmes, 'our intellectual Declaration of Independence' – the cutting of the cultural umbilical cord with England. All the same, once the Lyceums were available, English celebrities, such as Thackeray and Dickens, were soon being paid enormous sums by Yankee impresarios to work the American lecture circuit.

The process has been going on ever since. Indeed, it amazes me how many Americans are still prepared to turn out of an evening to hear someone expound. Last autumn, when I gave a course of lectures on the history of the United States at the Pierpont Morgan Library in New York, the hall, which held, I think, about 200, was filled to capacity by a ticket-only audience, and we had to accommodate an overflow. This was a tribute not so much to my appeal as to the sheer intellectual appetite of the Big Apple's culture-vultures. At Denver, in the Rockies, I found myself holding forth in a sports stadium to 2,000 people or more – an eerie experience. There is a lot of money to be made by lecturing in the United States, and not just by the ultra-celebrities in the Kissinger class who can command fees of $50,000 a time. Americans will pay top movie-house prices to hear all kinds of people, and audiotapes are mass-marketed; $27.95 for three hours (three lectures) on tape is typical.

Europe, normally eager to imitate American cultural patterns, has been slow to recover the lecture habit. The last great spasm of lecture-going occurred during the war, when both the British and the Germans enthusiastically attended, especially at lunchtime. Those organised by Sir Kenneth Clark at the National Gallery – there were wonderful concerts too – were the most famous and best remembered. Of course Clark was an outstanding lecturer himself. The courses he gave not long after the war, at the Ashmolean in Oxford, on Rembrandt and Tintoretto, were the best I have ever heard – and there was some stiff competition in those days, not least from C.S. Lewis, A.J.P. Taylor, C.M. Bowra and Lord David Cecil.

In France, too, there was a wartime revival of lecturing which continued for a while into the peace. Jean-Paul Sartre first became a celebrity with a course on the novel he gave in the Rue St Jacques in the autumn of 1944. Then, on 29 October 1945, he launched the European phenomenon of existentialism by a famous or notorious lecture he delivered in the Salle des Centraux at 8 Rue Jean Goujon, 'Existentialism is a Humanism'. The lecture was so popular that there were people fighting in the streets outside to get in, chairs were smashed, women fainted, and proceedings started an hour late. The next day virtually every word was printed in all the main Paris papers. Those were the days!

Unfortunately, radio and television, while keeping people at home, and thus killing the evening lecture, have so far failed to develop an electronic version of the traditional lecture style. The only man who succeeded in doing it, entirely by his own efforts, was A.J.P. Taylor (Clark's great *Civilisation* series was a filmed documentary, something quite different). It has always seemed to me a great pity that BBC Reith Lecturers are picked exclusively for their subjects irrespective of whether they can deliver a lecture or not – the last one, an architect, was literally a turn-off. But now that television is in headlong decline, especially among the chattering classes, and people are coming back to the lecture room, we have a new chance to develop the lecture as the ideal audio-visual art-form for the elite.

I look forward to the day when *le tout Londres* goes to a lecture once a week as a matter of course, and the right question to ask is: 'Who's spouting tonight?'

3 June 1995

The feminist world war has begun

The War of the Women entered a new phase last week. Germaine Greer started her counter-column on the *Times*, and her enemy Suzanne Moore, by way of a pre-emptive strike – and in answer to Germaine's taunt that she is only capable of writing about pop-music and similar grunge topics – produced a long piece about The Needs of Yoof. As might have been expected, it was dead boring (to use one of her expressions). Germaine was fine in the *Times*, where she has replaced a dreadful socialist called Anne Robinson, whose sole claim to attention is that she looks a bit like Barbara Castle.

However, I would rather have Ms Greer in the *Guardian*. It is her natural habitat, just as Mogg belongs in the *Times* and Perry in the *Sunday Telegraph* and Melanie in the *Observer*. The *Guardian* is my favourite morning paper. I disagree with virtually every word in it but I know it is not meant to be taken too seriously – Hugo Young likes a glass of the Widow with his Beluga just like everyone else – so, of the six or seven papers I buy each day, it is the one I turn to most eagerly, if only to work myself up into a healthy morning rage.

No *Guardian* contributor gave me more satisfaction than Greer. My only complaint was that she appeared once a fortnight rather than once a week. To begin with, her command of language, ranging from the lightest of persiflage to downright vulgar abuse, is unrivalled. No journalist alive is more skilled in the planting of venomous verbal arrows in human flesh, except of course the great Keith Waterhouse. Then again, Greer, unlike most of our tribe, is educated. She has read much, and thought about what she has read. She is unique among us scribes in her ability to resurrect a much-thumbed text – *Romeo and Juliet*, for instance – and give it new life and excitement by the sheer creativity of her imaginative insights. Moreover, she can argue. The perversity of her conclusions beggars belief, but the sinewy skill with which she reaches them is fascinating to follow. It is like listening, mesmerised, to one of those brilliant speeches in which Tony Benn proves that we should all stand on our heads.

For all these reasons I was disturbed to hear that she had resigned from the *Guardian*. So I phoned its new editor, Alan Rusbridger, who has improved the paper enormously since poor Peter Preston was kicked upstairs, and said I was afraid he was about to make his first mistake. 'Oh, there's nothing I can do,' he said. 'Germaine is beside herself with fury and you know how unreasonable she is even when calm.' Yes, said I, but all good writers are lunatics and it is an editor's job to humour them.

I spoke from experience. When I took over as editor of the *New Statesman* in 1964 I found that J.B. Priestley had had a row with my predecessor, John Freeman, and was refusing to write for us. As Freeman was reason personified, the row was unquestionably Priestley's fault. But that was not the point. The point was that he was a contributor of genius – no one wrote a better 'middle'. So I set about sending him a flattering letter. My mother, who was Lancashire to the core and detested Yorkshiremen – her motto was Foreigners Begin at the Pennines – always used to say, 'If you want to flatter a Yorkshireman lay it on thick. Their skins are not exactly sensitive and they love it.' So I did lay it on thick, and I wish I still had a copy of that radiantly insincere letter. Priestley was mollified. 'I always thought you were a perceptive sort of chap,' he replied. Not only did he return to the fold: he became a very good friend of mine and remained one till he died on the eve of his 90th birthday. So I told Rusbridger he should write Germaine a cunningly effusive letter and he agreed to do so.

Unfortunately, that evening Ms Greer appeared on a television chat show and laid into the *Guardian* as only she can – and its editor felt honour left him no alternative but to react violently. It was rather like the beginning of an old-fashioned world war. He published not one but two leading articles denouncing Greer, who thus took precedence over Bosnia, the Irish Troubles, China etc. – proving that, for once the *Guardian* has a proper sense of priorities. Moreover, he added the final insult by referring to her as 'Dr Greer', something calculated to wind her up still further. Then the other nations – I mean columnists – began to join in. Simon Jenkins, writing on behalf of establishment opinion, felt that Germaine, being older and wiser, ought to have his considered support. Julie Burchill weighed in heavily on the side of Suzanne Moore, believing that grunge columnists should stick together, and also feeling, as a newly self-outed pseudo-dyke, that she ought to back the younger woman. Minette Marrin, Mary Kenny, Peter McKay, Taki, Lord Deedes, Frank Johnson etc. have all been taking sides or indicating that they are open to offers, rather like Italy and Romania in 1914. Kenneth Rose has not yet informed us of the view taken of the conflict in the Diplomatic Corps and the College of Heralds – I rather think they will back Germaine, eventually, if only because she is, despite all her efforts, a lady – and we are still waiting to hear from the delicious and brilliant Zoë Heller whether the United States intends to remain isolationist or join in. But no one can possibly doubt that the conflict will continue and spread. This is not a war which will be 'over by Christmas'.

Meanwhile, what of those expletive-deleted shoes? That term was new to me, and to many others, I imagine. It certainly came as a surprise to my Italian friend Carla Powell, who has the largest collection of shoes in London, 96 pairs at the latest count, and who is rightly annoyed that all her high-powered cobbler advisers have left her in ignorance of this important new trend. What does Ferragamo think he is doing? Why is Bally invisible? Is Northampton asleep? As Carla says, 'A pair of dees shoes I must 'ave.' I am still not quite clear what they are, and it is not easy to find out. One can hardly go up to someone at a party and say, 'Excuse me, but those shoes you are wearing, could they accurately be described as —?' 'No, they could *not!*' Again, 'a bird's-nest hairdo' was also new to me. But in this case I can guess what it means, and how to bring it into the conversation. 'I say, what a splendidly outrageous bird's-nest hair-do you have!' 'So it bloody well should be – cost me a hundred quid at John Frieda's.'

That is why I like these rows. Just as world wars speed up the development of technical inventions, so a public exchange of views between talented ladies does wonders for one's vocabulary.

10 June 1995

Forgotten beauties resurface in a concrete hell

Landscapes of France at the Hayward is the most important exhibition to be held in London for some time, as well as the most enjoyable. It confirms my view that the whole of the historiography of art in the second half of the 19th century will have to be rewritten. The

Hayward must be the ugliest gallery in Europe and is notorious for swallowing works of art alive. But even its hideous concrete interiors are overcome by the power and splendour – and the luminous delicacy – of the immense canvases now hanging there.

For the first time in London we can see the work of great artists like Français and Busson, Pelouse and Chintreuil, Guigou, Saïn and Ségé. It is a revelation. I have already been to the gallery three times and intend to go again as often as I can, before the show finally closes at the end of August.

You may say: who are these people we have never heard of? A good question. The French themselves are largely unaware of their existence. Whereas the Americans, despite all the ravages of artistic fashion, cherish their outstanding 19th-century landscapists like Church and Bierstadt (the latter was the subject of an enormous exhibition in Brooklyn in 1991), and the Australians are rightly proud of their own masters, Tom Roberts and Arthur Streeton, the French have buried their best painters from the Second Empire and the Third Republic for nearly a century. Their works languish in places like Angers, Caen, Avignon, Morlaix, Chartres and Béziers, and these provincial dumps seldom display them now.

Even when the splendid Musée d'Orsay opened in 1986, only one or two of these forgotten artists were resuscitated for an international public. Little or nothing by Charles Busson has been shown in Paris for half a century, though his 'Le Village de Lavardin' is a masterpiece which recalls Constable at his best. Go and see it for yourself.

The cause of this neglect, which has denied entire generations of art-lovers the chance to make up their own minds about such painters, is to be found once again in that huge imposture known as Modern Art. The argument, for many decades axiomatic, runs as follows. In the 1860s, art throughout Europe languished in the philistine pits of the Paris Salon and the Royal Academy. Buried beneath bourgeois money, establishment painters forgot what colour was or how to look at nature, and great artists like Claude Monet could not get their work displayed at all, even in the Salon des Refusés. These unknown geniuses finally got together to hold the first Impressionist Exhibition in 1874, and gradually their rediscovery of light and colour penetrated the dim vision of even the French bourgeoisie. So Impressionism triumphed, and there followed the even greater achievements of Post-Impressionism and the Fauves and the Cubists and – and – and – all the tremendous glories of 20th century art from Lucian Freud's matchless studies of the vagina down to the brilliant bath-plug sold in London last week for £35,000.

The argument is false, as a whole and in every single particular. Indeed its impudent effrontery never ceases to astonish me. It is simply not true that the Impressionists rediscovered the art of painting light and learned to take their colour direct from nature. I became aware of the falsity of this assertion some time ago when I saw the big exhibition at the New York Metropolitan, *The Impressionists Before Impressionism*. The poignant lesson of this show was that Camille Pissarro and Monet were much better painters in the days when they were still trying to get into the Salon and taking a lot of trouble. Once 'freed' by Impressionism, they became lazy and careless and soon repetitive and mechanical. Monet, an observant and delicate painter in the 1860s, eventually set up a splodge-and-dot factory churning out three pictures a day, which now cover the galleries of the world like wallpaper. The last time I was at the Fine Arts in Boston I complained to the management that the vast numbers of virtually identical Monets on display meant there was no room to put up the pictures I had come to see.

The Hayward exhibition enables one to examine the best land-scapists of the Salon, from the 1860s to the 1890s, in rooms adjoining a representative selection of Impressionists. What becomes immediately clear is that the 'traditional' painters, who took their work with professional seriousness, were much closer to nature in all its manifestations than the Impressionists. Busson showing us pale sunshine after rain, Saïn conjuring up the blinding white light of Provence, Chintreuil on the First Dawn, René Billotte on winter fog, Ségé displaying the immensity of the Beauce, or Pelouse taking us into the dense thickets of an evening wood in Seine-et-Oise – here is the exciting reality of French nature brought to life in the Hayward's brown concrete rooms by prodigies of skill and devoted labour.

By comparison, even Pissarro, the least corrupt of the Impression-ists, looks jejeune, and Monet seems crude, inaccurate, unsubtle and monotonous. The colours are brash, the light is merely switched on and off like electricity, and most of the Impressionist canvases on show smell of lamp-oil rather than *plein air*. After I immerse myself in Pelouse and Français, I find poor Renoir's landscapes merely ridiculous – but then he did not pretend to be a landscape painter. The real victim of this exhibition is the overrated Paul Cézanne, whose endless metallic greens are an offence to the eye, once you have seen how true artists can create the real thing.

The painters on display at the Hayward were products of the

immensely strong French studio training which also benefited foreigners who came to Paris in those days. John House of the Courtauld,
who has organised the show, sensibly includes examples, notably
'Shower in the Rue Bonaparte' by the American master Childe
Hassam, and Stott of Oldham's strangely moving 'The Ferry', which
I have seen reproduced many times but never before in its magical
reality.

The Impressionists, with their practice and encouragement of
amateurism, set in motion the catastrophe which destroyed French
studio discipline, and until it is restored, in France and everywhere,
the central realist tradition of western art will not be able to resume
its majestic progress, halted these many lost decades. But there are
indications that sanity is returning at last, and the grand canvases
on display at the Hayward are premonitions.

8 July 1995

The North London cocktail circuit

The Bishop of Oxford was a happy man at the annual British Library
party. 'Ho, ho!' he boomed at me. 'You media fellows certainly took
a pasting in the Major election thing. And I tell my right reverend
brethren in Christ that there's a lesson in it for the dear old C of E –
in future we should simply ignore what the media tell us to do.'
'Quite right, Bishop,' I replied, 'though I hope you don't continue to
ignore what Almighty God tells you to do.'

The bishop is one of a number of elite figures who appear to believe
that John Major's 'victory' was scored over the Tory press as well as
over John Redwood. It is the line taken by the broadcasting duopoly
and the left-wing press, *Guardian, Independent* and so on. The flaw in
the argument is that Major actually lost the election, having made
sure of only 170 votes by the Tuesday morning. He only now clings
to office by virtue of the 'corrupt bargain' he did with his bitterest
enemy, Michael Heseltine, later in the day. This is the real stuff of
raw politics and has gone unreported by the broadcasters and
journalists who don't want to believe what happened.

Among those journalists is the curious figure of Sir Nicholas Lloyd.
He was quoted by the *Observer* as boasting, 'It was the *Express* wot

won it for Major', which rather implies that he had personally brokered the Major-Hezza deal. No such thing, of course: Major may welcome the support even of the *Daily Express*, and periodically invites Lloyd to a condescending drink at Number 10, but he does not share his confidences with the man. Lloyd, as I say, is an odd figure who does not quite fit into the Fleet Street rogues' gallery of archetypes. In the days when the *Express* was a great newspaper, its owner, Lord Beaverbrook, often rang it up late at night and bellowed, 'Who's in charge of the clattering train?' The answer today would be: 'A booby.'

The best thing about Lloyd is his wife, Eve Pollard, who has all the brains, style and guts of the family. She was running the poor old *Sunday Express* remarkably well when she fell foul of its pseudo-proprietor, Lord Stevens. I say 'pseudo' because Stevens, a sort of minute financial person of Welsh origin, controls the group while owning the merest sliver of its equity. He enormously values his invitations to Number 10, and when Ms Pollard's vigorous presentation of the news put them in jeopardy, he squeezed her out. Meanwhile, her husband continues to toe the Major-Stevens line, whatever that may be, and the circulation of the *Express* continues to fall, faster than that of any other national newspaper on record. As a direct result, this week the *Express* announced that it would have to sack 15 per cent of its workforce. Some years ago, Lloyd asked me to write a column in his paper, and I agreed to give it a try because I felt sorry for him. But after a month or so I asked to be excused: no one I knew ever read the thing and it was like dropping pebbles into a bottomless well – no splash. It is now many years since I came across an *Express* reader, though such people apparently exist, albeit in rapidly dwindling numbers. The interesting point is that while the anti-Major papers have been consistently putting on readers, the few pro-Major ones, such as the *Evening Standard*, are losing them in droves.

Lloyd is a former editor of the *News of the World*, promoted, or perhaps demoted, to edit the *Express*, and he has a rather edgy attitude to journalists who he considers have had more 'advantages' than he. In this he resembles Andrew Neil, who has a conspiracy theory about what he calls 'the Garrick Club Mafia'. Lloyd does not believe in that particular fantasy. He has one of his own called 'the North London Cocktail Circuit'. He thinks William Rees-Mogg is a member of the Circuit, and Dominic Lawson and Simon Heffer. Not only do I too belong to it but I 'spend [my] time there, high on champagne and zealotry'. I relish this vision of the Circuit, which in some ways sounds even more exciting than the Garrick Mafia.

'Where are you off to, old boy?'

'The Circuit, of course.'

'Lucky you. What's on tonight – champagne or zealotry?'

'Both, old bean.'

'I say.'

Alas, alas, I never set foot in North London – or drink champagne – any more than I have ever belonged to the Garrick. It is a vague area for me, though I suppose I must have driven through it. I think Lloyd is confusing me, and the others, with the famous Henry Fairlie, who was a notorious seducer of young suburban housewives and who often boasted, 'I can get a hot-cooked supper anywhere in North London.'

The Left's rallying to Major is an interesting example of the maxim 'My enemy's enemy is my friend.' The operation of this impulse is powerful, as I rediscovered for myself recently when the French locked horns with Greenpeace. Much as I dislike Frog governments, I loathe Greenpeace even more and found myself raising a feeble '*Vive la France!*' when its beastly boat was captured. Hatred of the Tory press operates in the same way. No one, not even Hugo Young of the *Guardian*, can actually admire Major for his talents or sparkling personality – but as a victim of the Tory press barons he has almost Baldwin-like sanctity.

Of course there are shrewder fellows who back Major for more solid reasons. Stewart Steven, the cunning editor of the *Evening Standard*, is a Labour supporter and is anxious for Major to remain in power as he is the easiest Tory leader to beat. Tony Blair thinks the same. Indeed there are even rumours – perhaps originating on the North London Cocktail Circuit – that Major's triumphant Question Time just before the leadership election was made possible because Blair's office fed the Prime Minister in advance with the supplementaries Blair intended to put.

However that may be, we live in a degenerate age. As the great Queen Elizabeth I put it in her twilight years, 'Now the wit of the fox is everywhere on foot, and hardly a virtuous or faithful man may be found.' But not everyone in John Major's corrupt Britain is a con-man or a twister, a larrikin or a hobbledehoy. There are still politicians of honour on both sides of the house, and still more outside it, and it may be that their time is at hand. For those of us who want to get back to honesty and rectitude in British politics, the election cannot come a second too soon.

22 July 1995

Apotheosis of a well-dressed poet

We live in a vale of tears made bearable by friendship. But the trouble with friends is that they die, leaving great, jagged holes in one's defences against the world's battalions of sorrows, holes that can never be filled. The truest observation Dr Johnson ever made was that 'friendship should be kept in constant repair'. He used the word in its collective sense: you should add to your friends deliberately to make good the inevitable losses of time. But this becomes more difficult with age, as old friends die faster and new ones are harder to come by.

Sometimes, however, there is an uncovenanted stroke of fortune, when a new friendship is made which acquires almost instant maturity so that, by the second encounter, it already has a patina of understanding. This happened to me a few years back with Stephen Spender. We had nodded to each other periodically over 30 years or more, but now, staying in the same house on the shores of an Italian lake, we suddenly became friends, and a great new delight entered my life.

To say that Stephen had a gift for friendship is to understate: he had a genius. Disparities in age, generation gaps, nationality, race, gender meant nothing to him, except as rich subjects for laughter – he reached a delicate tendril across them all to grasp the essence of his interlocutor. He struck the perfect balance between being a good talker and a good listener. He told his anecdotes with enviable skill, but his relish for your own was heartening. He asked questions. He listened hard to the answers. He made you feel he was learning something valuable from you. And his own memory was full of treasures, intimate stories about the great which went back to the second half of the Twenties, shrewd reflections on literature, views of living panjandrums which had the necessary salt of an almost imperceptible malice but which were never cold or cruel or unfair.

And all this was pervaded by his quintessential characteristic –

modesty. I never met a man less inclined to boast, to push himself forward or to peacock. Elderly giants of letters, in my experience, are inclined to be resentful of the thrusting young, or broody about honours withheld. There was none of that about Stephen. He was genuinely astonished at the lustre of his name, felt he had received more than his fair share of laurels and had not a whisper of envy. All his best stories were self-depreciative, showing himself bossed or humiliated by Auden, outwitted by Isherwood, snubbed by T.S. Eliot, even made to feel small by the sly and dishonest Dylan Thomas. I never knew Stephen tell a tale from which he emerged victorious.

Yet there was something godlike about the man. He has been criticised for saying, when very young, that he wished 'to be a poet'. The right expression, it is argued, is 'I wish to write poems.' But Stephen merely spoke the truth, as he always did. He made no claim to poetic genius but he wanted to devote his life to poetry, to serve the muse with devotion and industry – and that he did, throughout his long and full life. I hesitate to judge his work. But all I heard, I liked.

At his memorial service last week. Harold Pinter read a fine poem of Stephen's describing a lowland farm of his youth, images overlaid on a Wordsworthian palimpsest of the high Lakeland fells. Stephen read his own poetry superbly, not with any panache or flourish but with clarity and simple assurance. Not long ago he insisted on attending an *Evening Standard* literary lunch because he had promised to do so, though he had had a slight heart-attack only the day before. His address was hesitant and nervous and I feared he might break down. But once he began to recite a poem of his, a delightful thing about his beloved grandchildren, his voice grew confident and the audience was rapt. It was a magic moment, and young people present will recall it half a century hence.

Last year, despite his venerable age, he was made the object of a vicious plagiarism by one of those sub-sects which infest the American literary scene. I was able to spring to his defence in these pages, and shame Penguin, who were about to publish the offending book, into disowning its impudent author. Stephen was grateful because he was the last man on earth to wield a claymore on his own behalf. He was vulnerable and sensitive, just as he was sensitive to the feelings of others and specially delicate in dealing with those he knew, instinctively, to be vulnerable themselves. His chief concern on this occasion was that the attack on him would hurt his devoted wife

Natasha. No one I ever knew had stronger or more tender feeling for his family.

But to list Stephen's virtues does not quite convey the man. There was something else, a metaphysical factor, which lifted him over the rest of us. He had the true charisma of the good man. The ancients believed – it is an axiom of the Old Testament – that, just as all men are made in God's image, so the best of them have a singular bodily grace. Stephen was not just a handsome man, he was beautiful. Not small, either, in the tradition of poets like Pope, Keats and Shelley, but a big Norse god or a radiant golden knight from the *Nibelungenlied*. It was his physical glamour as well as his ardent poetic aspirations which made him a welcome guest at Garsington and in Bloomsbury when he was only 18, so that he got to know the literary titans from 1927 on, years before Auden and Co entered the competition.

This striking beauty he retained right to the end of his life. Indeed, it seemed to me that, in his very last years, he became even more beautiful – and younger – as though the splendour of his noble features was undergoing a premonitory apotheosis. Then, as always, Stephen was totally unconscious of his allure. Clothes were of no importance to him. Oddly enough, in his last phase, his amazing son-in-law, Barry Humphries – who as a showbiz paladin attached significance to dress – insisted on buying him some magnificent suits. Stephen wore them with initial trepidation, then with growing pleasure.

It was a rich source of amusement to him that at long last, on the threshold of eternity, he had attained the distinction of a Well-Dressed Man. I saw him thus adorned a week or so ago, at Mrs Drue Heinz's annual lunch in Mayfair. Standing next to him was the Duke of Devonshire, also exquisitely dressed, two pre-war gentlemen of the old school, the poet and the aristocrat, each a model of good manners, of consideration for others, and of modesty. I thought to myself: thank God for England. Now Stephen is gone, but his memory is safe in our hearts.

29 July 1995

Can France repel American verbal boarders

The latest sign of French official despair at the state of their language is a preposterous proposal from Maurice Druon, perpetual secretary of the Académie Française, that the French and English should make common cause against the threat posed to them by Americanisms, and that we should signify our new solidarity with the frogs by creating an English Academy. Monsieur Druon is a nice old boy and probably quite harmless but his proposal strikes me as cheek. Indeed, it reminds me of the plea from Paul Reynaud, the French Prime Minister in June 1940, that the British should fling all the resources of the RAF into the Battle of France, already manifestly lost, instead of reserving them for the Battle of Britain.

The cause of the French language as an instrument of state policy is a forlorn one. When Cardinal Richelieu instituted the Académie 361 years ago in 1634, he had a clear aim in view. Spoken and written French was still fairly chaotic, with few agreed grammatical rules and little uniformity of spelling. All that had to be clarified and ordered, and gradually it was done. Equally important – probably more important to His Eminence – was the fact that barely a majority of the inhabitants of what was then France, and less than half of those living within France's modern borders, actually spoke French.

The aim of French policy was to Frenchify all the area between the Pyrenees in the south, the Alps to the east, and the Rhine to the north-east. In Richelieu's day, and for long after, 'the French' spoke a variety of tongues, and it was not until the second half of the 19th century that speaking French became the norm throughout the territory of metropolitan France. French failed to advance as far as the Rhine, and the battle for supremacy between French and Flemish in Belgium is still raging – liable, indeed, to explode in violence any moment. The French eventually, after much bloodshed, won the battle against German in Alsace, but in the Saarland they finally lost it, quite recently. On the whole I think it can be said that Richelieu's long-term demotic strategy succeeded.

Richelieu, however, did not foresee the threat from modern mass-communications, especially radio, pop, movies, television and magazines, which have allowed English – not even a competitor in the 1630s – to carry out an airborne invasion of French. Ordinary speech is not merely demotic, it is democratic. It is an area where the masses decide and their decision is transmitted upwards, not the other way round. The Anglo-Saxon tongue beat French in England finally in the 14th century, though originally French had all the resources of the state and the ruling class behind it. Now Anglo-Saxon is moving, on the airwaves, across the Channel.

The Académie's efforts to fight the invasion are likely to prove counter-productive. In trying to curb popular trends, it has always lost every set-piece battle, usually demoralising its own supporters in the process. In the years 1815–30, for instance, it waged a full-scale campaign, under its ferocious perpetual secretary, Louis-Simon Auger, on behalf of entrenched classicism in literature, against the advancing forces of Romanticism, led by the works of Byron, Scott, Goethe, Schiller *et al.* On 24 April 1824, Auger delivered a monumental speech at the Académie, accusing the foreign romantics, and their fifth column in France, of subverting the laws of French literature and dividing the national genius. Five years later, it was apparent to all that the Académie's campaign had failed utterly, and Auger committed suicide in despair.

The French young are not going to take any notice of the Académie, whose absurd antics on behalf of 'official' French are an embarrassment to French traditionalists who deplore the growth of Franglais. Last year, the Académie backed a vicious law which tried to use France's enormous public sector to punish the use of banned Anglo-Saxon words by huge fines. The French constitutional court ruled it unlawful on the ground that it infringed the Declaration of the Rights of Man (1789). But the law would have been defied anyway. The French young are introducing English words even for common nouns, verbs, adjectives and adverbs because they find them more expressive and exciting than the old French terms: they are new, modern, 'in'. The only way the invasion can be repelled is by France producing great writers who use the traditional tongue even more compellingly. No sign of that, however: French literature is now crushed beneath the dead weight of state subsidies, the largest in the world.

We find no comparable threat from America. Many Americanisms are, in fact, attractive and are skilfully employed by the best young English writers, just as they seize on the many good Australianisms. World English literature and language is a system of mutual colonisation. We influence America just as much as she influences us. I lecture a lot to American audiences, commercial, political and academic, and, having taught myself to articulate in a way they can understand without effort – a lot of British speakers in America don't trouble to do this – I find them appreciative. They often congratulate me on the 'purity' of the way I speak and pronounce English. If anything, it is now the British who are colonising the American media, especially in its upper reaches.

As for Britain founding an academy on French lines, that would collapse at the first hurdle: choosing the 'Forty Immortals'. Imagine what a hash John Major would make of it. Who would he appoint the first perpetual secretary – his friend Jeffrey Archer? The English have always opposed French-style cultural centralisation and state bullying. William Hogarth, who virtually created the English school of painting, was even opposed to the foundation of the Royal Academy – and who can now say that he wasn't right? There is currently an attempt, by the modern-art dictator and brickie-in-chief Nicholas Serota, to create a suspiciously froggy type of centralised empire controlling all the national museums of art. I shall be writing about this shortly and I am quite certain it will eventually be defeated by the English spirit. As for an English Academy of Letters, laying down the law about split infinitives and dressing up in uniforms with gold braid and swords and fancy hats, with a few token women and a statutory black – let us laugh that one off the stage.

12 August 1995

Bruisers in mortarboards

A word of protest about the cult of gratuitous rudeness. Let me be quite clear what I mean. A certain terseness of repartee, a well-merited rebuke, a skilfully delivered dart in the entrails of the self-important, the insufferably pedantic, the bigoted or the obtuse has always had an honoured place in civilised English discourse. Here, Dr Johnson was the master, though occasionally his thunderbolts fell on unsuspecting innocents. But plenty of others, in the age of good conversation, were capable of well-deserved verbal admonishment. Even the mild Mr Bennett in *Pride and Prejudice* occasionally delivered what his wife called 'one of your put-downs'. That is not what I mean.

What I mean is rudeness for the sake of being rude. There are punch-up personalities about these days, especially in the media, who make a point of declaring to the world, in effect, 'This is how I put the boot in.' No particular cause is being served. Often there is no real animus, as when a yobbo says, 'There's nothing personal' to the victim he has just clobbered to impress his grinning mates. Behind these verbal head-butts there is usually a hint of class rancour, a whiff of pseudo-radical politics, but that is not the real motive. The object is simply to inform society, but especially the urchin's peers: 'I have a talent for being nasty.'

Not long ago I was rung up by a man from the *Guardian*, Cunningham by name. He said he was writing a profile of the editor of this journal and would I help him? He seemed polite. Having ascertained that he was not a gossip columnist, I agreed to answer his questions. It may be said: more fool you. But it is an agreeable principle in life to assume that everyone, even a journalist, is innocent until proved guilty. When I was a young man and making my way, I received enormous kindness and help from all kinds of busy people, including senior journalists who took a lot of trouble to 'fill me in', as they put it. So now I do the same, especially for the young, answering the phone as politely as work permits and seeing people at my house from all over the world. Considering I have a naturally irritable temperament, I am amazingly patient with them, as my wife Marigold wonderingly remarks, unless they bore me out of my senses, in which case I simply wander off out of the room.

So I answered Mr Cunningham's queries as fairly and truthfully as I could and gave him some good quotes. He seemed effusively grateful. When his profile appeared, I read it to ensure I was not grievously misreported and have no complaint on that score. But I was taken aback to see myself described, quite irrelevantly because except as a mere witness I did not come into the story at all, as 'a toad in a turncoat'. The man has never met me and seems to have plucked the phrase out of the air in exactly the same way as a young thug kicks a harmless old lady with his bovver boots – just to show he can do it.

However, Cunningham is not a young thug but a more or less literate person employed by a celebrated newspaper. He has certainly not learned his rudeness on the football terraces. I rather suspect academia is to blame. Disgruntled dons seem to have started the

rudeness cult in the years between the wars to distinguish themselves
from traditional Oxbridge charm. They saw themselves as outsiders,
out to 'get' the Establishment, oust 'the Old Gang'. Lewis Namier was
one, a genuinely ill-bred man, and 'Professor' Lindemann another.
But the outstanding example, as his gruesome centenary celebrations
have reminded us, was old Leavis. Former pupils have fallen over
themselves in recent weeks to recapture his unique blend of bare-
knuckle abuse and snarling bitterness. They admire it, you see, and
copy it when they dare. What they like is that Leavis's verbal
dismissals of everyone in sight, living or dead, had no pretension to
wit or elegance or felicity of phrase. Amazingly, for someone who
spent his life teaching Eng. Lit. Crit., Leavis could not write English,
or speak it either. A long reminiscence in the *TLS* showed him, aged
77, having forgotten nothing and forgiven nothing, still spitting out
gobbets of spleen at colleagues, rivals, former friends – no: he had no
friends – former followers or allies. His hatred of literature, and those
who practised it, was absolutely sincere: there was no subterfuge in
that grim, bony old face and shining bald head, stuck on a neck like
a stalk emerging from its defiantly open-necked shirt, like an old-style
Israeli politician. Leavis taught cultural grudges masquerading as
scholarship. A pupil of his, asked which poets he enjoyed, replied
smugly, 'Poetry is not meant to be enjoyed. It's meant to be *ee-val-u-
airted.*'

Centenary pieces by Leavisites expressed particular admiration for
his crude polemic against C.P. Snow. This struck me at the time as
having largely missed the drift of Snow's Two Cultures argument,
and as being so pointlessly venomous as to suggest an ancient
personal hurt. No doubt Snow had once done him a kindness – as
he did many people – for Leavis was the scowling embodiment of the
adage: 'No good deed ever goes unpunished.' Snow's response to
Leavis's unprovoked assault was a model of gentlemanly restraint.
That must have infuriated Old Fireworks still further. However, from
his centenary perch he must be rejoicing in the way his literary shin-
kicking and eye-gouging has now spread, not least among academics.
There is, for instance, one from the LSE, a fierce little man, a sort of
tall dwarf, who has achieved a mini-national reputation by being
rude to people on *The Moral Maze.*

Perhaps, since more and more of the young are going to university
as an alternative to starting work, there are enough viewers around
to justify an academic soap opera about a permanently apoplectic
don who goes around administering verbal sockings to high and low.

John Cleese, who once did a mad headmaster brilliantly, might be induced to play the Leavis character. And Simon Gray, now that he has done knocking the stuffing out of poor Stephen Fry, could do the script: if anyone knows about boiling point, he does. There are good laughs to be had from High Table Billingsgate and tutorial tantrums. I'm even willing to throw in, *gratis*, the title: *Nightmare Spires*.

19 August 1995

Clearing up the mystery of a love affair 40 years ago

Just occasionally a document comes to light which throws a brilliant ray of illumination into a dark corner of the past and solves a mystery which has been nagging one for decades. This happened to me the other day when I got a copy of *Between Friends*, the correspondence of Hannah Arendt and Mary McCarthy, 1949–1975. I bought it after reading a scathing review by David Pryce-Jones in this journal and expected, like him, to be entertained by the unconscious humour of these two self-important left-wing ladies chewing over the Cold War cud. Instead, I was treated to the touching, indeed tragic, solution to a puzzle which had intrigued me since 1955. The question was: did my old friend John Davenport have a spectacular love affair with Mary McCarthy or not?

Perry Worsthorne, who had been taught English by Davenport at Stowe, claimed that the romance was a reality and had gone on 'for years'. The late John Raymond, on the other hand, said it was a complete fantasy, one of many in which Davenport indulged. All of us enormously admired Davenport for his wit and erudition. We used to meet every Saturday morning in a dingy King's Road pub called the Commercial (now tarted up and renamed the Chelsea Potter). However early we arrived, Davenport was always ahead of us, seated at a table and 'clearing up', as he put it, 'my correspondence'. Many neat little envelopes were spread out on the table, addressed in his exquisite hand, and as we arrived he gathered them to himself and put them away, but not before we had had ample opportunity to read who it was he had been writing to: 'The Duke of Wellington

KG', 'Dylan Thomas Esq', 'HRH Princess Louise of Bourbon-Parma', 'T.S. Eliot OM' and other names to conjure with. For a time, letters addressed to Mary McCarthy also figured in this collection, and inquiries about her were met with meaningful evasions and sly hints.

John Raymond maintained that Davenport's entire correspondence was fantasy and all the envelopes scattered on the table had been addressed to impress us and were never sent. Why, he asked, should the McCarthy envelopes be any different? However, Billy Hughes, a rich lawyer who also belonged to our circle, used to insinuate darkly that there was more to it than that, and he might have a tale to tell were he not bound by professional confidentiality etc. (a device he often employed when he wished to lay claim to knowledge he probably did not possess). That Davenport, a muscle-bound, almost square, middle-aged man (he had been an all-in wrestler or boxer at one time), with a brick-red face, heavily married and much tortured by debts, drink and lack of productivity, should have enraptured McCarthy, then still good-looking and at the height of her fame, seemed improbable. But we were never quite sure. Asking Mary herself, who popped up in London from time to time, was out of the question: she was liable to be snarky at the best of times.

Now the answer is plain for all to see. She did indeed fall in love with Davenport, having met him in Rome, at the Hotel D'Inglaterra, in May 1956. They had an affair. As both were married, concealment was necessary, and McCarthy went secretly to London later in the summer to resume it, reporting ecstatically to her correspondent: 'Dear Hannah, it's been wonderful, more so than I could conceive, abstractly.' But during the winter of 1957, when they were separated by the Atlantic, Davenport had stopped replying to her letters, so when McCarthy returned to London in spring 1957, she took advantage of an airy Davenport aside: 'I'll give you the number of my cousin, Billy Hughes, in case you find it hard to get hold of me.'

A letter McCarthy wrote to Arendt on 21 May tells the rest of the story. 'I called up the cousin, the lawyer in Belgravia, who said, Yes, he would fix up a rendezvous that afternoon at his flat.' A telegram would be sent 'the Davenport phone being shut off for lack of payment', and if the telegram got no response, Hughes would send his housekeeper to fetch him. McCarthy arrived at the 'very elegant Belgravia flat' at 5.45, to find 'Mr Hughes, a tall dark man in white tie and tails', waiting for her. The housekeeper was sent off in a taxi to fetch Davenport. In 30 minutes, Hughes said, he had to leave for an official dinner attended by the Duke of Edinburgh, so he must not be late. Meanwhile, they talked about Davenport.

McCarthy's first shock came when Hughes corrected her reference to Davenport being his cousin. ' "Cousin? Did he tell you that?" And he laughed rather irritably. "I'm not his cousin. I'm no relation to him." ' Then Hughes added, 'I think I'd better tell you that John is a pathological liar.' McCarthy commented, 'Well, Hannah, that's how it all started. His ancestry. All that was lies about him and his "gentle birth".' Hughes told McCarthy that Davenport's father was 'a drunk who was a writer of song lyrics' and his mother 'an actress who played chars' but that Davenport pretended 'to be related to everyone in *Debrett*'. As for his drinking, 'it was much worse than I could possibly imagine'. He spent all his time in pubs getting 'bestially drunk'. Nothing could be done for him because of his lying. He also stole – 'books and small objects', such as Hughes's silver ash-trays. 'He stole books from the *Observer* and sold them, all the reviewers in London knew it.' And, said Hughes darkly, 'he *bragged*'. He had been boasting about his affair with her. The fortunate thing, said Hughes, was that he was known to be such a liar that in this instance nobody believed him.

By this point, McCarthy related, she was 'almost fainting'. The housekeeper, whom she called Evans but who was in fact named Walsh, arrived back without Davenport. She looked upset, and Hughes commented, 'She's afraid of [Davenport] I think.' Hughes added that he was a violent man. His wife had had a breakdown 'trying to bring up his children under these fearful conditions'. Instead of trying to help her, 'John goes around London telling people she's mad'. They both left in a taxi, Hughes to his dinner, McCarthy to her hotel.

McCarthy reported to Arendt: 'The truth is, I still care about him, just as much as ever, though perhaps this feeling would not last if I saw him in actuality. This caring, of course, is really hopeless now. Hughes says he *is* hopeless, and I believe him.' At any rate, the affair came to an abrupt end. Why Billy Hughes disillusioned McCarthy quite so brutally I do not know. He did tend to be jealous of his friends' happiness, though in general he was a good sort. And of course most of what he said was true. It is a sad little tale. Those involved are dead now. But it is a relief to have the mystery cleared up.

26 August 1995

The monstrous regiment of feminists

The United Nations Fourth World Conference on Women in Peking promises to be an ugly conjunction of all that is most objectionable in the modern world of Admass – to use that useful word J.B. Priestley coined to denote the systematic attempt to drown the truth in loudspeaker voices. The conference is supposed to be about 'rights'. That, presumably, is why it is being held in Peking, capital of a country where human rights, including the most elementary one of all – the right to live – are denied on a scale never before seen in history.

The Peking regime, let us never forget, has 20 million people in its gulag – more than Stalin at his worst – and is chewing up and digesting the entire Tibetan people, destroying for ever their ancient religion, culture and way of life. It is soon to engulf and obliterate the free society of Hong Kong and announces its intention to do the same for the highly successful democracy of Taiwan, if necessary by force. It treats women primarily as beasts of burden, forces them by law to abort and kill their unborn children and, if they somehow evade this diktat, persecutes them with relentless ferocity. One of the worst aspects of the regime, which is run entirely by men, usually very old men, is the way in which it brainwashes (a process invented by it) women into becoming agents of its odious purposes. One has only to read an account of a visit by a government female 'enforcer' to a Chinese village for the purpose of investigating its reproductive record to see exactly why Peking is the last place on earth for a conference on women's rights.

That, however, is only the beginning of the moral problems raised by this sinister event. What troubles me more, because it is less obvious, is the totalitarian assumption underlying the conference itself. Why is it necessary or desirable to hold a Conference on Women? We would not dream of holding a Conference on Men. No one would have the effrontery to proclaim that they spoke for men throughout the world and could be faithfully entrusted to represent their interests. Why, then, should a group of 'delegates' (delegated by whom?) claim to speak for all the world's women? Here, indeed, we have patronising paternalism at its worst – and fraudulent to boot. None of those going to Peking represent the interests of women, for they have no conception of what those interests are, or how most women want their interests identified and pursued. They are there to advance quite different interests, usually those of the government which appointed them. Many of the worst Third World dictators have sent their wives as head of delegation, a bad example followed by President Clinton.

A great many pressure groups and businesses which exploit women or prey on the 'women's market' are also out in force. I read in the *Evening Standard* an article by Anita Roddick called 'Why I believe women should go to Beijing'. It is perfectly clear why she is going – to advance the interests of her firm, The Body Shop. She says as much. But, she adds, with breathtaking effrontery, that she and the Body Shop people will also be 'taking with us the voices of women who cannot attend'. It is as though the chairman of Marks & Spencer went to an international gathering and claimed the right to speak on behalf of M&S's 30 million customers.

This brings me to my main point – the assumption, behind all these propaganda activities, that women, making up 52 per cent of the world's population, think broadly alike on a whole range of key issues. There is no evidence at all of this, and much evidence to the contrary. Women did not even agree about getting the vote – some of the most vociferous opponents of the Suffragettes were women. The fiercest opponents of married clergy are women and always have been, beginning with Queen Elizabeth I, in some other respects a notable proponent of women's rights. Women who actually go to church, as opposed to worshipping at the foot of the columns of the *Guardian* and *Independent*, are bitterly divided over women priests. On abortion, the most important issue of all, women hold the entire spectrum of views, forming the bulk of the militants on both sides but expressing every imaginable doubt and nuance in between. There is no such thing as the Woman's View on anything, least of all those issues where feminists claim to speak for the entire sex.

Nor is this surprising. It has often struck me, both as a student of historical texts and a journalistic observer of how people behave today, that women are much less easily categorised than men. They have, in fact, an anti-herd instinct. A woman, attending a reception, is mortified if she finds she is wearing the same outfit as some other woman. A man, by contrast, is mortified if he is *not* dressed like the other men. All over the world, dances are held at which all the men dress exactly alike and all the women dress differently. Even highly intelligent men are uneasy if they fail to conform, at least on the surface. By contrast, women positively want to appear egregious. Men who flourish in our orderly societies are admired for being 'sound', a 'safe pair of hands'. What women of spirit ever strove to be sound or safe?

Countless generations of physical subservience have quite failed to break a certain quiet determination in women to think for themselves. It is characteristic of the sex that a woman was the first to be recorded laughing. Sarah, Abraham's wife, has a cynical chortle to herself when she overhears the men – God, her husband, two male-sounding angels – discussing their plan for her to have a child. 'What,' she laughs, 'after I am waxed old shall I have pleasure, my lord being old also?' The men overhear her chuckles and are furious. But this has not stopped women from laughing behind men's backs ever since, even – perhaps especially – in tightly controlled, ultra-masculine societies like Japan's. This kind of distinctive women's laughter began to break the surface in Jane Austen's day, and is now popping out all over the place. But, just at the very moment when women are at last getting the chance to play their individualistic roles openly, along come the feminist totalitarians with their plans to turn the sex into regimented progressive zombies.

But it won't work. The genie of woman is now out of the bottle for good. The picnic at Peking will end as it deserves, in bickering, and the derisive laughter of women who aren't there.

2 September 1995

What is the Oxford atheist scared of?

Why have the atheists got cold feet? Having proclaimed for a century that the arguments for the existence of God had only to be brought out into the light of common day – and public discussion – for them to collapse ignominiously, why have they begun to panic about their own arguments? Why, having been brazen in their know-all arrogance, have they suddenly turned yellow? I ask this in the light of Richard Dawkins's craven refusal to come out of his safe academic burrow and debate with me, in an open forum, under agreed rules and neutral chairmanship, the existence or non-existence of God. If the head of Britain's anti-God lobby, and the occupant of Oxford's first Chair of Atheism – yes, I know it's officially about explaining science but we are all aware what Dawkers is really up to – is not willing to stand up for his beliefs, then we have to conclude there is something seriously wrong with them.

I brush aside Dawkins's ostensible reason for refusing – that my challenge is motivated by self-interest. We all know that is not the real reason he is scared. After all, according to the author of *The Selfish Gene*, everyone is motivated by self-interest all the time and any other motive would be unnatural or illusory. Needless to say, I do not subscribe to this depressing view of mankind, and I find myself pitying the Professor for thinking it impossible for a human being to be driven by a faith, a cause, a genuine desire to enlighten society or – the chief object in my case – a burning wish to share the precious gift of belief in God with as many fellow-mortals as possible. One of the truly dreadful consequences of being a materialist like Dawkins is that you are obliged in logic to deny the existence of metaphysics, and the world of the spirit is a no-go area for you. You are forced to imprison yourself in a one-dimensional existence, with no significant past and no personal future, where the only things that matter are material objects pushed around by hoggish genes. But as I say, Dawkins's professed reason for funking a debate is not the real one.

I suspect there are three main reasons why Dawkins won't compete. One is the intellectual laziness characteristic of Oxbridge prima donnas. After all, if you are accustomed to playing the smart-alec academic panjandrum in front of goggling gaggles of freshmen, or lecturing to tame audiences who copy down your words as if they were holy writ, or lording it as the resident lion in the provincial society of North Oxford drawing-rooms, it's a bit of a shock to go out into the real world where people answer back and proofs are demanded and academic waffle gets you nowhere. Outside the protected environment of the common rooms and lecture halls, there is no such thing as secure intellectual tenure. Dawkins knows this. It is one thing to go to London to deliver a few sound-bites in a television studio, quite another to face a live audience for two hours under real Queensberry rules.

Then again, I suspect Dawkins is genuinely worried by the poverty of his arguments. In the 19th century the positivists had it easy in one way: they could point to the absurdities of what theologians had

said in the past – angels dancing on the head of a pin, for example –
without being burdened by a similar body of archaic idiocies on their
own side. That is no longer true. Articulate atheism now has a long
history and a spectacularly silly one. The *obiter dicta* of earlier scientific
materialists, all of them in their own day at least as eminent and
confident as Dawkins, make hilarious reading today. Thus Emile
Littré defined 'the Soul' as 'anatomically the sum of the functions of
the neck and spinal column, physiologically the sum of function of
the power of perception in the brain'. By contrast, Ernst Haeckel
asserted: 'We now know that ... the soul [is] a sum of plasma-
movements in the ganglion cells.' Hippolyte Taine laid down: 'Man
is a spiritual automaton ... vice and virtue are products like sugar
and vitriol.' Karl Vogt insisted: 'Thoughts come out of the brain like
gall from the liver or urine from the kidneys.' Jacob Moleshot was
equally certain: 'No thought [can emerge] without phosphorus.' Once,
all the atheists had to do was attack. Now they have a lot to defend –
or repudiate. I can well believe that Dawkins is scared that on a
public platform he could well end by getting his plasma-movements
twisted in his ganglion cells.

Thirdly, unlike their predecessors, present-day atheists have it easy.
The whole grain of society – in academia, in the media, in public
discourse, in common parlance – is in their favour, as it once was in
favour of the Christians. As I know from my own experience, for
someone today to insist on bringing God into the argument – in a
television studio, round a dinner-table, in a public discussion – is
now a social solecism, causing uneasiness, disquiet and embarrassment. God is a three-letter word, not to be pronounced except in
a certified God-slot. An unthinking agnosticism is taken for granted
everywhere, so atheists are seldom called on to put their case *ab
initio*. They have almost forgotten what it is.

It was not always thus. Thomas Henry Huxley had to fight it out
all his life with militant bishops and self-confident Christian politicians,
and was a first-class controversialist in consequence – he makes
Dawkins seem naff. George Bernard Shaw and H.G. Wells were
constantly on public platforms debating God, religion and the possibilities of an after-life with the likes of Hilaire Belloc and G.K.
Chesterton. They too were brilliant at fighting their corner. Bertrand
Russell defended his own brands of rationality against all-comers for
three-quarters of a century and knew exactly how to do it. And I
don't recall Freddie Ayer ever ducking a fight either. But Dawkins
doesn't know whether he can do it. He is unsure of his arguments,

his cause and his skills. He is scared he would make a fool of himself in front of the world and, not least, in front of his academic colleagues, who whatever they believe or disbelieve would of course be delighted to see King Atheism take a tumble. So he skulks in his New College tent, afraid to put on his armour and venture forth. As the poet Chapman put it, there is something contemptible about the inactive scoffer:

> O incredulity: the wit of fools,
> That slovenly will spit on all things fair,
> The coward's castle and the sluggard's cradle.

16 March 1996

No ta-ra-ra-boom-de-ay this decade

We are living in the Grey Nineties. The greyness oozes relentlessly out of the stratosphere, enveloping all five continents in its dingy murk, dimming colour, killing glamour, extinguishing adventure. Hundreds of millions are unemployed, the banks aren't lending, the big spenders are in low-profile mode, Trump is silent, Maxwell dead, Bond finished, Maggie and Lord King in huffy retirement, the Queen is wondering where her next yacht is coming from, and her daughter is moving into a flat in Dolphin Square. Communism is extinct, capitalism not feeling so good, Russia is a black hole, America's broke, the curtain's come down on Sweden's welfare utopia, the European ideal buried in a sepulchre of bureaucracy and corruption, Africa's heart has returned to darkness, even the Japanese are retrenching.

Bill Clinton's mop has turned perceptibly greyer since he took over, as he piles on the ho-hum. He has his first 'human resource development session' with his staff at Camp David, to swap confessional stories about their inadequacies. The President admits 'about how he was this fat kid when he was five or six, and the other kids taunted him'. His Human Services Secretary, Ms Donna Shalala, insists it was 'fun'. Our own monochrome man, John Major, defiantly proclaims his greyness down to the last jot and tittle. As one lady put it, 'I'm so sorry it wasn't true about Clare Latimer, it's the first interesting thing I've ever heard about him.' Striking a different grey note, the fallen Arts Minister, David Mellor, argues that the De Sancha episode proves he is rather like Palmerston and Gladstone. Somehow, we don't believe him.

Even our children are being educated to grow up into a grey world where everyone is equal, no one fat, thin, tall, tiny, clever, stupid, poor, privileged, good, bad, blonde, brunette, black or white, lucky, unhappy or special. Little Black Sambo and Ferdinand the Bull are non-persons, pigs are unclean, lawns don't exist, and tales must be woven about small, good-tempered giants, huge, socially conscious dwarfs, benevolent witches, genial ogres and fairies who can't fly but take the bus to work like everyone else. 'What shall we play today?' 'Gollywog-hunting.' 'No, gender-bending.' 'Fascist!' 'Homophobe!'

Looking back from our iron-grey decade, it's not exactly clear why the 1890s were called 'the Gay Nineties'. There were hard times, stingy banks and countless unemployed then too. William Booth published *In Darkest England*, in case anyone thought it didn't exist. Across the Atlantic, the New York writer, Jacob Riis, wrote an equally sensational tract, *How the Other Half Lives*. It was a decade when high-minded, upper-middle-class youths from public schools and Oxbridge founded East End 'missions', when Hardy, Zola and Gissing were spreading literary gloom. It must have been the music-hall and the *bal-dansant* which supplied the note of gaiety. But Sickert's paintings of Katie Lawrence packing them in at Gatti's Hungerford Palace of Varieties evoke, if anything, plushy, flea-bitten discomfort, and Toulouse-Lautrec's posters, which began in 1891, show La Goulue, Yvette Guibert, Jean Avril and May Belfort hustling themselves not to Elysium but to TB, absinthe-poisoning and general paralysis of the insane. It is true that in 1892 one Lottie Collins had a sensational London hit by bawling out the new wedding-march, 'Ta-ra-ra-boom-de-ay'. But what did it mean? What explosion of joy, what noisy intimation of bliss was Lottie announcing? The year before, just as Lautrec was finishing his earliest theatrical lithographs, Sherlock Holmes and Dr Watson made their first appearance. But when they stepped into their hansom-cab and clip-clopped off to London Bridge station, their minds were not on high jinks but on mayhem, murder and gruesome conspiracy. Who, exactly, was being gay? Even 'gays' had a hard time: in 1893 Tchaikovsky, with rumours circulating about him, conveniently died from drinking infected water, and two years later Oscar Wilde went to gaol.

I suspect that what made the decade of the 1890s exhilarating was not the absence of poverty, horror, crime and despair, but the residual feeling that you could, at a pinch, get away from it all. My 12-year-old father, unhappy with his step-parents, simply ran away to sea, something you were still allowed to do then, and sailed all over the world. The open spaces were still wide. He told me that, arrived in New York, he perched on a high stool in a bar which advertised 'Free Eats' and was served with hot corned-beef hash. 'And what'll ya have to drink, kid?' 'Oh, I don't drink.' The barman's comment was: 'Wa-al, I'll be damned!' In the 1890s, 3,000 immigrants poured into New York alone every week. They went straight to tenements in the Lower East Side, which had the highest recorded human density in history; but the average stay there was no more than two months – then they moved on to prosperity and happiness, real or imaginary. When the 1890s opened, the frontier had not yet been closed, the Sioux were still fighting, you could still stake a gold claim in Colorado's Cripple Creek, let alone the Yukon. At the other ends of the world, pioneers were pouring into the Rand and Rhodesia, a few were starting to explore Kenya's Happy Valley, and Melbourne had the world's highest living standard.

What makes our planet such a grey place today is not just the recession but the feeling you are stuck with what you've got. There is nowhere else to go which is allowed, or is not the same, or worse. Shangri-la has disappeared under a pile of colour mags. Kathmandu is overcrowded. There are empty tins on the top of Everest and at the South Pole. California is a busted flush. The Riviera is smeared with suntan and reeks of diesel. If you flee London, you run into crime waves in Cheltenham or Maidstone or Taunton. A Cotswold cottage is as likely to be burgled as a terrace in Kensington or Camden Town. New Wavers are despoiling the Brecon Beacons and the Mendips. Bath has been infested with the evil-smelling Crusties, who award seniority to those who have gone longest without a wash. We know there's nothing at the end of the rainbow: everyone has been there to look. The world has become a gigantic time-share, heading straight for bankruptcy. President Clinton, meet Premier Major; Hillary, meet Norma. If everything else is in short supply, there are plenty of grey days to go round and everyone is going to get his or her fair share.

13 February 1993

Wimps, mediocrities, nonentities
and rogues

It is fashionable to deplore the low state of American politics by pointing to the competing inadequacies of the various presidential contenders, Republican and Democrat. It is true they are a sorry lot. I have never thought much of George Bush and have been agreeably surprised by how comparatively well he has done. During the Gulf war, he even looked, for a day or two, a major statesman, though I think it should be remembered that it was Margaret Thatcher who argued him into a tough stance on the Kuwait invasion as far back as August 1990; all flowed from that early decision.

He has been a lucky president in that events, above all the collapse of the USSR, have flowed his way, but he has rarely looked in charge of them. As a domestic leader, he is indecisive, unimaginative and lacking in convictions of any kind. It is a commentary on the feeble hold he has on Republican loyalties that a man like Pat Buchanan, who has no ideas except Protection, should make such a dent in the Bush following.

As for the Democrats, it is a daunting thought that they may have to choose between Bill Clinton and Paul Tsongas, with the even more disturbing possibility that the sinister and unattractive Mario Cuomo, a so-called Catholic who has sold the pass on every issue, could snatch the nomination by a late entry. Bush, I imagine, will beat any of them, but it is little consolation that the world's first sole superpower will be under his hesitant control for the next four years.

However, it has to be recognised that the odds are often against the best man getting to the White House. There have been long periods in American history when the country has been ruled, or rather not ruled, by mediocrities and even nonentities.

The point is disguised by the undoubted fact that the new Republic got off to a fine start. George Washington was a great and wise man, an outstanding example for all times and places of how a newly independent ex-colony should be steered. Then there was a distinguished succession from Massachusetts and Virginia: John Adams,

Thomas Jefferson, James Madison, James Munroe, John Quincy Adams, all civilised, well-read men of strong principles, though sometimes marred by personal faults. They had the further advantage, for a young state, of being drawn from the ruling establishment and so possessing a definite sense of public obligation. General Jackson, the first *parvenu*, who reached the White House in 1829, was a born leader who proved a president of iron will if sometimes confused notions.

After that it was downhill all the way to the Civil War. Jackson's successor, Martin Van Buren, was a dapper New York politico known as the Little Magician, who could swing things how he liked in his own state but who never mastered national politics and took the United States into deep recession. The two outstanding men of the age, Henry Clay and Daniel Webster, never got to the White House. In 1840, Clay was told by the party bosses that he was simply not popular enough to get the Whig nomination. Instead they picked a successful soldier, William Harrison (American presidents are nearly always lawyers or generals), who compounded his inadequacies by promptly expiring within weeks of taking office, thus letting in a second-rater called John Tyler. The next man, James Polk, was no better. Then came another lacklustre general, Zachary Taylor, who also died in office, producing the presidency of the ridiculous Millard Fillmore. The two last presidents before the War Between the States, Franklin Pierce and James Buchanan, did nothing to avert it.

There followed the outstanding presidency of Abraham Lincoln, and the more one studies what that remarkable man said and did the more one admires his intelligence, courage and wit. But he was a bright episode in a melancholy procession. Andrew Johnson, who took over when Lincoln was murdered, was so tactless he wrecked the great man's inheritance and nearly got himself successfully impeached. General Ulysses Grant was a fine general with little political judgment who allowed his White House to be infested by crooks. The quality of presidents from the Civil War to the early years of the 20th century was so low that, between Lincoln and Theodore Roosevelt, the best of them was Grover Cleveland, and that is not saying much.

In the 20th century it is true that the US presidential system has produced a much better roll-call. Woodrow Wilson's record of legislation and national leadership was of the highest standard until his health collapsed. Harry Truman, Dwight Eisenhower and Ronald Reagan all made fine national leaders, judicious and decisive. I would add to their number Calvin Coolidge, a particular favourite of mine, and I suppose some people would still include Franklin Roosevelt and J.F. Kennedy. It can also be argued that Lyndon Johnson and Richard Nixon, both brought low by events over which they lost control, were men of formidable ability with huge achievements to their credit; and few men in US history have understood its system better or worked it so well.

However, I suspect that the tortuous procedures whereby Americans now elect their leader and the horrible snakes-and-ladders game each is forced to endure are shifting the result back in the direction of mediocrity, or worse. Bush is beginning to look more in the tradition of Taft or Harding, Hoover or Carter; indeed, he has actually begun to sound like Hoover. The Democratic contenders in recent years have been so bad as to revive memories of Polk and Fillmore.

The truth is that the Americans expect too much of their presidents: absolute integrity, in a political system where multi-million personal fund-raising is essential; monk-like chastity in a permissive age; political correctness of an anodyne subservience which can only be maintained by suppressing precisely those opinions and quirks which make a politician interesting; and, furthermore, a willingness to be fiercely interrogated on all these and other issues by tinpot media Grand Inquisitors. Many men of decency, character and ability, however strong their sense of public service, will not submit to these conditions, and quite rightly. They would have been found unacceptable by all of America's first seven presidents. A media democracy like the United States, where the public demands the right to know everything, illustrates the principle that the best is the enemy of the good. You cannot get perfect presidents any way, and this way you do not even get good ones.

A surge of grassroots opinion can still propel forward an unfancied outsider like Reagan – dismissed by smart Georgetown opinion, I well remember, as 'impossible' as late as spring 1980 – but the more likely product is going to be an inadequate man like Bush. Or, quite possibly, a plausible rogue.

22 February 1992

The Queen's Shangri-La

An item of news which arrested me last week was an announcement in the *Times* that the Queen's favourite place in the whole wide world is the Hodder Valley in Lancashire, and that she would rather like to end her days there. This surprised and intrigued me. Surprised because I have never seen myself as someone with similar tastes to the Queen. I am an average Englishman, almost a statistical archetype of English ordinariness, with no taste for grandeur, ceremonial, racing, horses or, since the death of my never-to-be-forgotten Parker, dogs. Yet the intriguing fact is that the Hodder Valley is my favourite place too. I am unlikely to superannuate there, for my wife Marigold is a Londoner who believes civilisation begins to collapse somewhere north of Watford. On the only occasion I took her to the Hodder Valley she said, 'I had no conception that anywhere could be so *cold*.' So I will not end up there. Nor, for that matter, will the Queen – the Duke will see to that. But we can both have our dreams. It is *our* country.

It is mine in two senses. When people ask where I come from I say I was born in Manchester, but bits of my family originate in the Trough of Bowland. No one ever knows where that is. The Forest of Bowland – forest in the sense it was once a protected range for deer: there are few trees there – is a vast tract of indescribably wild and romantic country in the western Pennines, some miles east of places like Morecambe and Lancaster. Few people go there. Why should they? There is nothing to do except walk and listen to the silence and the brown burns flowing and the haunting cries of the moorland birds. The Hodder has its source in the northern reaches of the forest, behind Wolfhole Crag, skirts round to the east, trickles through a mountainy hamlet called Staidburn, heads south alongside a Roman road, and eventually bumps into and circumnavigates a formidable ridge called Longridge Fell. Then it tumbles into a peaceful valley and joins a placid stream called the Ribble and so to the sea at Preston.

All this country is familiar to me because I walked over it and painted it for many years while I was at school. Stonyhurst is a magnificent Elizabethan-Jacobean house surmounted by twin towers on which sit fierce golden eagles. It was built by remote Catholic squires who never surrendered their faith to the Southerners. They finally yielded their house in 1794 to the Jesuits, who had hitherto been obliged by the wicked penal laws to educate the sons of the papist gentry abroad. It is not strictly true that no Protestant has ever set foot in the place – Cromwell had his HQ there immediately before the murderous battle of Preston – but certainly in my time it was hard to find one within a range of five miles. The school was on the slopes of Longridge Fell, and the finest stretches of the Hodder were at our feet. I spent the years 1940 to 1946 there and loved almost every minute. They say that Jesuit schools were harsh in those days, and certainly some of the weaker boys whined a little. Gerard Manley Hopkins was unhappy there too, but to me it was a paradise.

The Hodder is both a sombre and cheerful river, depending on the weather. On sunny days it crashes and thunders through countless rapids and cataracts, rattling immense dark-chocolate brown boulders, sending up rainbows of spray and creating miniature Niagaras and deep golden-brown pools at their foaming feet. These 'roughs', as we called them, make natural bathing-places, with water-chutes galore and full-fathom-five depths to dive in. Especially in the summer term, grand feasts of the Church were celebrated by what were known as Good Days, in which we took cooking picnics to the Hodder, built roaring fires and fried sausages and bacon on its banks before plunging into its icy waters. These cataracts were spine-chilling and bruising and, I suppose, dangerous, but they were hugely exciting and we did not care. In those days children were not pampered and fussed over by social workers or legislated about. We knew the Jesuits loved us and were answerable to God for our well-being. We trusted them and they allowed us to enjoy the wilds and to roam all over the fells where, almost within living memory, there had been wolves and wildcats.

Across the rich valley where the Hodder joins the Ribble lay not indeed a mountain, but what Dr Johnson would have called a 'considerable protuberance' known as Pendle Hill. It is a haunted place and was rightly made the focal point of Harrison Ainsworth's novel *The Lancashire Witches* (1848), which is set in these parts and introduces some of the nearby crumbling old homes of the ancient Catholic squirearchy, such as Houghton Hall. I must have drawn Pendle Hill in watercolour as often as Cézanne painted Mont Ste-Victoire. It has an osmotic and elusive profile, rather like the Matterhorn, difficult to get exactly right. Indeed it is mysterious altogether, because, if you climb it, the monumental bosom of the hill suddenly dissolves into flat fields and you never, as it were, get to the top. But from its highest point northern Lancashire, that misty, chilly world of persecution and suffering and fidelity, of priests' hiding-holes and hanging raids at dawn, of masses said furtively in cellars and attics, of the secret whiff of incense and the muffled chink of Holy Communion bell, of the ever-waiting rack and gibbet – all this is spread at your feet. And wandering through it is the silvery ribbon of the Hodder, most blessed of streams to me. It is, perhaps, a surprising world for the Queen of England, Supreme Governor of the Anglican Church and, I suppose, the leading secular Protestant on earth, to wish to dwell in while preparing to meet her God. But in my view her instincts are sound and it could well be that in this delectable valley a celestial light will illuminate her thoughts and lead her back to the true faith.

27 January 1996

The Ur-documents of the School of Mud

The unanimity of critical and editorial opinion about the ridiculous Cézanne exhibition at the Tate Gallery reflects the extent to which our sad, art-ignorant nation has been brainwashed by the Brickies. Cézanne is a key figure for those who have turned high art into mere fashion. He was the son of an Aix moneylender and, to his credit, wanted to do something nobler with his life. For half a century he struggled to render nature as he saw it, against all the odds – lack of natural skill, inadequate training in a second-rate art school, an explosive temper which meant he had no friends and so could not learn from other artists, and a compulsive fear of women which prevented him drawing from life. He failed: there was nothing he did which had not been done better by many other painters. But he was nonetheless successfully hyped by the commercial galleries even in his lifetime, and so provided first proof positive that art and skill had parted company. His works became the Ur-documents of the School of Mud. The racketeers moved in and gradually captured all the positions of power in the art world, which they have held now for over 50 years. Ambitious and unscrupulous and self-deluded artists learn that they can win acclaim and even make fortunes without any need for talent, let alone genius, provided they have a nose for fashion. Indeed, today in most art schools it is not thought necessary for students to acquire skills of any kind, except in self-promotion.

Oddly enough, in all the hundreds of thousands of breathless words published in the last week about Cézanne's 'masterpieces' it is nowhere explained why, precisely, they are worth admiring. Nor is this surprising. It cannot be done. Even Ernst Gombrich failed, though to be fair to him his attempt was only half-hearted because he loves beauty in art and hates a racket. Virtually everything ever written about Cézanne is pretentious waffle or pseudo-theory. I recall Tom Boase, who had been head of the Courtauld and then became president of Magdalen, trying to brainwash me in 1949, in front of 'The Cardplayers', with stuff about 'reverse perspective' – all nonsense, as I told him at the time. No one has ever been able to explain why we should like Cézanne's women bathers, some of whom were copied from the painter's old life-drawings of male models, or from prints cut out of magazines, and who are, without exception, misshapen, grotesque and hideous. The only person whose liking for them was genuine was Henry Moore, who frankly admitted he had a perverted taste for enormous, brutal women-shapes and who persuaded a weak director of the National Gallery, Sir Philip Hendy, to spend half a million – a colossal sum in 1964 – on buying the worst painting in the whole misbegotten series. These dreadful daubs compel the Stakhanovites of the waffle industry to break even their records. Thus the *Times*, in a leading article (forsooth) of staggering idiocy, salutes them as 'strange, huge women of quite compelling mansuetude'. To be sure, these monstresses have a certain relevance to an age of transvestites, shemales, sex-ops, transsexuals and gender-bending.

Why, then, since the Brickies have so successfully brainwashed the nation, as reflected in the media, are they still running scared? For they are – dead scared. It is as though they are terrified that the entire outrageous imposture of Modern Art is about to collapse, suddenly and irrevocably, just as Soviet communism did after seven decades of triumphant tyranny. I have drawn attention before to this Brickie nervousness. It explains why they cannot tolerate any dissenting voice whatever. In the past 40 years, there have been only four outstanding art critics in Britain. John Berger now lives in Swiss exile. Peter Fuller is dead – and the Brickies have had the superb lectures held in his honour discontinued. Giles Auty, who wrote in this journal with such admirable courage, roundly rejecting all the false gods of modernism, has been forced to go to Australia to make the living denied to him here. And Brian Sewell, who has denounced Brickie excesses in the *Evening Standard* to brilliant effect, was made the object of the most concentrated campaign of venom ever launched against a British critic. The Brickies wanted him sacked and his voice silenced. His editor, despite much pressure, stood by him. But Sewell, an unworldly figure whose life is entirely devoted to aesthetic ideals, was obviously shaken by the hate and vehemence of his persecutors.

Now a new phase begins. The object of their pre-emptive attack is the Royal Academy. This time the Brickie-in-Chief Nicholas Serota, who normally leaves guerrilla warfare to underlings, has chosen to show his hand. His personal power is already greater than that of any official in the entire history of painting in England. He controls the Tate exactly as he wishes and his trustees rubber-stamp all he decides. He is soon to straddle the Thames with his triumphalist Brickie palace at Bankside, the vast expense of which is to be met from the Lottery pence of the poor. His tentacles stretch to the Liverpool Tate in the North and the St Ives Tate in the West. I have no doubt he has much higher ambitions, though he denies it, and would like to be the British equivalent of the French art-supremo who, in true Napoleonic tradition, has ultimate control over every state museum in the country. A Serota dictatorship of British art is a sinister possibility.

In the meantime the Brickies seems to have targeted the Royal Academy. This royal but independent foundation, run by its Members and Associates, has put up in recent decades only a feeble line of resistance to Brickie ideology. Indeed, the last president of the RA who stood up to the modernist juggernaut, Sir Alfred Munnings, resigned as long ago as 1949. Abstracts, daubs and other rubbish have been admitted to the RA's summer show in growing quantities. But the RA, in its own limited way, still displays works which demonstrate skill and devoted hard work as well as a belief that painting is a noble calling and not just a commercial racket and a power quest. That is what raises the fury of the Brickies. The RA, for all its lack of self-confidence, is still an outpost of the civilisation they wish to destroy. So the Brickies are mounting what looks suspiciously like a putsch. With the help of the fifth column within the RA, they are calling a meeting which could well end by putting the summer exhibition firmly in Brickie hands. The meeting is to be chaired by Julia Peyton-Jones, who runs the Serpentine Gallery, the Brickie fortress in Hyde Park. It looks like being one of the most totalitarian occasions since Hitler's notorious exhibition of Degenerate Art. Anyone who really cares about painting and sculpture – and there are a growing number of us, despite the ceaseless brainwashing – should press the RA to throw the meeting open to the public.

17 February 1996

The new republicanism and how to deal with it

The Prince of Wales has achieved something at last: he has recreated the republican movement in Britain. Despite Tony Blair's best efforts, more and more Labour MPs are voicing anti-royal sentiments privately, and we must expect their views to become increasingly public. The *Independent* and the *Guardian* have both turned republican. I expect the bulk of the broadcasting media to follow suit in due course: not officially but in the kind of comment and material they put out.

The English are still overwhelmingly royalist. So are the Ulster Unionists in their own odd way. But a majority of the Scots and the Welsh, I suspect, now reject royalty, or at any rate the present dynasty. This movement of opinion is bound to grow as the disreputable behaviour of some of the Windsors continues, and as ordinary people realise it is no longer taboo to express anti-royal views.

The Prince of Wales is to blame because it was his original decision to try to run his wife and his old mistress in tandem. Princess Diana turned out to be a much stronger woman than he calculated and would not put up with such treatment. Therein lies the origin of the dynasty's present troubles. Princes Charles, instead of seeking a reconciliation with his wife, which she would have welcomed, and which would have restored his popularity, now insists on a formal dissolution of their marriage, thus compounding his original mistake. It is going to be one of the messiest divorces of all time. The Princess will fight every inch of the way and exact her full rights, as she is morally as well as legally entitled to do.

Nor will the public acrimony end with the divorce. The Windsors, with all their power, money and arrogance, cannot take one thing away from her: she is the mother of a future king – a first-class mother too, and a wise and determined one, loved by young Prince William almost to the point of idolatry. So she remains a central player in the royal game. The dynasty cannot treat her as they treated the Duchess of Windsor and reduce her to an exiled non-person. They are stuck with her, and if they behave cruelly she will become the focus of republican discontent.

If the throne is to be saved, some hard decisions ought to be taken soon. The difficulty is that the Queen has no one to turn to for sound, disinterested advice. And she needs it. She is an excellent constitutional monarch when it comes to routine matters, but experience shows she cannot handle her own family. She has no imagination or originality and cannot think constructively about the long term. All she wants is to bury her nose in her red boxes, hoping trouble will go away. It is no use turning to John Major. He is a simpleton in such matters and anyway can think of nothing except how to stay in office a bit longer. The family has no elder of note. The Duke of Edinburgh has long since washed his hands of policy, having been rebuffed and snubbed savagely in the past, not so much by the Queen but by those who surround her.

Earl Mountbatten is much missed. He may have been frivolous in many ways but in others he could be imaginative and long-sighted – after all, he predicted that Charles, unless properly led, would get into deep trouble and might even 'go the same way as his great-uncle David'. But 'Dickie' is dead and has had no successor. None of the courtiers is much good. The last clever one was Martin Charteris and no one, I fear, takes much notice of him now. So the royal coach trundles on without direction, the victim of haphazard events, and is in danger of leaving the road.

Ordinary English people of all classes instinctively want the monarchy to stay and their instinct is constitutionally sound. The key argument in favour of a Crown as opposed to an elected president is that the Crown inspires deference even in the mighty. A prime minister may have an overwhelmingly popular following, all the charismatic gifts and a will of iron, but the monarchical principle forces him to humble himself, bow the knee and submit to the forms of obedience in front of a humdrum figure whose status derives from birth. The most potent commoners in our history – Pitt the Elder, Gladstone and Winston Churchill – accepted this as axiomatic and no one was more deferential to the throne than these three.

The constitutional monarchy is, by its nature, a valuable defence against authoritarianism. This is something the British Left has never been able to understand. If, by some horrible series of events, we were to send royalty packing, it would not be a simple matter of putting in its place a retired politician as a formal head of state. We would have to redesign our entire political system, introduce a written constitution, fixed terms and a president elected by universal suffrage. We would end up with something like the American set-up. Very few would like this, least of all the unhistorical idiots now clamouring for a republic.

Far better to fine-tune the present system by altering the succession. We are not obliged to perpetuate the present dynasty. There are plenty of potential candidates among the older nobility of Plantagenet, Tudor or Stuart descent. Parliament has an undoubted right to prefer their claims if it decides the Windsors are hopeless, just as it put their Hanoverian forebear, George I, on the throne in the first place. But we do not need to be so drastic as to change the dynasty. One solution is for Parliament to jump a generation and appoint Prince William as the Queen's successor. That would eliminate the foolish and unpopular Charles and might prove a winner with the public. Another is for it to pick one of the women candidates from the middle generation – Princess Anne or Princess Alexandra would make excellent constitutional sovereigns, and it is a fact that the country has always done well under queens-regnant.

There are many different possibilities which ought to be considered and debated. What we should not allow to continue is the present aimless slide to disaster, with members of the royal family scratching each other's eyes out, egged on by an unrestrained and irresponsible media. That can benefit only the republicans.

9 March 1996

The battle for God as the millennium looms

One of the most fascinating aspects of history is not so much the things that happen as the things which obstinately refuse to happen. Seemingly irresistible forces suddenly come to an unexpected stop. Powerful trends evaporate. Crumbling relics survive. Yesterday's men go on, and on, and on. The great non-event of the 20th century was the Death of God. Late-19th-century intellectuals did not quite agree with Nietzsche that God was already dead, but they were fairly confident that he would be by the year 2000. During the 20th century they assumed that belief in God would largely disappear in the West and that only backward societies would retain religious 'superstition'. Yet here we are at the end of what was supposed to be the first century of atheism, with God alive and well and reigning in the hearts of billions all over the world. Partly as a result of the growth of population, to be sure, more people believe in God today than in 1900. I don't doubt there are more agnostics too. What there are not more of are atheists. The number of those prepared to declare, flatly, that there is no God has actually declined since the heyday of organised atheism in the 1880s. It is characteristic of Oxford University, the home of lost causes, that it has just appointed Richard Dawkins its first Professor of Atheism.

Indeed, at the end of the 20th century, the prospects for God are excellent. It could turn out to be His century. In the 19th century we worshipped Progress. It was real, visible, fast-moving and on the whole beneficent. But it came to a juddering halt in the catastrophe of the first world war. The human race felt that Progress had let them down. They turned instead to Ideology – to communism, fascism, Freudianism and even darker systems of belief. The 20th century was the Age of Ideology just as the 19th century was the Age of Progress. But Ideology failed its human adherents too and finally came crashing down at the beginning of the 1990s. One thing history teaches about human beings is that they do not relish believing in nothing. A credal vacuum is abhorrent. It may well be that God, who had to struggle to survive in the 20th century, will fill the vacuum in the 21st and so become the residual legatee of those dead titans, Progress and Ideology.

I have been thinking about this prospect because I am about to publish a little book on God. *The Quest for God: A Personal Pilgrimage* is not primarily a work of piety. It is an inquiry, and not a wholly successful one, as I am the first to admit. I wrote it to satisfy what I think is a common need. When the conversation turns to what we believe in now, as it often does, and I ask people, 'Do you believe in God?' the answer is usually 'Yes'. But if I press the point and ask, 'What exactly do you mean by that?' answer comes there none, or the query is pushed aside by a jest: 'These are deep waters, Watson' or 'I require notice of that question'. People do not like to say 'I don't know' or admit that they have put off pondering what they mean by God or by their acceptance of His existence. They fight shy of thinking about God just as they would prefer not to think about death – their own in particular. And even if they try to think about God, they do not know how to do it. So I decided to write a book, sorting out my ideas about God, in the hope that reading it would help other people to sort out their ideas. I cover most of the difficult topics, such as who God is, why He created the universe, and how He runs it – if He does run it – and why He permits evil to flourish. I discuss animals and their possible souls and the earth and its future, the chances of life on other worlds and how this would affect the notion of *our* God. I deal with the Four Last Things: death, judgment, hell and heaven, and, finally, with prayer, the most important subject of all, because it is our way of communicating with this mysterious Being.

Writing the book proved more difficult than I had imagined because I discovered areas of ignorance and bottomless depths of uncertainty within me. I thought I had most of the answers and found I had very few, and had to think everything out all over again and do a lot of reading. But I am glad I made the effort because I am now much clearer in my own mind than I was. I am stronger in faith too and, most of all, I take enhanced delight in the fact that through all the vicissitudes of six decades, I have somehow managed to retain, virtually intact, the beliefs taught me by my parents. Faith in a just and all-powerful God is the greatest of gifts. We may wish to be born handsome or rich or clever or fascinating, but faith is a more valuable inheritance than any of these endowments. When I am in London at the weekend I attend the 11 o'clock mass at the Carmelite Friars in Kensington Church Street. It is a sung mass in Latin, with a simple homily, and the entire congregation takes communion – Catholicism at its best and most pleasing. Afterwards I usually have coffee nearby with my old friend and fellow historian Antonia Fraser. We often say to each other, 'How lucky we are to be Catholics and have access to this unique spiritual sustenance.' It sounds like complacency but it is not, it is humble gratitude. Our faith is a suit of armour which, whether we deserve it or not, is a marvellous protection against the slings and arrows of the world. Within it we feel secure, warm, privileged.

I would like every human being to have a similar garment. I do not proselytise but I pray for the conversion of those I love and indeed for the whole world. And I am willing to take on, in fair debate, the paladins of the other side. If Richard Dawkins wants to argue with me about the existence of God, on Channel 4 or BBC 2 or Radio Three or any other public platform, I am ready to meet him. These are indeed deep waters, Watson, but we must all plunge into them sooner or later. I suspect that, as the millennium approaches, the religious ferment which has already begun will rise. Most religious revivals, such as the Great Awakenings in America, have sprung from the depths of society. Christianity itself started as a religion of the poor, of women, the underprivileged and outcasts. It may again be so this time, but I have a hunch it will be ignited – in this country at least – among the higher classes, and among the intellectuals and the educated. So in my judgment we are in for an exciting time during the next few years, at the dawn of a century when God may come into His own again. The battle will be fierce and I shall be in the front line if I can.

10 February 1996

An Oxford meditation under the spell of Magdalen tower

The first Saturday in Lent. February fill-dyke doing its worst: torrential downpours punctuated by spells of spotty showers and a shaft or two of deceptive sunlight. Can even Oxford charm in such conditions? Yet it can – it does. I sat under a leaking exotic in the Botanical Gardens to draw the great towers of Magdalen.

As my pen traced the structure of this miracle of late Perpendicular, all the old magic came back instantly. There was the pride of my old college, exactly as I used to draw it nearly half a century ago, refurbished and cleaned in the 1970s perhaps, but still confidently asserting the faith of medieval Oxford in Almighty God and scholarship. It was completed in the first decade of the 16th century, on the very eve of the Reformation, when the world of old Oxford fell apart. For it was Cambridge which opted for Protestantism and power – and it was Cambridge men who ran Elizabethan England: their Queen, as it were, was a Cambridge girl.

Never mind, Cambridge has nothing to match Magdalen tower. It was the one thing I loved above all when I came up at the age of 17, and truth to tell I hardly need to look at it to draw it: I know every rib and pinnacle by heart. But I sometimes feel guilty that, as a youth, I did not appreciate Oxford as it deserved. I can't remember ever setting foot in the Botanical Gardens, for instance, founded in 1621 as the first herbiary in England. A generation or two later it was superbly adorned in memory of the martyred king, Charles I, by Danby, a rapacious ruffian and the only politician ever to be impeached twice by the Commons, but a man of taste nonetheless. He loved Oxford. What makes its old stones so hypnotic is that they radiate back to you the affection of so many generations of clever and gifted men – often of dubious character like Wolsey and Harley and Laud, whose overwhelming passion for the university was the redeeming expiation of their lives.

As the rain had stopped, I dodged the traffic pouring over Magdalen Bridge to look round the college again. People complain that Oxford has been destroyed by cars and progress but I do not agree. The old core is largely intact, the finest conglomeration of buildings in Europe, still riddled by little alleys like Magpie Lane and Catte Street and the Turl, still with little shops which seem eternal. I bought some ties at Hine's, at the bottom of the High, and could almost swear that the gentle old man who served me was the same who sold me my first college tie in 1946.

True, a generation or so ago the fellows of Magdalen built an abomination across the river called the Waynflete Building, where two of my sons served sentences. But the college has redeemed itself by a new quadrangle at Longwall, a masterwork of well-contrived traditional modernity. The deer-park is exactly as I knew it in the 1940s when, leaning companionably against the railing, Gilbert Ryle pointed out to me a dapper figure paying a visit to the New Buildings: 'That's Freddie Ayer. Might have been a great philosopher. *Ruined by sex.*' I passed through the Cloisters and by Kitchen Staircase, where poor Oscar Wilde once had a magnificent abode crowded with his exquisite bric-à-brac. In my day it was still an undergraduate set – if you could afford it. Now it is a 'Function Room'.

Addison's Walk, exactly a mile round the college water-meadows, is much the same. A proto-Pugin 'improver' wanted to gothicise it in 1801, putting in a hermitage or two, but ancient-minded fellows resisted him and they have continued to fend off those who would turn this enchanting wilderness into a Heritage Trail. At Oxford, the heritage is all in the mind, where it belongs. Not that Addison himself was other-worldly or anti-urbane. He boasted in the *Spectator* in 1711, 'I have brought philosophy out of Closets and Libraries, Schools and Colleges, to dwell in Clubs and Assemblies, at Tea-tables and in Coffee-houses.' I was taken round his walk by C.S. Lewis, a kindly man always anxious to impart information, who told me what an astonishing difference it would have made to English literature if Wordsworth and Coleridge had been at Oxford instead of Cambridge. And I used to walk here on my way to attend tutorials with A.J.P. Taylor at a then isolated college house called Holywell Ford, across the stream. In the garden was a caravan, where Taylor's naughty wife Margaret cavorted with the poet Dylan Thomas, who sponged there in repellent ingratitude. Taylor hated him, as well he might, though he did not show it at the time. In those days adultery, and the bitterness it engendered, were carefully shrouded – though I do recall having pointed out to me Dr Martin Ridley, deprived of his Balliol fellowship 'for being caught *in flagrante delicto* on college premises' – it was the last circumstance which damned him.

I looked in at the college chapel, which was empty save for an organ scholar practising. There is a tale that Oliver Cromwell stole the college organ and used it for his private delight at Hampton Court, where he lorded it as Protector. But the college got it back and in due course it was played on by Sir John Stainer, choirmaster at the college in the 1870s, when he got the idea for my favourite Easter oratorio, 'The Crucifixion'. In the ante-chapel are tombs and plaques of dusty old fellows. Magdalen is famous for its long-lived presidents, such as Sir Herbert Warren, elected to the post in 1885, who survived in it till 1928, a reign of 43 years. When I was up, some of the dons still remembered him, vividly and not always with affection, 'though he got us the Prince of Wales, you know, in 1911. That was one in the eye for Balliol and the House!' An even longer tenure was Martin Routh's, president for 63 years until his death in 1854, who staggered Macaulay by referring to the Glorious Revolution of 1688 as 'the late Troubles'.

But then, what is wrong with very old dons who remember better times? What Oxford is about is the reconsideration of the past through the prism of modern *mores*. Waiting in the pitiless February rain, I enjoyed hearing one woman jogger say to another, 'It's *unbelievable!* I wonder what Kant would have said about *her!*'

2 March 1996

INDEX